TRUSTS

TRUSTS
FOURTH EDITION

Rob Foxall

This edition published 2024 by
The University of Law
2 Bunhill Row
London EC1Y 8HQ

© The University of Law 2024

All rights reserved. No part of this publication may be reproduced, stored in a retrieval system, or transmitted, in any form or by any means, without the prior written permission of the copyright holder, application for which should be addressed to the publisher.

Contains public sector information licensed under the Open Government Licence v3.0

British Library Cataloguing in Publication Data

A catalogue record for this book is available from the British Library.

ISBN 978 1 80502 129 2

Preface

This book is part of a series of Study Manuals that have been specially designed to support the reader to achieve the SQE1 Assessment Specification in relation to Functioning Legal Knowledge. Each Study Manual aims to provide the reader with a solid knowledge and understanding of fundamental legal principles and rules, including how those principles and rules might be applied in practice.

This Study Manual covers the Solicitors Regulation Authority's syllabus for the SQE1 assessment for Trusts in a concise and tightly focused manner. The Manual provides a clear statement of relevant legal rules and a well-defined road map through examinable law and practice. The Manual aims to bring the law and practice to life through the use of example scenarios based on realistic client-based problems and allows the reader to test their knowledge and understanding through single best answer questions that have been modelled on the SRA's sample assessment questions.

For those readers who are students at the University of Law, the Study Manual is used alongside other learning resources and the University's assessment bank to best prepare students not only for the SQE1 assessments, but also for a future life in professional legal practice.

We hope that you find the Study Manual supportive of your preparation for SQE1 and we wish you every success.

The legal principles and rules contained within this Manual are stated as at 1 May 2024.

Author acknowledgments
We would like to thank Russell Binch, the previous author, for his considerable work in the writing of this book.

Contents

Preface		v
Table of Cases		xv
Table of Statutes		xvii

Introduction			1
	SQE1 syllabus		1
	Learning outcomes		1
	A.	What is equity?	2
	B.	Maxims of equity	2
	C.	Ownership of property	2
	D.	What is a trust?	3
	E.	Who is involved?	4
	F.	Trust property and how it is owned	4
	G.	Why use a trust?	7
	H.	Classification of trusts	8
		H.1 Express trusts	8
		H.2 Implied trusts	8
	I.	When trusts can be created	9
		I.1 Lifetime trusts (inter vivos trusts)	9
		I.2 Will trusts	10
		I.3 The residuary estate	10
		I.4 The statutory next-of-kin	11
	J.	Scope of this manual	11

PART 1	**CREATION OF TRUSTS**		13
Chapter 1	**Express Trusts: Declaration of Trust**		15
	SQE1 syllabus		15
	Learning outcomes		15
	1.1	Introduction	16
	1.2	Fixed interest trusts and discretionary trusts	16
		1.2.1 Fixed interest trusts	16
		1.2.2 Discretionary trusts	17
	1.3	The three certainties	17
		1.3.1 Certainty of intention	18
		1.3.2 Certainty of subject-matter	19
		1.3.3 Certainty of objects	21

	1.4	The beneficiary principle		24
	1.5	Perpetuities		24
		1.5.1	Remoteness of vesting	24
	1.6	Formalities relating to the declaration of trust		24
	1.7	Summary flowchart		26
	Summary			27
	Sample questions			27
Chapter 2	**Express Trusts: Constitution of Trusts**			**31**
	SQE1 syllabus			31
	Learning outcomes			31
	2.1	Introduction		32
	2.2	Settlor declares themselves to be trustee		32
	2.3	Settlor appoints a third party to be trustee		32
		2.3.1	Land	33
		2.3.2	Shares	33
		2.3.3	Money	34
		2.3.4	Chattels	34
	2.4	Equity will not assist a volunteer		34
	2.5	Exceptions to the maxim 'equity will not assist a volunteer'		35
		2.5.1	The 'every effort' test	35
		2.5.2	The rule in *Strong v Bird*	36
	2.6	Settlor declares themselves and third party to be trustees		37
	2.7	Summary flowchart		38
	Summary			39
	Sample questions			39
Chapter 3	**Beneficial Entitlement**			**43**
	SQE1 syllabus			43
	Learning outcomes			43
	3.1	Introduction		44
	3.2	Capital and income		44
	3.3	Fixed interest trusts: vested, contingent and successive interests		45
		3.3.1	Vested interests	45
		3.3.2	Contingent interests	46
		3.3.3	Successive interests	46
	3.4	Discretionary trusts		47
	3.5	The rule in *Saunders v Vautier*		48
		3.5.1	Bare trusts	48
		3.5.2	The extended rule of *Saunders v Vautier*	49

		3.6	Summary table and flowchart	51
		Summary		52
		Sample questions		52
Chapter 4		**Charitable and Non-Charitable Purpose Trusts**		**55**
		SQE1 syllabus		55
		Learning outcomes		55
		4.1	Introduction	56
		4.2	Purpose trusts	56
		4.3	Validity rules for the declaration of trust	57
		4.4	The beneficiary principle	57
		4.5	Rule against perpetuities	58
		4.6	Charitable trusts	58
			4.6.1 Charitable purposes	59
			4.6.2 Public benefit	59
			4.6.3 Exclusively charitable	61
			4.6.4 Summary of charitable trusts	63
		4.7	Valid non-charitable purpose trusts	63
			4.7.1 *Re Denley* trusts	63
			4.7.2 Trusts of imperfect obligation	64
		4.8	Summary flowchart	65
		Summary		66
		Sample questions		66
Chapter 5		**Resulting Trusts**		**69**
		SQE1 syllabus		69
		Learning outcomes		69
		5.1	Introduction	70
		5.2	Presumptions of resulting trust and advancement	70
			5.2.1 Presumption of resulting trust	70
			5.2.2 Presumption of advancement	73
			5.2.3 Rebutting the presumptions	74
			5.2.4 Summary flowchart	75
		5.3	Resulting trusts when the beneficial interest is not completely disposed	75
		5.4	Do any formalities attach to a resulting trust?	77
		Summary		77
		Sample questions		78

Contents

Chapter 6	Trusts of the Family Home		81
	SQE1 syllabus		81
	Learning outcomes		81
	6.1	Introduction	82
	6.2	Ownership of the family home	82
		6.2.1 Joint ownership	82
		6.2.2 Sole ownership	83
		6.2.3 Regimes dealing with separating couples	83
	6.3	Express trusts of the family home	83
	6.4	Resulting trusts of the family home	84
	6.5	Common intention constructive trusts of the family home	84
		6.5.1 Home is jointly owned	84
		6.5.2 Home is solely owned	85
		6.5.3 Summary flowchart	89
	6.6	Proprietary estoppel	89
		6.6.1 Stage 1: Establishing the equity	90
		6.6.2 Stage 2: Satisfying the equity (remedies)	91
		6.6.3 Summary flowchart	92
	Summary		93
	Sample questions		93
PART 2	ADMINISTRATION OF TRUSTS		97
Chapter 7	Trustees: Appointment, Removal and Retirement		99
	SQE1 syllabus		99
	Learning outcomes		99
	7.1	Introduction	100
	7.2	Who can be a trustee	100
	7.3	Minimum and maximum number of trustees	100
	7.4	Appointment, removal and retirement of trustees by express power	100
	7.5	Retirement of trustees	101
	7.6	Removal of trustees	102
	7.7	Appointment of additional trustees	103
	7.8	Death of a trustee	104
	7.9	Appointment of an attorney	104
	Summary		104
	Sample questions		105

Chapter 8 — Trustee Powers: Maintenance and Advancement — 109

SQE1 syllabus — 109

Learning outcomes — 109

8.1 Introduction — 110

8.2 Express powers in the declaration of trust — 110

8.3 Power to apply income for beneficiaries who are minors — 110

8.4 Duty to pay income to certain beneficiaries — 112

8.5 Power to pay capital to or for beneficiaries — 112

8.6 Summary flowchart — 115

Summary — 116

Sample questions — 116

Chapter 9 — Trustees' Duties When Running a Trust — 119

SQE1 syllabus — 119

Learning outcomes — 119

9.1 Introduction — 120

9.2 Differences between powers and duties — 120

9.3 Express provisions in the declaration of trust — 121

9.4 Duty of care — 121

9.5 Duties when starting out as trustee — 121

9.6 Duty to act impartially between beneficiaries — 122

9.7 Duty to act personally and unanimously — 122

9.8 Duty to exercise discretions properly — 123

9.9 Reasons for the exercise of a power — 124

9.10 Disclosure of information — 124

9.11 Summary flowchart — 125

Summary — 125

Sample questions — 126

Chapter 10 — Trustee Duties: Investment — 129

SQE1 syllabus — 129

Learning outcomes — 129

10.1 Introduction — 130

10.2 Investments, objectives and strategy — 131

    10.2.1 Objectives — 131

    10.2.2 Investment types — 132

10.3 Express provisions in the declaration of trust — 133

10.4 Authorised investments — 133

xi

10.5	Duties when purchasing investments		134
	10.5.1	Statutory duties	134
	10.5.2	Non-statutory duties	136
10.6	Delegation		136
10.7	Summary flowchart		138
Summary			139
Sample questions			139

Chapter 11 Fiduciary Duties — 143

SQE1 syllabus			143
Learning outcomes			143
11.1	Introduction		144
11.2	Who can be a fiduciary		144
11.3	The core fiduciary duty		144
11.4	When trustees can make a personal profit		145
11.5	Breaches of fiduciary duty		146
	11.5.1	Self-dealing	146
	11.5.2	Competition with the trust	147
	11.5.3	Remuneration of trustees	147
	11.5.4	Incidental profits: commission	148
	11.5.5	Incidental profits: director's salary	148
	11.5.6	Use of information or opportunity	149
11.6	Remedies		150
11.7	Summary flowchart		151
Summary			151
Sample questions			152

PART 3 BREACH OF TRUSTS AND EQUITABLE REMEDIES — 155

Chapter 12 Remedies Against Trustees: Personal Claims — 157

SQE1 syllabus		157
Learning outcomes		157
12.1	Introduction	158
12.2	Personal claims	158
12.3	Breach of trust	159
12.4	Which trustees can be the subject-matter of a personal claim?	160
12.5	Causation	160
12.6	The value of the personal claim	161

	12.7	Defences	162
		12.7.1 Exemption clauses	162
		12.7.2 Knowledge and consent of the beneficiaries	162
		12.7.3 Section 61 of the Trustee Act 1925	162
		12.7.4 Limitation and laches	163
	12.8	Indemnity and contribution	163
		12.8.1 Equitable indemnity	164
		12.8.2 Contribution	164
	12.9	Summary flowchart	165
	Summary		166
	Sample questions		166
Chapter 13	**Remedies Against Trustees: Proprietary Claims**		**171**
	SQE1 syllabus		171
	Learning outcomes		171
	13.1	Introduction	172
	13.2	Proprietary claims	172
	13.3	Trustee holds original trust property	173
	13.4	Trustee holds substitute property	173
	13.5	Trustee mixes trust property with other property	174
		13.5.1 Mixed asset (trust + trustee funds)	174
		13.5.2 Withdrawals from a mixed bank account (trust + trustee funds)	175
		13.5.3 Mixed asset (trust + trust funds)	180
		13.5.4 Withdrawals from a mixed bank account (trust + trust funds)	181
		13.5.5 Withdrawals from a mixed bank account (trust + trust + trustee funds)	183
	13.6	Proprietary claims against other fiduciaries	185
	Summary		185
	Sample questions		186
Chapter 14	**Remedies Against Third Parties**		**189**
	SQE1 syllabus		189
	Learning outcomes		189
	14.1	Introduction	190
	14.2	Third party claims	190
	14.3	Intermeddling	192
	14.4	Equitable personal recipient liability (knowing receipt)	192
	14.5	Equitable proprietary claims	194
		14.5.1 Wrongdoing tracing rules	195
		14.5.2 Innocent tracing rules	196

14.6	Equitable personal accessory liability (dishonest assistance)	197
14.7	Claims arising out of a breach of fiduciary duty	199
14.8	Summary flowchart	200
Summary		201
Sample questions		201

Appendix 1 Equitable Remedies	205
Appendix 2 Charitable Purposes	209
Glossary	213
Index	215

Table of Cases

A	Ali v Khan [2002] EWCA Civ 974	71

B	Bank of Credit and Commerce International (Overseas) Ltd v Akindele [2000] 4 All ER 221	193
	Barlow Clowes International Ltd (in liquidation) v Vaughan [1992] 4 All ER 22	182–5, 196, 200
	Barlow's Will Trusts, Re [1979] 1 WLR 278	21
	Bartlett v Barclays Bank Trust Co Ltd [1980] 2 WLR 430	136
	Boardman v Phipps [1967] 2 AC 46	149–50
	Boyce v Boyce (1849) 16 Sim 476	22
	Bray v Ford [1896] AC 44	145
	Bristol and West Building Society v Mothew [1998] Ch 1	144–5

C	Choithram (T) International SA v Pagarani [2001] 1 WLR 1	37
	Clayton's Case (1816) 1 Mer 572	181–5, 187, 196, 200, 203
	Coulthurst, Re [1951] Ch 661	59

D	Denley's Trust Deed, Re [1969] 1 Ch 373	63–5
	Diplock, Re [1948] Ch 465	197, 200
	District Auditor, ex p West Yorkshire Metropolitan CC [1986] RVR 24	23

F	Foskett v McKeown [2001] 1 AC 102	177, 179

G	Gill v Thind [2023] EWCA Civ 1276	24
	Gilmour v Coats [1949] AC 426	60
	Grant v Edwards [1986] 1 Ch 638	86

H	Hallett's Estate, Re (1880) 13 Ch D 696	175–9, 183–6, 195, 200
	Hodkin v Registrar General of Births, Deaths and Marriages [2013] UKSC 77	59
	Hooper, Re [1932] 1 Ch 38	65
	Hudson v Hathway [2022] EWCA Civ 1648	25, 86, 87
	Hunter v Moss [1994] 1 WLR 452	20

I	Independent Schools Council v Charity Commission [2012] Ch 214	61
	IRC v Baddeley [1955] AC 572	60–1

K	Knight v Knight (1840) 3 Beav 77	17

Table of Cases

L	Le Foe v Le Foe [2002] 1 FCR 107	87
	Lloyds Bank plc v Rosset [1991] 1 AC 107	86
	London Wine Co (Shippers), Re [1986] PCC 121	20
	Lyell v Kennedy (No 4) (1889) 14 App Cas 437	192
M	Macadam, Re [1946] Ch 73	149
	Manisty's Settlement, Re [1974] Ch 17	24
	McGovern v Attorney General [1982] Ch 321	61
	McPhail v Doulton [1971] AC 424	23
N	Nestle v National Westminster Bank plc [1993] 1 WLR 1260	161
	Neville Estates v Madden [1962] Ch 832	60
O	Oatway, Re [1903] 2 Ch 356	178–9, 183–6, 195–6, 200
	Oppenheim v Tobacco Securities Trust Co Ltd [1951] AC 297	60
P	Palmer v Simmonds (1854) 2 Drew 221	20
	Paul v Constance [1977] 1 WLR 527	18
	Pauling's Settlement Trusts, Re [1964] 1 Ch 303	113
	Pennington v Waine [2002] EWCA Civ 227	36
R	Roscoe v Winder [1915] 1 Ch 62	179–80
	Royal Brunei Airlines v Tan [1995] 2 AC 378	198
S	Saunders v Vautier (1841) 4 Beav 115	43, 48, 53, 76, 117–18
	Schulman v Hewson [2002] EWHC 855 (Ch)	163
	Shaw, Re [1957] 1 WLR 51	57
	Speight v Gaunt (1883) 9 App Cas 1	121
	Strong v Bird (1874) LR 18 Eq 315	36–7, 39–40
T	Taylor Fashions Ltd v Liverpool Victoria Trustees Co Ltd [1982] QB 133	89
	Twinsectra Ltd v Yardley [2002] UKHL 12	198
W	Warren v Gurney [1944] 2 All ER 472	74
	Watts v Storey (1983) 134 NLJ 631	90
	Williams v Barton [1927] 2 Ch 9	148

Table of Statutes

A	Administration of Estates Act 1925	11

C	Charities Act 2011	
	s 3(1)	59, 62, 66, 68
	Civil Liability (Contribution) Act 1978	167, 168, 188
	s 1	164
	Companies Act 2006	144

E	Equality Act 2010	
	s 199	74

L	Law of Property Act 1925	
	s 52	33
	s 53(1)(b)	25–7, 30, 33, 38, 57, 65, 77, 83, 94
	s 53(2)	77, 84
	s 60(3)	71, 80
	Law of Property (Miscellaneous Provisions) Act 1989	
	s 1	33
	Limitation Act 1980	166
	s 21	163

M	Matrimonial Causes Act 1973	83, 87

S	Stock Transfer Act 1963	
	Sch 1	34

T	Trustee Act 1925	110, 140
	s 18	104
	s 25	104, 107, 123
	s 31	111, 112, 117, 118, 162
	s 32	112, 114–17, 118, 126, 141, 168
	s 36	101, 102, 103
	s 36(1)	101–3, 106
	s 36(6)	103
	s 39	101
	s 40	101, 102, 103
	s 41	102, 103
	s 61	162, 163, 164, 165, 168

Table of Statutes

Trustee Act 2000	136, 140, 147, 153, 159, 163, 167
s 1	135
s 3	133, 141
s 4	134
s 5	135
s 8	133–4, 141
s 23	137
s 31	148
Trusts of Land and Appointment of Trustees Act 1996	101
s 19	102, 103, 105–6

W

Wills Act 1837	10, 24

Introduction

A.	What is equity?	2
B.	Maxims of equity	2
C.	Ownership of property	2
D.	What is a trust?	3
E.	Who is involved?	4
F.	Trust property and how it is owned	4
G.	Why use a trust?	7
H.	Classification of trusts	8
I.	When trusts can be created	9
J.	Scope of this manual	11

SQE1 syllabus

This section introduces you to some of the key concepts and people involved in trusts. A good working knowledge of these matters will enable you to achieve the SQE1 assessment specification in relation to functioning legal knowledge as it relates to trusts.

Learning outcomes

By the end of this introduction you will be able to:

- understand the fundamental structure of a trust;
- recognise the importance of a trust; and
- understand the widespread use of trusts and the people involved.

A. What is equity?

Historically, equity was a distinct system of English law that was developed and administered separately from the common law. The purpose of equity was primarily twofold:

- To mitigate the rigours of the common law. The rules of the common law were sometimes applied universally and inflexibly, which could result in injustice and unfairness in certain cases. Equity would be called on in such cases to do justice between the parties. It would often do so by focusing on the consciences of the parties – was one party seeking to engage in conduct that was unconscionable or unfair?

- To provide the victim of a wrong with more options for redress. Generally speaking, the only remedy available at common law was damages. Equity developed new remedies to better protect the innocent party. Such remedies are available at the discretion of the court and usually only awarded when damages would be inadequate. A number of these equitable remedies are covered in other **University of Law SQE1 Manuals**, but a brief overview can be found in **Appendix 1**.

Equity and the common law are now administered by all courts, but equity conceptually remains a distinct body of rules and principles, whose role is largely to achieve the two purposes set out above.

The most important and well-known invention of equity is the trust.

B. Maxims of equity

In cases and textbooks, you will frequently see references to the 'maxims of equity'. These maxims are statements that embody the core principles of equity, eg:

(a) 'He who comes to equity must come with clean hands'. This refers to the fundamental idea of doing justice between the parties and examining the conscience of the parties. Put simply, if the claimant has done something untoward, they may not be granted a remedy in equity. It would be contrary to the principles of justice and fairness if a wrongdoer could benefit from a remedy granted by equity.

(b) Another important maxim that we will consider in more detail in this manual is that 'equity will not assist a volunteer'. We will address this maxim in **Chapter 2**.

C. Ownership of property

'Property' encompasses all sorts of things. It can include money, shares in companies, land and personal possessions, such as jewellery, paintings and furniture. Most of the property you own – such as your smartphone, clothes, jewellery etc – you own outright.

When someone is the outright owner of property, they have both the legal and equitable ownership in the property. This means that the property is entirely theirs and they can do what they like with it.

⭐ Example

Andrew owns shares in McDowell Properties Limited. The company regularly declares a dividend on these shares. Andrew no longer needs this revenue stream, so decides to gift the shares to his adult daughter, Bea.

Andrew is the absolute owner of the shares and can do what he wants with those shares, including gifting them to someone else. Once Andrew complies with the relevant formalities relating to the gifting of shares, Andrew will no longer have any interest in the shares. Bea will become the new absolute owner. An important consequence of this is that the company will now pay any dividends to Bea.

However, it is possible for one person to hold the legal interest in property and someone else to hold the equitable interest in property. This is where the concept of the trust arises.

 Example

Charlotte also owns shares in McDowell Properties Limited. As with Andrew, she no longer has any financial need for the dividends declared on the shares but would like future dividends to be used to pay for her granddaughter's education. Her granddaughter, Danielle, is aged 12 years. Charlotte thinks Danielle might to be too young to own shares absolutely. Charlotte therefore asks her solicitor, Elliot, to hold those shares for the benefit of Danielle.

In this situation, Elliot appears to the outside world to be the absolute owner. He will be the registered owner of the shares and the dividends will be paid to him. However, an absolute owner can do what they want with the property they own, and clearly Elliot cannot in this situation – he must hold the shares for the benefit of Danielle. He must use the dividends to pay for Danielle's education. He must also ensure that the shares continue to produce a dividend stream that can pay for Danielle's education and, if this is not the case (eg because McDowell Properties Limited is not doing very well), he must sell the shares and purchase some other form of property that will do so.

In this situation, we say that Charlotte has created a trust. Elliot, as the trustee, must hold property for the benefit of Danielle, who we call the beneficiary. Elliot is the legal owner of the shares, but Danielle is the equitable or beneficial owner of the shares.

There is both legal and equitable ownership in any property (the terms 'equitable ownership' and 'beneficial ownership' generally mean the same thing and will be used interchangeably in this manual).

Where someone is an absolute owner, they have both the legal and equitable ownership, and so can do what they like with the property. In these cases, the equitable interest has no legal or practical significance.

However, the equitable interest *does* become significant where the legal and equitable ownership is in separate hands, because in this situation, both parties have rights in the property.

D. What is a trust?

At its most simple, a trust is an arrangement where a trustee holds property for the benefit of another.

Broken down, a trust involves:

- a duty imposed on (a) trustee(s);
- to deal with property over which the trustee has control;
- for the benefit of beneficiaries who can enforce the duty.

The creation of a lifetime trust is often represented by the diagram in **Figure Intro.1**.

Figure Intro.1 A lifetime trust

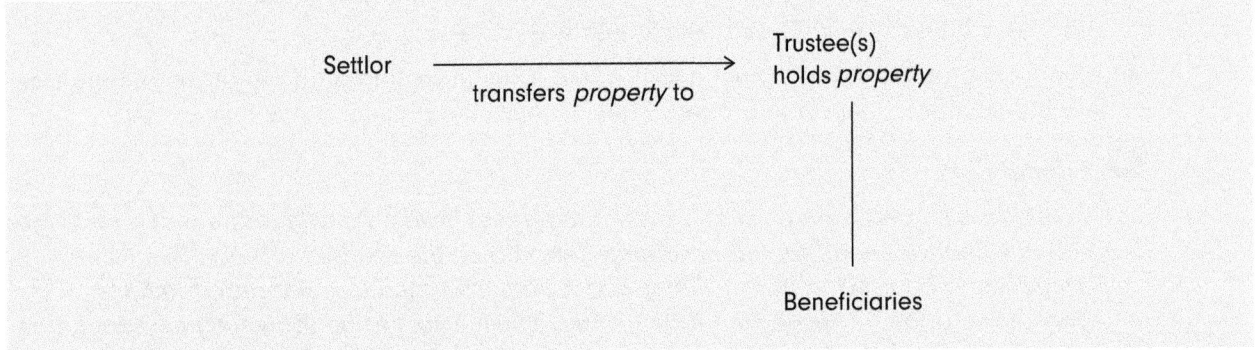

The settlor (the person who creates a trust) can either select a third party to be a trustee or they can select themselves to be a trustee.

 Example

Fiona says to her nephew, Garry, that from now on she is holding her shares in McDowell Properties Limited for him. She has created a trust where she is the trustee and Garry is the beneficiary.

E. Who is involved?

The following people are involved in a trust:

- Settlor – the person who creates a trust. The settlor selects the trustees, beneficiaries and the property that will initially be held in the trust, and lays down the terms of the trust (essentially, an instruction manual that trustees must then follow). The terms of the trust are often referred to as the declaration of trust, which, if put in writing, is also known as the trust deed or trust document. Once the settlor has set out the terms of the trust, they must ensure that the trustee gets legal title to the trust property. When this has all happened, the trust is complete and the settlor is no longer involved in the trust (unless they become a trustee or beneficiary, but note that in these situations, the settlor is no longer involved in the trust *as the settlor*).
- Trustee(s) – the person or people chosen to hold the trust property for the benefit of the beneficiaries. The trustee *must* follow the terms of the trust laid down by the settlor and manage trust property until such time as the beneficiaries become entitled to it.
- Beneficiaries – the people who will ultimately benefit from the trust and the property being managed by the trustee.

F. Trust property and how it is owned

The property held on trust can be almost anything and will often be a mixture of things, eg a house, company shares, cash, IP rights etc. The property held on trust is referred to as either the 'trust property', 'trust fund' or 'trust capital' (these terms will be used interchangeably in this manual).

When a trust is created, the ownership of the property held on trust automatically splits up:

- legal title goes to the trustee; and
- equitable or beneficial title goes to the beneficiary.

For instance, see **Figure Intro.2**.

This splitting up of equitable from legal title is important to the way a trust works.

It can be seen from **Table Intro.1** that the trustee is essentially the owner of trust property in name only. The real value of the trust lies in the equitable title that belongs to the beneficiary.

Figure Intro.2 Title to trust property

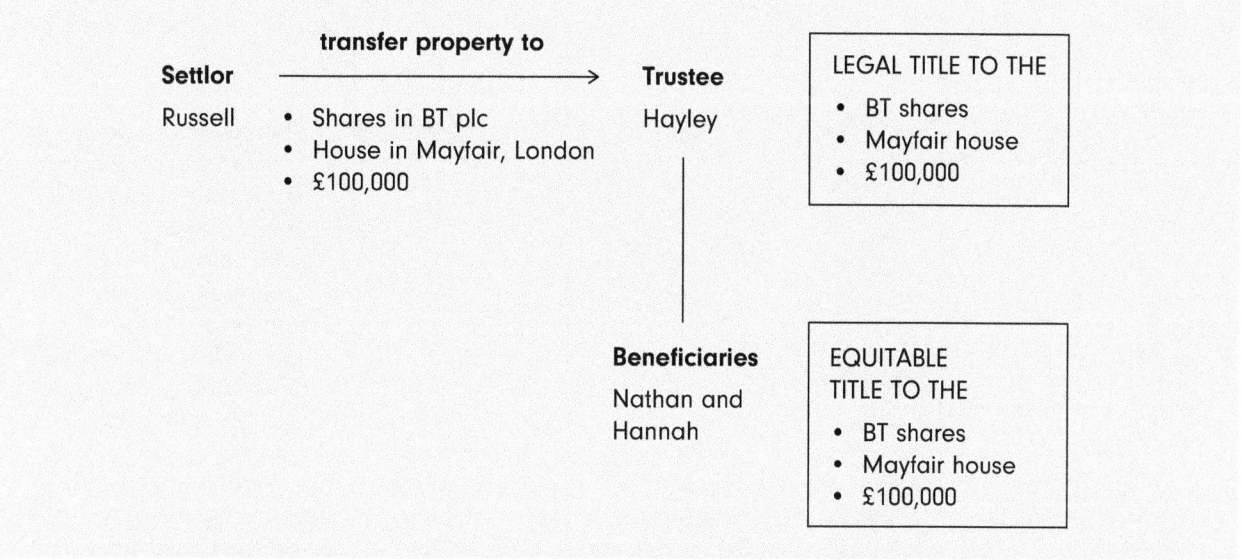

Table Intro.1 Characteristics of legal and equitable title

Legal title (held by trustee)		Equitable title (held by beneficiary)	
Characteristics	**Which means**	**Characteristics**	**Which means**
Looks like the absolute owner	As far as the outside world is concerned, the trustee owns the trust property, eg: • A bank account held on trust will be in the name of the trustee, to whom the bank will send bank statements. • Shares in a company will be registered in the name of the trustee, to whom information about the company will be sent. This gives the trustee the power to manage trust property.	Carries all the benefits of the trust property	The trust fund ultimately belongs to the beneficiaries. The beneficiary is therefore entitled to all the benefits of the trust without having to worry about the responsibility of managing the trust. As a result, they have a *proprietary* (or ownership) right in the trust fund itself. They also have a *personal* right to enforce the trustees' duties and seek compensation for any breach of trust.

5

Legal title (held by trustee)		Equitable title (held by beneficiary)	
Characteristics	**Which means**	**Characteristics**	**Which means**
Responsible for managing the property	The trustee must manage the property for the beneficiary.	Can be enforced against third parties	As the trust fund belongs to the beneficiaries, they can assert their proprietary rights against third parties, eg: • If a trustee goes bankrupt, the trust fund is not shared out amongst the trustees' creditors, but is preserved for the beneficiaries. • If the trustee wrongly gives trust property to someone who is not a beneficiary, the rightful beneficiaries can recover that property back.
Subject to onerous duties	To stop the trustee from misusing trust property, equity imposes very onerous duties on them, eg: • They must invest the trust fund with the aim of growing its value for the beneficiaries, but avoid unreasonable and speculative investments. • They must distribute the trust fund in accordance with the terms set down in the declaration of trust. • They must make good any loss in value of the trust fund caused by any breach of duty.	Can be sold or given away	Given that beneficiaries have a proprietary (or ownership) right, they can sell or gift their interests in the trust property, in the same way that any property owner can sell or give their property away.

One of the trustees' main duties is to look after the trust fund until the beneficiaries become entitled to it. However, this does not mean that they must just safeguard the property. If I own £10,000 absolutely and have no immediate need for that money, I would not just put it in my bank's current account. The value of money (and all property) is constantly being eroded by inflation. £10,000 today might only be worth around £7,500 in 10 years' time. Rather than locking my money away in a current account, I would probably think of investing it – buying some kind of property (eg shares, bonds or real estate) that might increase in value quicker than inflation.

Trustees are under a similar duty to consider investing and growing the trust fund for the benefit of the beneficiaries. As a result, at regular intervals trustees must consider whether to sell existing elements of the trust fund and purchase other forms of property that might be better suited for the beneficiaries. If the trustees are holding property for a long period, they may decide to purchase riskier forms of investments that are more likely to grow in value over time, whereas trustees who are holding property for a short period may decide not to gamble and instead purchase safer forms of investments to retain the value of the trust fund for the beneficiaries.

The form of property in the trust may therefore change over the duration of the trust and, once the trust finishes, the property held on trust might be very different from the property that was initially put in the trust by the settlor. Nevertheless, whatever form that property takes at a particular time, it will always be referred to generically as the 'trust property', 'trust fund' or 'trust capital'.

G. Why use a trust?

Trusts are commonly distinguished from gifts.

The owner of property decides that they want to give that property away – perhaps because they are already wealthy, and the property would be better used by a less fortunate friend or family member; perhaps because they are looking to reduce their inheritance tax bill upon death. If they were to gift that property to someone else, that property would completely belong to that third party, and the person who made the gift (called the 'donor') would have no control whatsoever over the property. That might be fine in some instances, but what if the person who receives the gift is too young, immature, vulnerable or unwell to make decisions about the property? What if the current property owner wants to give property to another, but wants to do something more sophisticated than the 'all-or-nothing' nature of a gift?

Trusts are more versatile and sophisticated than gifts. A trust ensures that property is controlled and managed by a trustee. The trustee is under a duty to maintain, and potentially increase, the value of the property held on trust for the benefit of beneficiaries. They will therefore make decisions in the best interests of beneficiaries who might be too young, immature, vulnerable or unwell to make those decisions themselves. In addition, the settlor can set down the *terms* on which the trustees hold trust property. These terms can allow the trustees to drip-feed money early to beneficiaries if the need arises or allow the settlor to delay the entitlement of beneficiaries or impose conditions on their entitlement.

⭐ *Example*

Harry wants to give £50,000 to look after his nephew, Ian, and to pay for his education. Ian is aged 10 years. Rather than give Ian the money now, Harry would be better advised to create a trust over the £50,000.

Harry also wants Ian to attend university and is concerned that if Ian gets the money when aged 18 years, Ian might decide not to go. So Harry decides that Ian should only become entitled to the trust property at the later age of 25 years. Ian's entitlement therefore is contingent (conditional) on him reaching the age of 25 years.

However, Harry is happy that some of the money be used now for Ian's education. He can therefore direct that the trustees can use the trust fund for Ian's benefit before he reaches the age of 25 years, such as to pay school and university tuition fees.

Trusts arise in a wide variety of different situations and solicitors come across them when working in a number of different practice areas:

- Private client – trusts are an important vehicle that allow people of all means to plan for the future (often referred to as 'estate planning').
- Land – houses that are owned by more than one person are owned in a trust arrangement.
- Charities – many charities are organised as trusts.
- Pensions – pension schemes are often established using trusts.
- Investments – many sophisticated investments take the form of trusts (such as unit trusts, which enable different people to invest in the same pool of assets by purchasing units in, or making a contribution to, investments).

Trusts are a vital legal tool whenever the management of property needs to be split up from the enjoyment of that property.

H. Classification of trusts

Trusts come in a variety of shapes and sizes but can be classified as follows.

H.1 Express trusts

These are trusts that the settlor *expressly* intends to create.

An initial distinction to make is between express trusts that will directly benefit individuals and express trusts that are designed to achieve a purpose.

H.1.1 Express trusts that benefit individuals

Here, the settlor creates a trust and directs that the trustees must (ultimately) distribute trust property to individuals. There are various examples of such trusts – including bare trusts, contingent interest, life interest and discretionary trusts – and we will consider these in more detail in **Chapters 1** and **3**.

H.1.2 Express trusts to achieve a purpose

The other main form of express trust is where a settlor leaves property on trust to achieve a purpose or attain an objective, such as putting money on trust to be used to build a gymnasium or putting money on trust to improve educational standards in a particular town. We will address whether such trusts are valid in **Chapter 4**.

H.2 Implied trusts

Trusts can arise even though there has been no express intention on the part of the settlor to set one up. Such trusts are *implied* – they come into existence because the law says they should.

There are two main types of implied trusts:

(a) resulting trusts; and

(b) constructive trusts.

H.2.1 Resulting trusts

A resulting trust is implied in situations where it is presumed that the settlor would have intended such a trust, if they had thought about it.

⭐ *Example*

Robert creates an express trust for such of Susan and Tia who reach the age of 30 years, and if both of them do, in equal shares. He appoints his brother to be the trustee.

If Susan dies aged 26 years, then her interest fails because she has failed to satisfy the contingency – as she did not reach the age of 30 years, she is not entitled to a share of the trust fund. The entire trust fund will then be held for Tia.

But what happens if Tia dies aged 24 years? This would mean that her interest would also fail, as she has not satisfied the relevant condition. So, neither Susan nor Tia would be able to take any share of Robert's trust.

In this situation, a resulting trust would arise. The brother would hold the trust fund for Robert. A resulting trust arises because, in the absence of any further information, equity presumes that Robert would want the property back. The resulting trust allows this to happen. We shall consider these types of trusts in more detail in **Chapter 5**.

H.2.2 Constructive trusts

A constructive trust is implied in order to achieve a fair result between the parties involved. It is often used where it would be unfair to allow the legal owner to have full enjoyment of the property they hold.

⭐ *Example*

Ulrich and Vivienne (an unmarried couple) decide to live together. They each contribute equally both to the initial deposit and to subsequent mortgage payments. However, the house is put in Ulrich's sole name.

No trust is expressly set up in Vivienne's favour. However, it would be unfair to give Ulrich sole rights over the house, bearing in mind Vivienne's contributions.

In these circumstances, equity would give Vivienne an equitable interest in the house. A constructive trust is imposed such that Ulrich has to hold the house on trust for himself and Vivienne. We shall consider these kinds of trusts in more detail in **Chapter 6**.

Figure Intro.3 provides an overview of these trust classifications.

Figure Intro.3 The 'family tree' of trusts

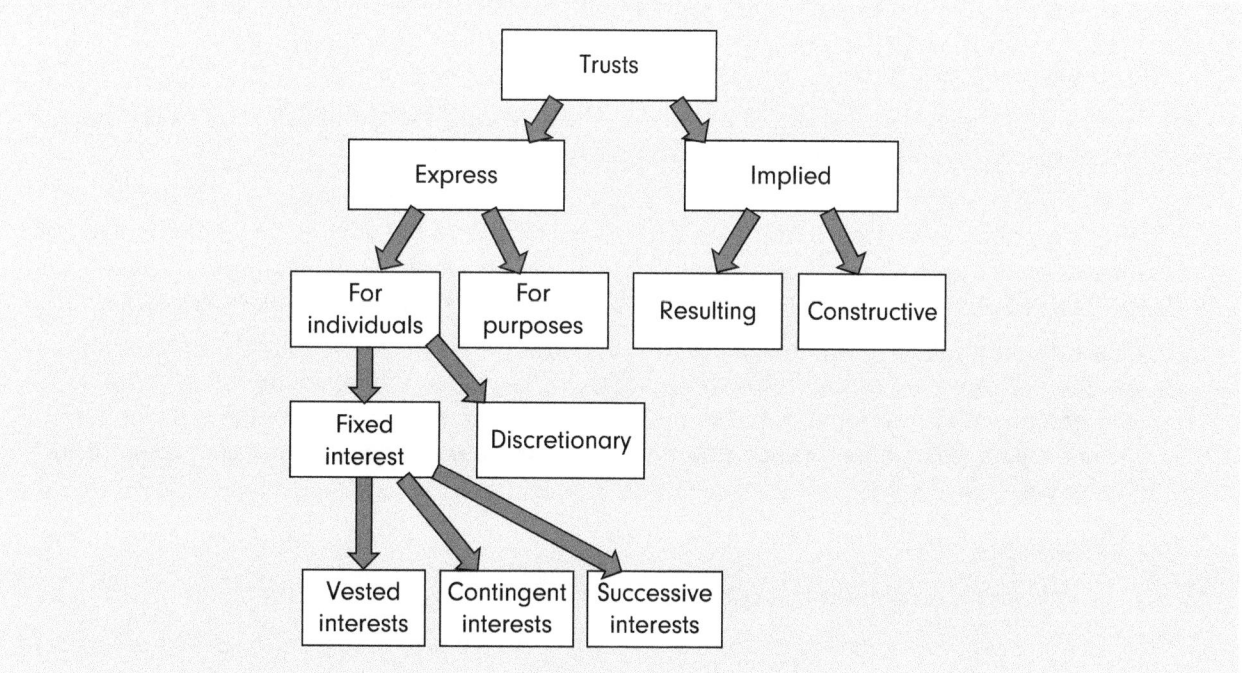

I. When trusts can be created

A trust can be created to take effect either:

(a) during the settlor's lifetime; or

(b) on their death in their will.

I.1 Lifetime trusts (inter vivos trusts)

A settlor can create a trust to take effect during their lifetime. In order to create a valid lifetime trust, the settlor must:

(a) make a valid declaration of trust. We shall consider this in more detail in **Chapter 1**; and

(b) ensure that property is put into the trust. Where the settlor appoints someone else to be the trustee, the settlor must ensure that trust property is transferred to the trustee. If a settlor creates a trust with themselves as trustee ('I shall hold my house in London on trust for my son'), once the settlor has made a valid declaration of trust, the settlor does not need to take any further steps – the trust property is already in the hands of the trustee (the settlor has converted themselves into a trustee by virtue of their valid declaration of trust). We shall consider this in more detail in **Chapter 2**.

When both steps are complete, we say that the trust has been 'constituted'.

1.2 Will trusts

A person can create a trust to take effect on their death. We call this person the 'testator' (if male) or 'testatrix' (if female).

In order to create a valid will trust, the testator/testatrix must:

(a) make a valid declaration of trust in a will that complies with the provisions of the Wills Act 1837. These provisions are considered in more detail in the **Wills and the Administration of Estates Manual** and are not considered further here; and

(b) direct (in a valid will) that title to the trust property will be put in the hands of the trustee.

1.3 The residuary estate

Whilst wills are considered in more detail in the **Wills and the Administration of Estates Manual**, one important concept will be briefly addressed here.

If a settlor attempts to create a lifetime trust, but something goes wrong, we have seen above that the equitable interest under the trust will result back to the settlor. But what if the settlor has already died? Where does the equitable interest go then? If the settlor has made a valid will, the equitable interest will go to the beneficiary of the settlor's residuary estate.

The residuary estate (or the residue of a will) is what remains of the settlor's property on death after payment of debts, tax and all specific legacies. The 'residuary beneficiary' is the person who is named to take the residuary estate under the terms of the will. The term 'residuary estate' can be misleading, as often it can be the largest parcel of property given under the will.

★ Example

William's will contains the following provisions:

- *'I give my paintings to Yasmin' – this is a legacy or bequest. It is a gift of property in a will.*

- *'I give £5,000 to Anita' – this is a pecuniary legacy, a gift of money.*

- *'I give all the rest of my estate whatsoever and wheresoever not otherwise disposed of by this my will to my husband, Bernard' – this is a gift of the residuary estate. Bernard is the residuary beneficiary.*

If a settlor attempts to create a lifetime trust, but something goes wrong and the settlor has already died, the equitable interest results back to the settlor's residuary estate and will belong to the residuary beneficiary.

★ Example

William created a trust over £100,000 for the benefit of Caitlyn should she reach the age of 25 years, appointing David as trustee. William died a year later. Caitlyn died shortly after at the age of 22 years.

As Caitlyn failed to satisfy the contingency in the trust, her interest fails.

That interest would ordinarily result back to William as the settlor. However, as William has died, the equitable interest forms part of his residuary estate and is now owned by Bernard as the residuary beneficiary. Bernard can now require David to transfer the trust property over to him.

Likewise, if a testator attempts to create a will trust, but something goes wrong, the trust property will belong to the residuary beneficiary.

I.4 The statutory next-of-kin

If a settlor attempts to create a lifetime trust, but something goes wrong and the settlor dies without leaving a will, the equitable interest will go to the settlor's statutory next-of-kin under the rules of intestacy. These rules determine who inherits property if someone dies without leaving a will.

⭐ *Example*

William created a trust over £100,000 for the benefit of Caitlyn should she reach the age of 25 years, appointing David as trustee. William died a year later without leaving a will (it is therefore said that William 'died intestate'). Caitlyn died shortly after at the age of 22 years.

As Caitlyn failed to satisfy the contingency in the trust, her interest fails.

*That interest would ordinarily result back to William as the settlor. However, as William has died, the equitable interest will go to his statutory next-of-kin as determined by the Administration of Estates Act 1925 (see the **Wills and the Administration of Estates Manual** for more information).*

J. Scope of this manual

This manual will follow the lifecycle of a trust by focusing on the three key stages when lawyers are involved:

- The creation of a trust
- Running the trust
- Resolving disputes relating to trusts

This will enable you to achieve the SQE1 assessment specification in relation to functioning legal knowledge as it relates to trusts.

The law of trusts has its own special vocabulary. To ensure that you feel confident in using this vocabulary, the manual has a glossary of key terms at the back.

PART 1
CREATION
OF TRUSTS

1 Express Trusts: Declaration of Trust

1.1	Introduction	16
1.2	Fixed interest trusts and discretionary trusts	16
1.3	The three certainties	17
1.4	The beneficiary principle	24
1.5	Perpetuities	24
1.6	Formalities relating to the declaration of trust	24
1.7	Summary flowchart	26

SQE1 syllabus

This chapter will enable you to achieve the SQE1 assessment specification in relation to functioning legal knowledge concerned with the following core principles:

- The creation and requirements of express trusts
- The three certainties of intention, subject-matter and objects
- Fixed interest trusts and discretionary trusts
- Formalities to create express inter vivos trusts

Note that for SQE1, candidates are not usually required to recall specific case names or cite statutory or regulatory authorities. Cases are provided for illustrative purposes only.

Learning outcomes

By the end of this chapter you will be able to apply relevant core legal principles and rules appropriately and effectively, at the level of a competent newly qualified solicitor in practice, to realistic client-based and ethical problems and situations in the following areas:

- identifying declarations of trust;
- establishing the three certainties;
- distinguishing between fixed interest trusts and discretionary trusts and knowing which tests for certainty of objects apply to which trusts;
- understanding perpetuity rules relevant to trusts that will benefit individuals;
- establishing whether the declaration of trust must be in writing; and
- advising on what might happen if the relevant rules are not followed.

1.1 Introduction

An express trust is a trust that the settlor expressly intends to create.

To be enforceable, a settlor must

(a) make a valid declaration of trust. We will look at declarations of trust in this chapter;

(b) put assets in the trust (or, to put it more accurately, put title to the property to be held in trust into the hands of the trustee, so that the trustee can manage that property going forwards, see **Chapter 2**).

A declaration of trust is essentially the instruction manual on how the trustees should run the trust and who will ultimately benefit from the trust. A valid declaration of trust must therefore (amongst other things):

(a) identify the trustees;

(b) identify the property that is to be held in trust;

(c) identify the beneficiaries (this can be done by name or by description); and

(d) identify the powers and duties that the trustees have in running the trust and administering trust property (although as we shall see in **Chapters 8** to **10** the general law sets out a number of default trustee powers and duties that will apply in the absence of any express provision in the declaration of trust).

As we shall see, the instructions given to the trustees must be sufficiently certain and clear so that the trustees know how to carry out their duties and know who ultimately will get what from the trust.

This chapter will therefore look at:

- the rules that dictate how much certainty and clarity the trustees need from a declaration of trust;
- what happens if that certainty and clarity is not provided; and
- whether the declaration of trust must be in writing or whether an oral declaration will suffice.

This chapter will focus on trusts where the beneficiaries are individuals. It is possible in certain circumstances to create trusts to promote a purpose or achieve an objective. These 'purpose trusts' will be considered in more detail in **Chapter 4**.

1.2 Fixed interest trusts and discretionary trusts

Before we consider the rules concerning the validity of declarations of trust, we must first make a distinction between two common types of express trust.

1.2.1 Fixed interest trusts

Under a fixed interest trust, the trustees have no discretion as to how the trust property is to be distributed between the beneficiaries. The settlor has stipulated once and for all who the beneficiaries are and the proportions in which they will share the trust property.

⭐ *Examples*

(a) *'I give my house Blackacres to my Trustees to hold on trust for my sister, Rachael'*

This is a fixed interest trust as I (the settlor) have fixed who the beneficiary is (Rachael) and what she will receive (Blackacres).

(b) *'I give £500,000 to my Trustees to hold on trust for my children in equal shares'*

This is a fixed interest trust as I have fixed who the beneficiaries are (my children) and what they will receive (each will get an equal share of the trust fund). Note that I do not need to identify the beneficiaries by name – identifying them as a group of individuals will be enough so long as that group can be identified with sufficient certainty. We refer to a group of beneficiaries as 'a class'.

(c) *'I give £500,000 to my Trustees to hold on trust for my children'*

This is a fixed interest trust. When a declaration of trust is silent on the shares that beneficiaries will take, it is presumed that they will share equally.

(d) *'I give £500,000 to my Trustees to hold on trust for such of my children that reach the age of 25 years – if more than one, in equal shares'*

This is a fixed interest trust. Again, I have fixed who the beneficiaries are and what they will receive. I have also introduced a condition, namely that each child will only get a share of the trust fund if they reach the age of 25 years (if they die before that age, they will have no entitlement to the trust).

1.2.2 Discretionary trusts

A discretionary trust gives the trustees a discretion as to the amounts any person may receive and/or whether particular people receive anything at all.

 Example

'I give my Trustees £500,000 to hold on trust for such of my children and in such shares as my Trustees think fit'

This is a discretionary trust because my trustees can choose which of my children will benefit from the trust fund and how much they will get.

In the above example, note that I (the settlor) have stipulated upfront the class of people who might benefit. The trustees cannot choose to benefit someone who falls outside the class, ie they could not choose to benefit someone who was not a child of mine. However, I have not fixed which of my children will get what – I have left that decision to my trustees.

Discretionary trusts can be useful in situations when it will be a while before anyone will benefit from the trust fund. In the above example, I might have four children all under the age of 8 years. I know I want them to be looked after when they grow up, but I do not know what their needs will be. Some of the children may require more assistance than others. A discretionary trust allows the trustees to respond to changes in circumstances when the time comes for the distribution of trust property.

1.3 The three certainties

A declaration of trust is only valid if there is sufficient certainty. The declaration of trust must satisfy three certainties (set out in *Knight v Knight* (1840) 3 Beav 77):

(a) certainty of intention (also known as certainty of words): it must be clear that the person making the declaration intended to create a trust;

(b) certainty of subject-matter: it must be clear what property is being held on trust and also what the individual interests of beneficiaries are (ie it must be clear how that property will be shared); and

(c) certainty of objects: it must be clear who the beneficiaries are.

These certainties are equally relevant to lifetime trusts and will trusts. For convenience, in this section, we shall refer to the person creating the trust as the settlor, but the same rules apply when thinking about a testator creating trusts in their will.

1.3.1 Certainty of intention

Someone who owns property might part with that property for different reasons. For instance, they might intend a gift, they might be transferring the property under a contract, or they might intend to put the property under trust. We therefore need to know what that person intended before we can say that a trust was validly created.

The essence of this rule requires that the settlor must have used words that impose a *duty* on someone to act as a trustee, ie the words must impose a duty on the trustee to hold property for someone else.

 Examples

(a) Anna writes to Barry, 'I am transferring my cottage in Cornwall to you to hold on trust for Charlotte'. In this example, it is clear that Anna wants to create a trust (she says so).

(b) Gerry says to Hayley, 'I give my collection of Grayson Perry vases to you to distribute a vase to each of my children'. In this example, whilst Gerry has not used the words 'on trust', the words 'to distribute' impose a duty on Hayley – she must hold the vases for someone else, ie the children to whom those vases will be distributed. A trust is therefore intended.

Whilst it is desirable therefore for a person creating a trust to use the word 'trust' to make it clear what they are doing, this is not necessary. All that is required is words (or sometimes even just actions) that impose a duty on someone to hold property for the benefit of someone else.

In Paul v Constance [1977] 1 WLR 527, Mr Constance, who had separated from his wife, began to live with Mrs Paul. Having received compensation for a personal injury, Mr Constance was advised to deposit that money in a bank account in his sole name. Further money representing joint bingo winnings of Mr Constance and Mrs Paul was paid into the account and Mr Constance frequently told Mrs Paul that the 'money is as much yours as mine'. Upon Mr Constance's death, his separated wife claimed that all the monies in the bank account were hers as Mr Constance had not made a will and she was still legally his statutory next-of-kin. However, the court held that it was clear from Mr Constance's words and actions that a trust over the bank account was intended and awarded Mrs Paul a half share of the bank account. Quoting from a leading practitioners' textbook, the court observed that '[n]o particular form of expression is necessary for the creation of a trust, if on the whole it can be gathered that a trust was intended ... A trust may thus be created without using the word "trust", for what the court regards is the substance and effect of the words used'.

1.3.1.1 Precatory words

Precatory words express a wish, hope or expectation. Such words do not create a trust. Obligatory or mandatory wording must be used if the settlor is looking to create a trust.

 Examples

(a) Iesha says to Janet, 'I am giving you my wedding ring in the hope that you will look after it for Katherine'. This does not impose a trust on Janet. There is no duty to look after the ring for someone else, merely an expectation that Janet will do so. As a result, all that Iesha is doing is gifting the ring to Janet, who becomes the absolute owner of the ring.

(b) Lionel says to Mark, 'I give you my collection of Grayson Perry vases trusting that you will give a vase to each of my children'. Notwithstanding that Lionel uses the word 'trusting', this imposes no trust on Mark. All that Lionel is doing is expressing a hope or expectation that Mark will distribute vases to his children. This is precatory wording. As a result, Lionel is taken to have gifted the vases to Mark, who takes those vases absolutely.

1.3.1.2 What if there is no certainty of intention?

As can be seen from the above examples, if someone transfers property to another using precatory wording, then it is likely that that person will be deemed to have made a gift.

If someone transfers property to another and there is no evidence of what they intended (whether through words or conduct), then the law has to rely on various presumptions to work out what should be the correct legal result (see **Chapter 5**).

1.3.2 Certainty of subject-matter

There are two aspects to this certainty:

(a) the trust property must be described with certainty; and

(b) the settlor must define the beneficiaries' interests with certainty.

1.3.2.1 Trust property must be certain

Trust property must be identifiable. If that were not the case, how would trustees know what property they had to hold and manage for the benefit of the beneficiaries?

Firstly, the thing being held on trust must constitute 'property'. As we have seen from the **Introduction**, most things are property. One exception to this, however, is 'future property', ie property that someone does not presently own but which they hope or anticipate will become theirs in the future. A trust can only be validly created over property (or an equitable right in property) that the settlor currently owns.

⭐ *Example*

Nigel says to Oscar, 'I have been told by Aunt Pauline that I am getting £50,000 under the terms of her will. I will hold this amount on trust for you'.

This is not a valid trust. Aunt Pauline is free to change her mind at any time about whether she wants to leave money to Nigel under her will or not. Nigel cannot put on trust something that he does not currently own. The trust therefore fails for lack of subject-matter.

As regards property that the settlor currently owns and wants to put on trust, the settlor must list out in the declaration of trust the individual items of property that will become the initial trust fund.

⭐ *Examples*

(a) A trust deed (a written declaration of trust) defines 'Trust Property' as being such property listed in the annex to the deed. The annex lists the 'Trust Property' as:

- the settlor's shares in BT plc (this is sufficiently certain because in the absence of anything to the contrary, it is assumed that this refers to all the settlor's shares in BT plc);
- the settlor's house in Mayfair, London (this is sufficiently certain assuming the settlor only has one house in Mayfair); and
- £100,000.

This is a sufficiently certain description of the property being held on trust.

(b) *'My Trustees are directed to hold the bulk of my estate on trust for my niece, Hannah'. This is not a valid declaration of trust because there is no way of knowing how big or small 'the bulk' will be, or what it does and does not include (Palmer v Simmonds (1854) 2 Drew 221). By contrast, directing my Trustees in a will that they hold the residue of my estate on trust for my niece Hannah is certain because the 'residue' of my estate can be calculated with certainty – it is that portion of the estate left over once all taxes and debts have been paid and all specific legacies have been made.*

Certainty of subject-matter can be a particular problem with trusts of part of a collection of items, eg 'I will hold some of my silver on trust for my cousin, Laurence'. This is not a valid declaration of trust because there is no way of knowing how much of my silver is being held on trust and how much is still owned outright by myself (which might therefore belong to someone else when I die).

In Re London Wine Co (Shippers) *[1986] PCC 121, a company had stocks of wine that people could purchase but which would remain stored at the company's warehouses. The company said that it held each customer's consignment of wine on trust for that customer. However, the company did not label or separate each customer's consignment from the rest of the stock in its warehouse – all the bottles remained in bulk storage. The company went into financial difficulty and proceedings were started to work out whether the wine belonged to the company (and therefore could be used to pay off its debts) or to the customers under various trusts. Although the company clearly intended to create trusts, the court held that there was insufficient certainty of subject-matter. The crates of wine were not labelled with any customer names, so it was impossible to identify which particular crate of wine was held on trust for which particular customer. All the wine therefore still belonged to the company. The company should have taken steps to physically separate (or label) each customer's consignment of wine from those of other customers.*

This case was distinguished in Hunter v Moss *[1994] 1 WLR 452, where the owner of 950 shares in a company said that he would hold 50 of those shares on trust for another. Whilst it was never made clear which 50 shares were being held on trust, the court held that there was nevertheless sufficient certainty of subject-matter. The 950 shares were all the same type – indistinguishable from each other – and it did not matter therefore which 50 shares were held on trust, so long as there were 50 shares available.*

It would therefore appear that you can create a trust over part of a collection of items, so long as the items in that collection are all identical. This is likely to be true only for intangible property, such as shares (and only then if those shares are truly identical, eg they have the same voting rights and dividend rights attaching to them). Items of tangible property – things that physically exist – might be ostensibly similar to other items but will nevertheless generally retain characteristics that distinguish them from each other. Bottles of wine (even of the same vintage) are not identical to each other and so it is essential for the settlor to specify exactly which ones are intended to be subject to the trust. The best way of achieving this is to segregate (physically separate) intended trust property from other property.

1.3.2.2 The beneficial interests must be certain

The trust will fail if the beneficiaries' shares or interests in the trust fund are not defined with sufficient certainty.

Examples

(a) *'I give £100,000 to my Trustees to hold on trust for my children in equal shares'. The beneficial interests here are certain. Each child will get an equal share in the trust fund.*

(b) *'I give £100,000 to my Trustees to hold on trust for my children'.* The beneficial interests here are also certain. As we have seen, if the declaration of trust is silent about the shares of each beneficiary, it is assumed that those shares are equal.

(c) *'I give £100,000 to my Trustees to hold on trust for such of my children and in such shares as my Trustees think fit'.* The beneficial interests here are again certain. The trustees are under a duty to decide who gets what – the decisions they make will provide the certainty needed.

(d) *'I give £100,000 to my Trustees to distribute generous amounts to each of my nieces and the rest to my sister'.* The phrase 'generous amounts' does not give enough guidance on how much each niece is to get (and how much therefore is left over for the sister). The beneficial interests here are uncertain.

In Boyce v Boyce *(1849) 16 Sim 476, the testator declared that of the two houses held on trust, the trustees should convey one to Maria 'whichever she might think proper to choose' and the other to Charlotte. Maria died before the trust took effect. The court held that Charlotte had no claim. She was entitled to that house which Maria had not chosen, but in the absence of Maria choosing, Charlotte had no entitlement. The trust property was certain – the two houses – but it was unclear who got what. The houses were therefore held on resulting trust for the testator's residuary beneficiary.*

1.3.2.3 What if there is no certainty of subject-matter?

This might result in the following circumstances:

(a) If the settlor intended to create a trust with themselves as trustee, but there is no certainty of trust property, then no trust is created. The settlor will remain the outright owner.

(b) If the settlor transfers property to a third party and declares that that person shall be a trustee over 'some of it' and that a gift is intended over the rest, then no trust is created. The third party will take the entire property absolutely, free from any trust.

(c) If the settlor has appointed a trustee and intended to create a trust for the benefit of individuals but does not specify the interests that those individuals will take, the trustee shall hold the trust fund for the benefit of the settlor under a 'resulting trust' (see **Chapter 5**).

1.3.3 Certainty of objects

The object of the trust is the beneficiary. The beneficiaries need to be identified with sufficient certainty so that the trustees know to whom they should distribute property. If they distribute property to someone who is not a beneficiary, the trustees will be in breach of trust.

There is generally no issue in identifying beneficiaries if those beneficiaries are named individually. Problems might arise, however, if the beneficiaries are described as a class. In this case, there are different certainty of objects tests for fixed interest and discretionary trusts.

1.3.3.1 Fixed interest trusts

The test for certainty of objects in a fixed interest trust is the complete list test. Under this test, it must be possible to draw up a complete list of each and every beneficiary.

Examples

(a) *'I give £500,000 to my Trustees to hold on trust for each of my nephews in equal shares'.* This is a fixed interest trust because I have spelt out who should benefit and in what shares, and the trustees have no discretion. My trustees need to draw up a complete list of my nephews. This is necessary because the amount each nephew will receive depends on how long the list is. If I have only two nephews, each nephew will receive a half share; if I have five nephews, each nephew will receive a fifth share. My trustees need to be able to draw up a complete list of my nephews, which should not be a problem.

(b) *'I give £500,000 to my Trustees to hold on trust for each of my deserving friends in equal shares'. This looks like a fixed interest trust. But can the trustees draw up a complete list of 'my deserving friends'? This trust does not meet the complete list test. The description of beneficiaries is conceptually uncertain. 'Conceptual certainty' requires that the settlor must describe the class using clear concepts – the class must be capable of objective description and definition.*

'Friends' is generally taken not to have an objective, universal definition (Re Barlow's Will Trusts [1979] 1 WLR 278) – does it mean those people I see on a regular basis, those people who I have friended on social media, those people listed in the contacts folder of my smartphone? Different people will have different views. Plus, what do we mean by 'deserving'? People who are in financial need; people who undertake lots of charity work? Different people will have different views.

The trust fails because the trustees have insufficient criteria to know what type of person they are looking for.

(c) *'I hold £500,000 on trust for all employees and ex-employees of Holtam's Hair Heaven Ltd equally'. The company started in 1985 but has no records of who was employed before 2010.*

This looks like a fixed interest trust, but again this trust does not meet the complete list test.

There is no issue this time around with conceptual certainty. The law defines who is an employee, so we have an objective definition that can be used to identify who is an employee (and therefore also an ex-employee). The problem is that we cannot draw up a complete list of beneficiaries because we have no idea of who was employed between 1985 and 2010. This trust fails because of a lack of 'evidential certainty' – we do not have the evidence needed to draw up a complete list.

(d) *'I give £500,000 to my Trustees to hold on trust for each of my grandchildren alive today in equal shares'. Five grandchildren are alive today, but one of them has gone missing.*

This time around there is no problem with uncertainty, whether conceptual ('grandchildren' is a clear concept) or evidential (we know that I have five grandchildren). The fact that it might be difficult or expensive to trace a beneficiary does not make the trust uncertain. My trustees can distribute a one-fifth share to each of the four grandchildren that are around and can then ask the court for guidance on what to do with the remaining one-fifth share if my last grandchild still cannot be located.

Fixed interest trusts therefore must satisfy the complete list test. If the beneficiaries are described as a class of people, in order to satisfy the test, we need:

(a) conceptual certainty – is the description of the class clear and objective? If the language used to describe the class is unclear and lacks precision, then the trust will fail; and

(b) evidential certainty – do we have the evidence to identify all the beneficiaries that will benefit under the fixed interest trust? If we do not have sufficient evidence to identify all the beneficiaries, then the trust will fail.

1.3.3.2 Discretionary trusts

The test for discretionary trusts is different. This is because the trustees do not necessarily have to draw up a complete list of possible beneficiaries before deciding how to exercise their discretion as to whom property should be distributed. What the trustees *do* need to do, however, is to ensure that they are distributing trust property to the right type of people.

> ⭐ *Example*
>
> *I create a trust for such of my cousins and in such shares as my Trustees in their discretion see fit. This is a discretionary trust because it is up to my Trustees to decide which of my cousins will take trust property and in what shares.*
>
> *My Trustees do not need a complete list of my cousins in order to start distributing property. They must identify that a particular individual falls within the class to be benefited (ie are they a cousin of mine) and consider whether distributing property to a particular cousin is appropriate, but they do not need a complete list of cousins for this.*

The certainty of objects test for discretionary trusts is therefore not the complete list test, but instead the 'given postulant' test (sometimes referred to as the 'given individual' test). This test asks: can it be said with certainty whether any given postulant (individual) is or is not a member of the class of objects? For the test to be satisfied, you need conceptual certainty – has the settlor laid down sufficient criteria when describing the class so that it is clear what sort of person will qualify? Evidential certainty is not a prerequisite, and the fact that it might be difficult to prove whether someone does or does not fall within an otherwise clear and objective class will not cause the trust to fail.

Discretionary trusts therefore must satisfy the given postulant test. In order to satisfy the test, we need conceptual certainty – is the description of the class (amongst whom the trustees will exercise their discretion) clear and objective? If the language used to describe the class is unclear and lacks precision (ie the trustees cannot say with certainty what sort of person they are looking for), then the trust will fail.

Administrative unworkability

Even if the class of people who might benefit under a discretionary trust is clear, the trust must also overcome a separate test of administrative workability. A discretionary trust will be administratively unworkable, and therefore invalid, if the class is so hopelessly wide as 'not to form anything like a class' (*McPhail v Doulton* [1971] AC 424). The primary objection seems to be that if the class is too large, the trustees may spend so much time and money thinking about whom to distribute property to that there will be no trust property left to distribute. Another objection might be that as the class is too large to survey, the trustees cannot identify whether distributing property to a particular individual is appropriate (compared to the competing needs of other people), and so cannot distribute property in a rational and sensible way.

> 📖 *In R v District Auditor, ex p West Yorkshire Metropolitan CC [1986] RVR 24, the Council created a discretionary trust of £400,000 for any of the inhabitants of West Yorkshire (about 2.5 million in number). It was held that the trust was invalid because the size of the class was too large, which rendered the trust administratively unworkable.*

There is no defined number of people over which a discretionary trust becomes administratively unworkable. This will be a question of fact in each case – much will depend on the size of the class compared to the size of the trust fund (the greater the trust fund, the greater the size of the class can be before it becomes too wide).

Administrative unworkability is not an issue for fixed trusts.

Capriciousness

Another hurdle that discretionary trusts must overcome is that the trust cannot be capricious. A discretionary trust may be capricious if there is absolutely no rational reason for the trust or absolutely no rational basis on which the trustees can exercise their discretion to distribute trust property (ie the terms of the trust require trustees to 'consider only an accidental conglomeration of persons who have no discernible link with the settlor or any institution'; *Re Manisty's Settlement* [1974] Ch 17). In most cases, this will not be a problem.

1.3.3.3 What if there is no certainty of objects?

If there is no certainty of objects (or, in the case of a discretionary trust, the trust is administratively unworkable or capricious), then there will be a resulting trust in favour of the settlor (see **Chapter 5**).

1.4 The beneficiary principle

In order to be valid, a trust must (subject to exceptions, which we shall consider in **Chapter 4**) be for the benefit of individuals. The express trusts considered in this chapter will automatically satisfy this requirement.

1.5 Perpetuities

Trusts are often used for 'forward-planning', with settlors trying to plan for what might happen many years into the future. English law, however, takes a dim view on people trying to lock away wealth into trusts for excessive periods of time. In a market economy, property must be freely alienable. Where property is held on trust for a long period of time, money does not circulate freely in the economy to the potential disadvantage of us all.

Therefore, the law will only tolerate trusts that last for an acceptable period, and it achieves this by subjecting trusts to rules against perpetuity.

1.5.1 Remoteness of vesting

When dealing with trusts for individuals, the relevant rule against perpetuity is known as the rule against remoteness of vesting. To be a valid trust, the beneficial interests under the trust must vest – ie must become unconditional – within the relevant perpetuity period.

For trusts created on or after 1 April 2010, the perpetuity period is 125 years. As a result, it is unlikely these days that any trust will offend this rule.

1.6 Formalities relating to the declaration of trust

For will trusts to be valid, the declaration of trust must be contained in a will that complies with the Wills Act 1837. In summary, the declaration of trust must be contained in a will that is made in writing and signed by the testator in the joint presence of two witnesses (who must then witness the testator's signature by signing the will in the testator's presence).

For lifetime trusts, most declarations of trust can be made orally, although this is not advised given that the trustees (and possibly the beneficiaries and the court in the case of any future dispute) will want to refer back to that declaration over the duration of the trust.

In the recent case of *Gill v Thind* [2023] EWCA Civ 1276, the Court of Appeal has clarified the difference between a declaration of trust made in a document and one made orally. Both require a two-stage analysis:

Documentary declaration	Oral declaration
If A asserts that B declared a trust in writing: (1) A has to prove that B had signed the document. (Question of fact) (2) A has to show that the document, properly interpreted, constituted a declaration of trust. (Question of law)	If A asserts that B made an oral declaration of trust: (1) A has to prove what B said. (Question of fact) (2) A has to show that this demonstrated an intention to declare a trust. (Question of fact)

According to the Court of Appeal, the key difference between the two scenarios is that evidence of B's subjective intentions and subsequent conduct are admissible for proving an oral declaration of trust (because the question of what was said and what was intended by it are both questions of fact) but inadmissible for proving a documentary declaration of trust. It was also acknowledged that it may not always be possible for the court to establish the exact words used by B, in which case the gist of B's words would be examined to ask whether, on the balance of probabilities, B's words demonstrated an intention to declare a trust.

However, declarations of trust over land must comply with s 53(1)(b) of the Law of Property Act (LPA) 1925. This requires that the declaration of trust must be 'manifested and proved by some writing signed by some person who is able to declare such trust'. This means that the declaration of trust must be evidenced in writing signed by the settlor. If a declaration of trust over land does not comply with this formality, the trust will be unenforceable.

The recent case of *Hudson v Hathway* [2022] EWCA Civ 1648 summarises how this applies to emails:

- An email is a written document.
- If a settlor declares the terms of an express trust over land in an email at the end of which they type out their name, the typing of their name will constitute a signature for these purposes. This is true whether the settlor types out their full name, last name prefixed by some or all of their initials, just their initials, just their first name or a nickname by which they are known.
- If a settlor declares the terms of an express trust over land in an email, that email will be signed where the settlor has previously inserted a signature block into their email settings which is then applied to all outgoing mail. This is particularly true where the settlor has typed a common salutation above that signature block (such as 'yours sincerely' or 'kind regards').
- However, the email address of the settlor, by itself, is not a signature. 'From joe.bloggs@aol.co.uk' is insufficient to comply with s 53(1)(b).

★ *Examples*

(a) Over dinner, Nazma tells her daughter, 'from now on, I am holding this house on trust for you'. The next morning, she writes to her solicitor telling him what she has done.

Nazma has satisfied the formality of s 53(1)(b) of the LPA 1925. Note that the declaration of trust does not need to be set out in writing – the declaration itself can be oral so long as it is subsequently confirmed in writing. Note also that the writing does not need to be in any particular form, so a letter would be sufficient. Note also that the signed, written document does not need to be sent to the beneficiary.

(b) During a telephone call, Rebecca asks Shairah (who agrees) to hold her cottage in Cornwall on trust for her daughter Teila, subject to her reaching the age of 30 years (she is currently aged 21 years). Rebecca then writes to her daughter to advise that she has set up a trust for her benefit with Shairah as trustee over the cottage in Cornwall but omits to mention that Teila will only become entitled to the cottage if she reaches the age of 30 years.

Trusts

The letter does not satisfy the formality of s 53(1)(b) LPA 1925 because the signed writing must contain all the material terms of the trust (who the trustee is, what the trust property is, who the beneficiaries are and what their interests are in the trust fund). By failing to record the contingency that attaches to Teila's interest, Rebecca has failed to sufficiently evidence the declaration of trust in signed writing.

1.7 Summary flowchart

Figure 1.1 Declaration of trust summary flowchart

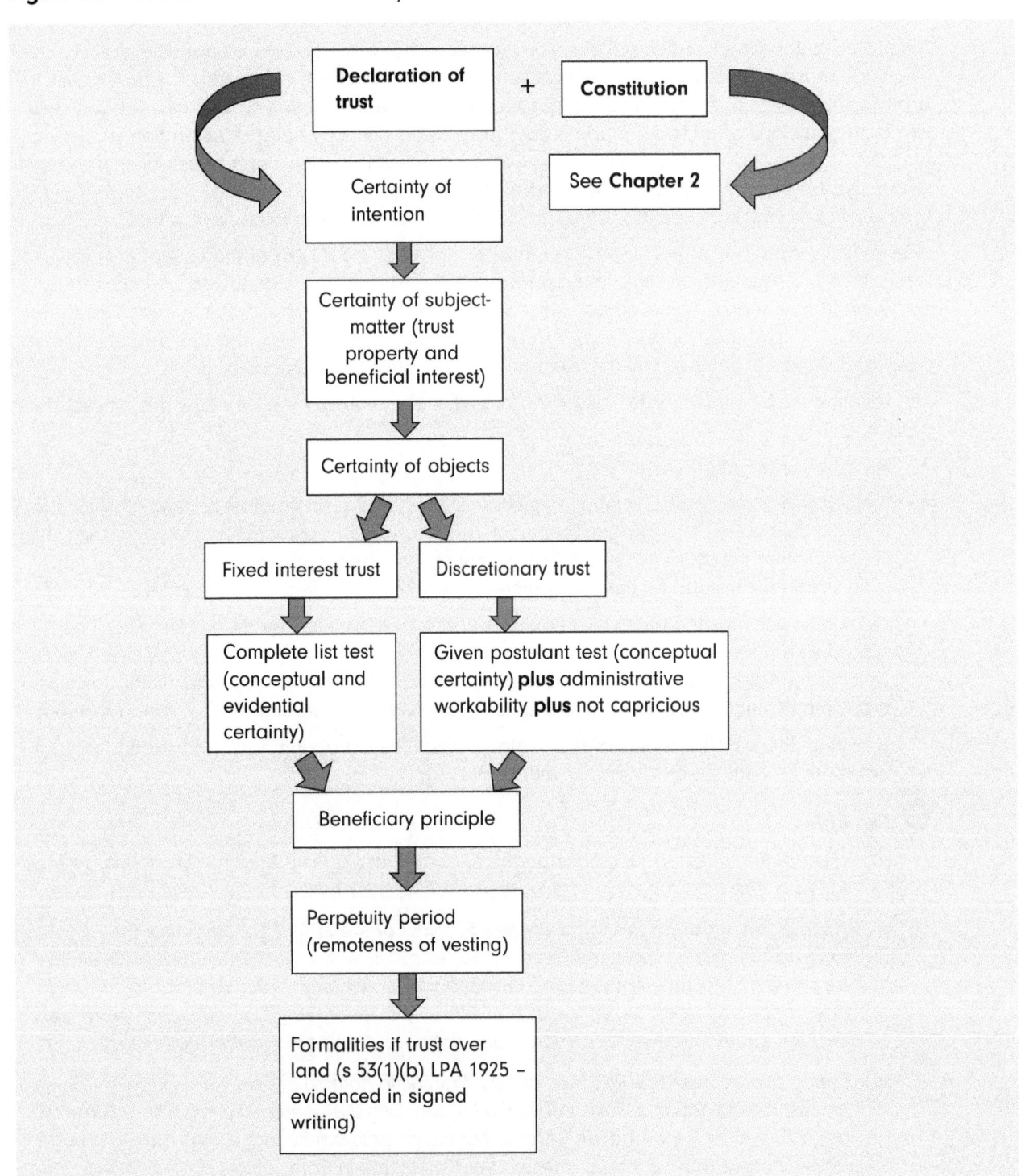

```
Declaration of trust  +  Constitution
                             │
         ┌───────────────────┘
         ▼                    See Chapter 2
Certainty of intention
         │
         ▼
Certainty of subject-matter (trust property and beneficial interest)
         │
         ▼
Certainty of objects
    ┌────┴────┐
    ▼         ▼
Fixed      Discretionary
interest   trust
trust
    │         │
    ▼         ▼
Complete   Given postulant test (conceptual
list test  certainty) plus administrative
(conceptual workability plus not capricious
and
evidential
certainty)
    └────┬────┘
         ▼
Beneficiary principle
         │
         ▼
Perpetuity period (remoteness of vesting)
         │
         ▼
Formalities if trust over land (s 53(1)(b) LPA 1925 – evidenced in signed writing)
```

Express Trusts: Declaration of Trust

Summary

In this chapter you have considered some different types of express trust for individuals (fixed interest trusts and discretionary trusts) and seen that in order to create a valid express trust you need to declare the trust and put assets into it.

You have considered the rules relating to the declaration of trust:

- *The three certainties.* The declaration of trust must satisfy the three certainties:
  - Certainty of intention – is it clear from the settlor's words (or conduct) that a trust was intended?
  - Certainty of subject-matter – is it clear what property will be held on trust and what the beneficial interests / shares in that property will be?
  - Certainty of objects – is it clear who the beneficiaries will be? We have seen that different tests apply depending on whether the settlor is trying to create a fixed interest trust or a discretionary trust.
- *The beneficiary principle.* This principle, which requires that a trust generally benefits individuals, is automatically satisfied for the trusts covered in this chapter.
- *Perpetuity rules.* A trust cannot go on for too long. With trusts for individuals, beneficiaries must have been selected (in the case of a discretionary trust) and/or must have become entitled to trust property (in the case of all trusts) within 125 years of the trust's creation.
- *Formalities.* For a lifetime trust over land, the declaration of trust must be evidenced in signed writing in order to comply with s 53(1)(b) of the LPA 1925. For lifetime trusts over other property, the declaration of trust can be oral, although a settlor who is properly advised should consider recording that declaration of trust in a trust document.

Sample questions

Question 1

Under the terms of a valid will, a woman appointed her son to hold her residuary estate on trust 'for such promising young tennis players living in Wales and in such shares as [my son] thinks fit'. The woman was a past Chair of a tennis club and grew up in Cardiff. Her residuary estate was made up of money held in various UK bank accounts.

The woman's son asks a solicitor whether this trust is valid. The son wants to carry out the woman's wishes as much as possible and has already put together a list of people who he thinks should benefit from the trust.

Is the trust valid?

A   Yes, because the son has identified people he thinks would benefit from it.

B   Yes, because it is not capricious.

C   Yes, because it is contained in a valid will.

D   No, because there is insufficient certainty of subject-matter.

E   No, because there is insufficient certainty of objects.

Trusts

Answer

Option E is correct. The trust is not valid because it lacks certainty of objects. The trust is discretionary and therefore must comply with the given postulant test. This requires that the description of the class of objects be conceptually certain. That is not the case here. For instance, it is unclear what is meant by 'promising' and 'young' (eg does the latter mean people under the age of 16, 18, 21 years or some other age?) The trust therefore fails.

Option A is wrong. Just because the son thinks he knows who might benefit under a trust does not mean that the trust is valid. If the son chooses incorrectly, he will be in breach of trust.

Option B is wrong. Whilst it correctly identifies that the trust is not capricious (there is a discernible link between the woman and the class she wants to benefit), this does not make the trust valid. If the trust is uncertain (as here), the fact that it is not capricious will not save it.

Option C is wrong. Whilst it correctly identifies that the trust is contained in a valid will, this does not make the trust valid. The declaration of trust must satisfy the three certainties (which it does not).

Option D is wrong because a trust over a residuary estate has certain subject-matter. The residuary estate can be calculated with certainty – it is whatever is left over once all debts, taxes and specific legacies have been met. This is not why the trust fails.

Question 2

During his lifetime, an accountant wrote a letter to a teacher, in which he said, 'I have decided to give you my holiday home in Bowness-on-Windermere. I would like you to think about giving this home to your daughter when she reaches the age of 18 years'.

The daughter is now aged 18 years. She has found a copy of the letter and she says that she is entitled to the home in Bowness-on-Windermere. The teacher fell out with his daughter two years ago. The teacher does not want to transfer the home to his daughter.

Must the teacher transfer the home to his daughter?

A Yes, because there was a trust over the home in the daughter's favour and, having reached the age of 18 years, the daughter is now entitled to the home.

B Yes, because the accountant has identified the home and the daughter with sufficient certainty.

C Yes, because the accountant created an express trust in favour of the daughter and that trust was manifested and proved in signed writing.

D No, because what the accountant said in this letter did not amount to a trust in favour of the daughter as there was insufficient certainty of intention.

E No, because the daughter is too young to hold legal title in land.

Answer

Option D is correct. What the accountant says is not sufficient to give rise to a trust, ie there is no certainty of intention. He used precatory wording – 'I would like you to think about ...'. There is no binding obligation on the teacher to give the home to his daughter. When the accountant transferred the home to the teacher, the teacher became the absolute owner of the home.

Option A is wrong. As the accountant's letter did not declare a trust over the home, the age of the daughter is irrelevant.

Option B is wrong. Whilst the accountant did identify the home and the daughter with sufficient certainty, a declaration of trust needs to comply with all three certainties and, in this case, there is no certainty of intention. The daughter therefore has no interest in the home.

Option C is wrong. The accountant's letter did not declare a trust over the home (for the reasons set out above).

Option E is wrong. A person aged 18 years or over can hold a legal estate in land.

Question 3

During a telephone conversation with a friend, a manager asked the friend whether she would look after her flat in Nottingham and transfer that flat to her friend's son when he turned 25 years of age. The son is currently aged 15 years. The friend agreed.

The manager then wrote to a solicitor who was looking after the manager's affairs. The manager advised the solicitor that, going forward, the friend would 'hold my flat in Nottingham on trust'.

Which of the following statements best describes why the trust is not enforceable?

A The trust is not enforceable because during the telephone conversation with the friend, the manager never used the word 'trust'.

B The trust is not enforceable because there is no certainty of subject-matter.

C The trust is not enforceable because the manager cannot delay the son's entitlement to the flat beyond the age of 18 years.

D The trust is not enforceable because the manager must have written to the friend to record that the flat would be transferred to the son.

E The trust is not enforceable because the manager has not set out all the material terms of the trust when writing to the solicitor.

Answer

Option E is correct. The manager is attempting to create a trust over land. She must therefore comply with the requirements of s 53(1)(b) of the LPA 1925, namely that the declaration of trust must be evidenced in signed writing. The letter to the solicitor does not satisfy this formality, as it does not record the material terms of the trust. For instance, it does not identify who the beneficiary is under the trust and when his interest will vest. The trust therefore is unenforceable.

Option A is wrong. Just because the manager did not use the word 'trust' when speaking to the friend does not make the trust unenforceable. It is clear from the wording she used that a trust was intended. The friend had to look after the flat and then distribute it to someone else. This describes the classic role of a trustee.

Option B is wrong. Assuming that the manager has only one flat in Nottingham (and there is nothing to suggest that this is not the case), then there will be sufficient certainty of subject-matter. Objectively speaking, we know what property will be held under trust.

Option C is wrong. The manager can delay the son's entitlement to the flat, so long as she does not offend the rule against remoteness of vesting. Given that the son's interest will vest after 10 years, this is not an issue.

Option D is wrong. Whilst s 53(1)(b) of the LPA 1925 requires that the manager record the material terms of the trust in signed writing, she does not need to send that written record to the friend (although clearly such a course of action would be prudent). Had the letter to the solicitor set out all the material terms of the trust, that would have been sufficient.

2 Express Trusts: Constitution of Trusts

2.1	Introduction	32
2.2	Settlor declares themselves to be trustee	32
2.3	Settlor appoints a third party to be trustee	32
2.4	Equity will not assist a volunteer	34
2.5	Exceptions to the maxim 'equity will not assist a volunteer'	35
2.6	Settlor declares themselves and third party to be trustees	37
2.7	Summary flowchart	38

SQE1 syllabus

This chapter will enable you to achieve the SQE1 assessment specification in relation to functioning legal knowledge concerned with the following core principles:

- Constitution of express inter vivos trusts
- The rule that equity will not assist a volunteer
- Exceptions to the rule that equity will not assist a volunteer

Note that for SQE1, candidates are not usually required to recall specific case names or cite statutory or regulatory authorities. Cases are provided for illustrative purposes only.

Learning outcomes

By the end of this chapter you will be able to apply relevant core legal principles and rules appropriately and effectively, at the level of a competent newly qualified solicitor in practice, to realistic client-based and ethical problems and situations in the following areas:

- identifying which lifetime trusts are constituted by a valid declaration of trust and those which are constituted by a valid declaration of trust *plus* the transfer of assets to the trustees;
- identifying the transfer of legal title in different types of property; and
- advising on what happens if the transfer of legal title is not properly carried out.

2.1 Introduction

For an express trust to be enforceable, the settlor must:

(a) make a valid declaration of trust (see **Chapter 1**); and

(b) put assets into the trust.

Once both steps are complete, the trust is said to be 'constituted'. Once the trust is constituted, the settlor cannot change their mind. If the trust is not constituted (ie the settlor fails to declare themselves trustee or property is not transferred to the intended trustee), no trust exists – the settlor remains the absolute owner of the property.

In general, there are two methods of constituting an express lifetime (or inter vivos) trust:

(a) the settlor appoints themselves trustee for the beneficiary by making a valid declaration of trust. We will briefly deal with this situation first; or

(b) the settlor appoints someone else to be the trustee by making a valid declaration of trust. In this situation, the settlor must also transfer legal title in the trust property to the trustee. We will deal with this situation second.

This chapter will therefore look at:

- the difference between trusts that are constituted by way of a valid declaration of trust and those which are constituted by way of a valid declaration *plus* transfer of property to the trustees;
- how legal title to different types of property is transferred;
- what happens if the settlor does not take all the steps required to transfer legal title; and
- whether a trust can be valid in equity even if the settlor has not taken all the steps required to transfer legal title.

2.2 Settlor declares themselves to be trustee

If the settlor declares themselves trustee, so long as the settlor has complied with the rules in **Chapter 1** concerning the making of a valid declaration of trust, the settlor has done everything necessary to create the trust.

Prior to the declaration of trust, the settlor owned the relevant property absolutely – they held both the legal and equitable title to that property. Following the declaration of trust, the settlor becomes the trustee. The trustee must have legal title to the trust property, but the settlor-trustee already has legal title, so nothing further need take place.

In these circumstances, the trust is constituted once the settlor validly declares themselves to be trustee.

2.3 Settlor appoints a third party to be trustee

If the settlor appoints someone else as trustee, then as well as making a valid declaration of trust, the settlor must take steps to put legal title to the trust property into the hands of that other trustee.

How the settlor does that depends on the type of property that will be held on trust. Different rules for the transfer of legal title apply to different types of property. We shall address some common forms of property:

Express Trusts: Constitution of Trusts

(a) Land
(b) Shares
(c) Money
(d) Chattels

There are other forms of property that can be put in trust. For instance, intellectual property can be put into a trust, but the transfer rules relating to these kinds of property are rather specialised and beyond the scope of this manual.

2.3.1 Land

If land is part of the trust fund, in order to transfer legal title to a third party trustee, the settlor must:

(a) execute a deed (LPA 1925, s 52). A deed is a document that satisfies s 1 of the Law of Property (Miscellaneous Provisions) Act 1989, ie:

  (i) the document is stated to be a deed or is stated to be signed as a deed; and

  (ii) the person making the deed signs the document in the presence of a witness who also signs it.

  Where the land is registered (which most land now is), Form TR1 is used – this satisfies the above definition; and

(b) give the executed deed either to the trustee (who will then pass it on to Land Registry) or send it to Land Registry direct.

Land Registry will then register the trustee as the new legal owner.

Legal title is not transferred until all steps have been completed and the trustee is the new registered proprietor of the land.

⭐ Example

Ursula appoints Vika to be a trustee of her cottage in Exmouth for the benefit of her nephew, Wojciech. Ursula needs to make a valid declaration of trust (which must be evidenced in signed writing in order to comply with LPA 1925, s 53(1)(b)), execute a deed (TR1) naming Vika as the new owner of the cottage, and send that deed to Vika, who will then send that deed to Land Registry for re-registration. Once Land Registry registers Vika as the new legal owner of the cottage, the trust will be constituted and will be enforceable by the beneficiary.

2.3.2 Shares

Legal title in company shares can be transferred either:

(a) within the CREST system – this only applies to certain shares in public quoted companies; or

(b) outside the CREST system – this applies to all other shares, especially shares in private companies.

2.3.2.1 Transferring shares within the CREST system

CREST is a computerised share transfer system. Shares in designated public quoted companies are recorded electronically and those shares can be transferred electronically and instantaneously without the need for paperwork (although note that CREST is voluntary and shareholders can still use the paper-based system set out below). Shares in CREST are generally managed by a stockbroker, so the settlor will need to instruct the stockbroker to make the necessary transfer.

2.3.2.2 Transferring shares outside the CREST system

For all other shares (especially in private companies – those companies whose names end in 'Ltd' or 'Limited'), paperwork is required. The owner of such shares will have a share certificate as evidence of their ownership, and that ownership is confirmed by the name of the owner being entered in the company's register of members.

If private company shares are to be part of the trust fund, in order to transfer legal title to a third party trustee, the settlor must:

(a) execute a stock transfer form – usually the settlor will execute the stock transfer form set out in Sch 1 of the Stock Transfer Act 1963; and

(b) give the executed stock transfer form and relevant share certificate either to the trustee (who will then pass it on to the relevant company) or send it to the company direct.

The company's secretary will then register the trustee as the new shareholder (and therefore the new legal owner) in the register of members.

Legal title is not transferred until all steps have been completed and the trustee is the new registered shareholder.

⭐ Example

William appoints Yuriy to be a trustee of his shares in Jarrett & Co Limited for the benefit of his daughter, Alecia. Having made a valid declaration of trust, William must then execute a stock transfer form naming Yuriy as the transferee of the shares, send that form and the share certificate to Yuriy, who will then send those documents to Jarrett & Co Limited for re-registration. Once the company registers Yuriy as the new legal owner of the shares, the trust will be constituted and will be enforceable by the beneficiary.

2.3.3 Money

Legal title to money generally passes with delivery:

(a) If the settlor hands over cash to a trustee, legal title to the cash passes upon delivery.

(b) If the settlor transfers money electronically from their bank account to the trustee's, legal title to the cash passes once the monies have arrived in the trustee's bank account.

(c) If the settlor hands over a cheque to a trustee, legal title passes once the cheque has cleared. If the settlor dies before then, the cheque can no longer be cashed.

2.3.4 Chattels

Chattels are anything else that is tangible in nature, eg jewellery, furniture, paintings etc. Title to chattels is passed by physical delivery of the asset to the trustee or by deed.

2.4 Equity will not assist a volunteer

A properly advised settlor who wants to create a trust and appoint people other than themselves as trustee will follow the rules for transferring legal title relevant to the property that will be held under trust. But what happens if the settlor does not follow the rules properly and completely?

The general rule is set out in the maxim of equity that 'equity will not assist a volunteer' (also known by the saying 'equity will not perfect an imperfect gift'). A volunteer is someone who has not provided consideration for the transfer of property. Whilst the property is being transferred to the trustee, it is the beneficiary who ultimately will want to enforce the terms of the trust (after all, the trust is being created for their benefit). Most beneficiaries do not pay the settlor to create a trust in their favour. Beneficiaries are therefore usually 'volunteers'.

It follows that the transfer rules cannot be 'bent' or overlooked in order to constitute a trust. If the settlor has not properly followed the transfer rules relevant to the property that was going to be held on trust, there will be no trust – equity cannot help, because equity will not assist a volunteer (the beneficiary).

2.5 Exceptions to the maxim 'equity will not assist a volunteer'

A strict application of the maxim might lead to harsh and unfair results. The settlor might have clearly intended to create a trust, and everyone involved was happy for a trust to be created, but one little formality was overlooked. Over time, therefore, various exceptions to the maxim have been developed. In these cases, equity will get involved and will help to create an enforceable trust.

2.5.1 The 'every effort' test

Where the settlor did everything they could to transfer legal title, the transfer may be regarded as complete in equity even though the transfer of legal title has not yet been completed. In order to take the benefit of this exception it is often said that the settlor must have passed the point of no return or put the property being transferred 'beyond recall'. The settlor must have completed all the steps they were required to take, ie the settlor took steps to properly execute and send out all documents relating to the transfer of the property. All that remains for the transfer to be completed is the act of a third party.

This rule is particularly useful in cases of private company shares and land. As we have seen above, the transfer of legal title to these types of property cannot be finalised without the involvement of a third party.

⭐ Examples

Ben wants to create a trust over his second home in Nottingham with Cassy as trustee and David as beneficiary. He validly declares the trust, executes a deed and gives that deed to Cassy, who sends them to Land Registry. The day after Cassy sends the documentation to Land Registry (but before she is registered as the new proprietor), Ben dies leaving everything to his civil partner, Elliot. There was no full and complete compliance with the transfer rules relating to land during Ben's lifetime – title did not transfer to Cassy because Cassy was not registered as the new proprietor of the house in Nottingham.

However, Ben did everything he could to transfer legal title – in particular, he executed all the documents he needed to and handed those documents on to Cassy. His actions satisfy the every effort test. The trust will be valid in equity, with the result that the house belongs beneficially to David and not to Elliot (who otherwise would have been entitled to the house).

(A good way of testing whether property has been put 'beyond recall' is to ask what has happened to the transfer documents that the settlor must execute. If those documents are still within the possession or control of the settlor, the settlor has not satisfied the every effort test. If those documents are no longer within the possession or the control of the settlor, the test has generally been satisfied.)

What if the settlor does not go far enough to satisfy the every effort test, but clearly did intend to create a trust and took some action to follow through on that intention? In those cases, equity *may* regard the trust as valid once the stage is reached when it would be unconscionable (unfair) for the settlor to back out of creating a trust. This is based on the case of *Pennington v Waine* [2002] EWCA Civ 227. However, this case involved a lifetime gift, and it is unclear how the factors set out in the case might be applied in subsequent cases, particularly in the case of trusts. The possible future application of this case is outside the scope of this manual.

2.5.2 The rule in *Strong v Bird*

When someone dies, people are appointed to administer and distribute their estate:

(a) if the person dies leaving a will, we usually call these people 'executors'; and

(b) if the person dies without a will (ie is 'intestate'), we call these people 'administrators'.

Executors and administrators acquire legal title to all of the assets that comprise the deceased's estate by means of the operation of a grant of representation (they need that legal title to administer, manage and distribute those assets, in the same way that a trustee needs legal title to administer, manage and distribute trust property). The grant of representation is covered in more detail in the **Wills and Administration of Estates Manual**.

If the settlor wanted to create a trust with someone else acting as trustee, but did not get round to transferring legal title during their lifetime, if that same person is then appointed as their executor or administrator, is the fact that that person has got legal title (albeit in a round-about way) sufficient to constitute the trust? Yes, if the conditions in *Strong v Bird* (1874) LR 18 Eq 315 are satisfied:

(a) the settlor intended to create an immediate trust with a third party acting as trustee;

(b) that trust was not immediately created due to a failure to comply with a relevant transfer rule;

(c) the settlor's intention continued up to their death; and

(d) the intended trustee acquired legal title to the trust property by becoming the settlor's executor or administrator.

⭐ Example

Megan, who was ill and unable to leave her house, said to Natalie, 'I want you to hold my wedding ring on trust for my granddaughter, Olivia. I will give you the ring the next time you visit.' Natalie was unable to visit Megan, and a week later, Megan died. In her valid will that she had executed some time earlier, she appointed Natalie as her executor (a female executor is often referred to as an 'executrix') and gave her entire estate to Oxfam.

It is likely that the rule in Strong v Bird *can be used to constitute the intended trust since:*

(a) Megan intended to create an immediate trust with Natalie acting as trustee;

(b) the trust was not immediately created as Megan had not delivered the wedding ring to Natalie (the ring is a chattel and Megan must therefore comply with the relevant transfer rules for chattels);

(c) there is nothing to suggest that Megan changed her mind before she died; and

(d) Natalie acquired legal title by becoming Megan's executrix.

By contrast, *if Megan had made her will two days after she spoke to Natalie and specifically left her wedding ring to her other granddaughter Polly, the rule in* Strong v Bird *could not be used to create a trust for the benefit of Olivia because it is clear that Megan had changed her mind about the wedding ring – she wanted to leave this to Polly rather than put it on trust for Olivia.*

2.6 Settlor declares themselves and third party to be trustees

So far, we have considered trusts where the settlor appoints themselves as trustee and trusts where the settlor appoints other people as trustee. What happens where the settlor appoints themselves *and* someone else to immediately act as trustee (eg 'I appoint myself and Qirat to act as trustees in relation to the Trust Fund')?

In these situations, the settlor must take steps to transfer legal title from their sole name into the joint names of the settlor *and* the other trustees. The settlor must comply with the relevant transfer rules set out above (eg with shares in a private company, I (the settlor) must sign a stock transfer form where I am the named transferor and Qirat and I are the named transferees).

What happens if I make a valid declaration of trust that myself and Qirat will immediately hold shares on trust for someone else, but I do not take any steps to transfer legal title into the joint names of myself and Qirat? In *Choithram (T) International SA v Pagarani* [2001] 1 WLR 1, Lord Browne-Wilkinson observed, 'There can in principle be no distinction between the case where the [settlor] declares himself to be the sole trustee ... and the case where he declares himself to be one of the trustees ... In both cases his conscience is affected and it would be unconscionable and contrary to the principles of equity to allow such a [settlor] to resile from his [trust].' In the absence of special factors, having made a valid declaration, it would be unconscionable for me to back out of the trust. I am one of the trustees. I am no longer free to do as I wish with the property. I cannot deny the existence of the trust. I must therefore give effect to the trust by transferring the trust property into the names of all the trustees (and, if I die before this can be achieved, then my executors/administrators must put the property into the names of the surviving trustees).

⭐ Example

Rabia sent a letter to her brother, Salman, which said 'I am hereby putting my shares in Tea and Cakes Ltd into a trust for Ursula. You and I will be trustees of the shares for her.' Rabia did not sign any documents before she died last week.

Rabia did not comply with the relevant transfer rules for shares in a private company. However, as soon as she validly declared a trust appointing herself and her brother as trustees, she was duty-bound to take the necessary steps to comply with the relevant transfer rules. As a result, the trust will be valid in equity, with the result that the shares will belong beneficially to Ursula.

Trusts

2.7 Summary flowchart

Figure 2.1 Constitution of trusts summary flowchart

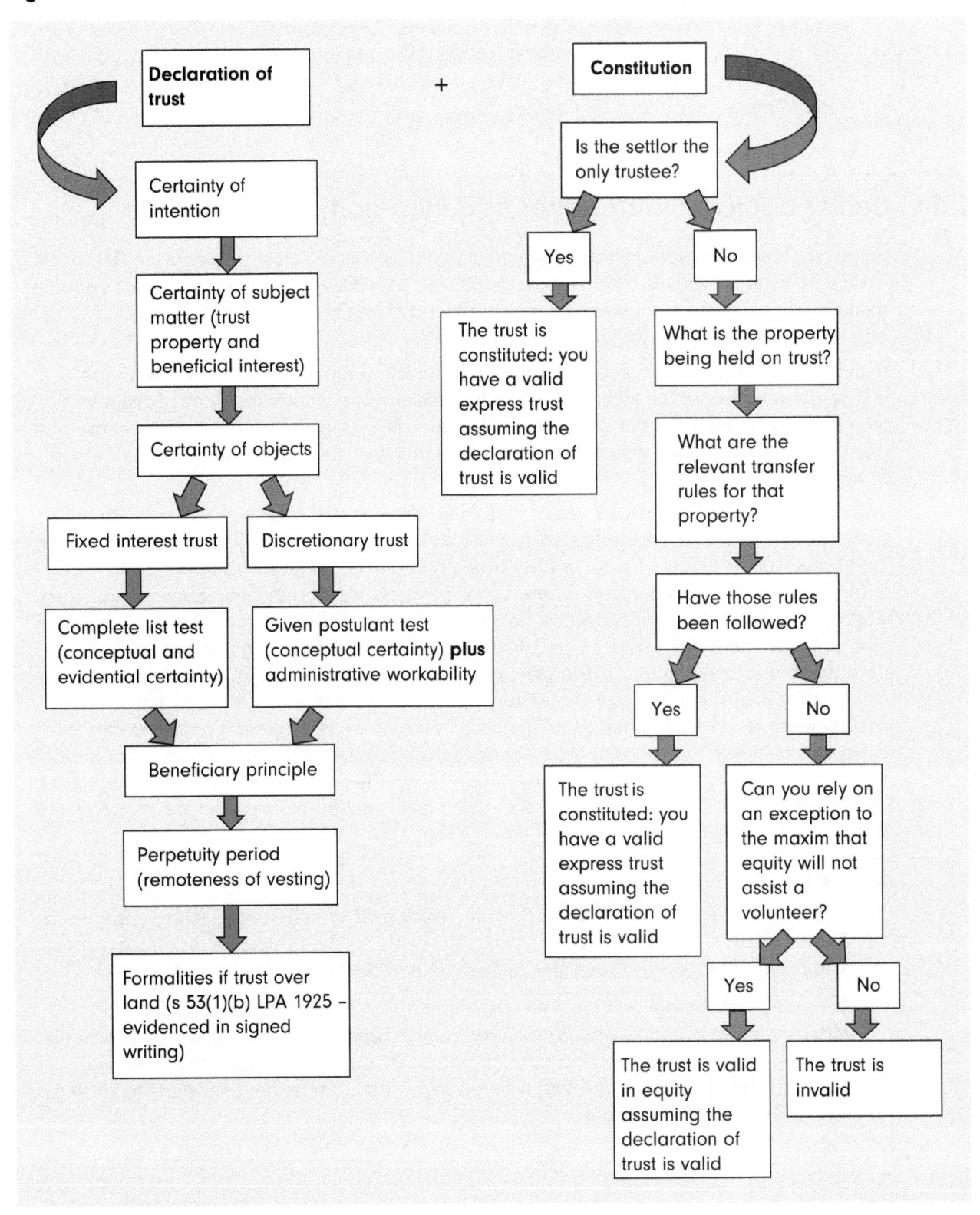

Declaration of trust

- Certainty of intention
- Certainty of subject matter (trust property and beneficial interest)
- Certainty of objects
  - Fixed interest trust → Complete list test (conceptual and evidential certainty)
  - Discretionary trust → Given postulant test (conceptual certainty) **plus** administrative workability
- Beneficiary principle
- Perpetuity period (remoteness of vesting)
- Formalities if trust over land (s 53(1)(b) LPA 1925 – evidenced in signed writing)

+

Constitution

Is the settlor the only trustee?

- **Yes** → The trust is constituted: you have a valid express trust assuming the declaration of trust is valid
- **No** → What is the property being held on trust? → What are the relevant transfer rules for that property? → Have those rules been followed?
  - **Yes** → The trust is constituted: you have a valid express trust assuming the declaration of trust is valid
  - **No** → Can you rely on an exception to the maxim that equity will not assist a volunteer?
    - **Yes** → The trust is valid in equity assuming the declaration of trust is valid
    - **No** → The trust is invalid

Summary

In this chapter you have identified that a trust must be constituted and considered how to constitute an express lifetime trust.

- *Self-declaration as trustee.* Where the settlor declares themselves to be the sole trustee, the trust is constituted so long as the declaration of trust is valid.

- *Appointment of third party trustees.* Where the settlor appoints other people as trustees, the trust is constituted so long as the declaration of trust is valid *and* the intended trust property is put into the hands of the trustees.

- *Transfer rules.* The steps that must be taken to correctly transfer legal title in property from a settlor to a third party trustee(s) differ depending on the type of property that is being transferred.

- *Equity does not assist a volunteer.* If the relevant steps have not been fully complied with, the general result is that the trust will not be validly created and therefore cannot be enforced by the beneficiary (who is usually a volunteer).

- *The exceptions.* There are some exceptions to the general rule where, even though legal title to the trust property has not vested in the name of the trustee, equity will still allow the beneficiary to enforce the terms of the trust.

Sample questions

Question 1

Last month, a woman wrote to a banker as follows, 'You will hold my house in Edale for my nephew, who shall become entitled to the house when he reaches the age of 25 years'. The woman executed a TR1 in favour of the banker.

The woman died two weeks ago. In her will (executed five years ago), she appointed the banker to be her executor. Everything in the will was left to the woman's daughter. When going through the woman's belongings, the banker found the TR1 in the hall sideboard in the woman's home. Land Registry have confirmed that the woman was still the registered proprietor of the house in Edale when she died.

Is the house held on trust for the nephew?

A Yes, because the woman executed a valid TR1 to transfer legal title to the banker.

B Yes, because the woman made every effort to transfer legal title to the banker.

C Yes, because the fact that the banker is the woman's executor in this case constitutes the trust.

D No, because the daughter is the sole beneficiary under the woman's will.

E No, because the woman failed to transfer legal title in the house to the banker while she was alive.

Answer

Option C is correct. The woman tried to create a valid lifetime trust with the banker as the trustee. This would usually require the woman to transfer legal title in the house to the banker while she was alive. However, as an exception to the rule that 'equity will not assist a volunteer', equity can constitute this trust using the rule in *Strong v Bird*. This is because the woman intended to create an immediate trust; that trust was not immediately created due to a failure to comply with a relevant transfer rule; there is nothing to suggest that the woman's intention did not continue up to her death; and the banker acquired legal title to the trust property by becoming the woman's executor.

Option A is wrong. The mere execution of a TR1 is not sufficient by itself to transfer legal title in land.

Option B is wrong. In order to satisfy the every effort test, the woman would have had to put relevant documents beyond recall, ie she would have had to send the TR1 to either the banker or Land Registry. She did neither.

Options D and E correctly set out what the general position should be given that the woman failed to transfer legal title to the house during her lifetime. However, given that the nephew can rely on the rule in *Strong v Bird* to constitute the trust in his favour, neither statement represents the best advice on the facts.

Question 2

An artist writes a letter to her brother saying, 'The two of us shall be trustees over the sum of money in my savings account for your daughter until such time as your daughter marries or turns 30 years of age (whichever is the earliest), when it will become hers'. The brother telephoned the artist to agree. The daughter is aged 21 years.

The artist dies two weeks later. The artist had taken no steps before her death to put the money into a joint bank account in the names of herself and her brother. In her will, the artist named the daughter as the executrix of her estate.

Which of the following statements best describes why the money in the savings account belongs beneficially to the daughter?

A   The money belongs beneficially to the daughter because the letter is a valid declaration of trust and it would be unconscionable for the trust not to take effect.

B   The money belongs beneficially to the daughter because the letter comprises a deed of transfer of that money to the brother, which constitutes the trust.

C   The money belongs beneficially to the daughter because the letter demonstrates that the woman made every effort to constitute the trust.

D   The money belongs beneficially to the daughter because of the rule in *Strong v Bird*.

E   The money belongs beneficially to the daughter because the artist wanted the brother to act as trustee and he is still alive and able to act as trustee.

Answer

Option A is correct. The artist intended to create a trust with herself and her brother as trustees. Ordinarily, the artist in this situation would have had to take whatever steps were required to put the legal title to the money into the joint names of herself and her brother. However, having made a valid declaration of trust, it would have been unconscionable for the artist to back out of constituting the trust. As a result, the trust is valid in equity and the money belongs beneficially to the daughter.

Option B is wrong. The letter is not a deed (as it will not have been witnessed by a third party) and, in any event, is not sufficient to constitute the trust.

Option C is wrong. The letter is not sufficient to satisfy the every effort test. The artist needed to take steps to open a joint account in the name of herself and her brother and transfer the money from her savings account into that joint account. The every effort test generally only applies in cases where land or company shares are being transferred.

Option D is wrong. The fact that the daughter is appointed to be the executrix is irrelevant to the operation of the rule in *Strong v Bird*. In order to constitute a trust using this rule, it is the trustee who must be appointed the executor/executrix, not the beneficiary.

Option E is not the best answer. Had the artist intended to create a trust with just her brother as trustee, the money would not belong beneficially to the daughter even if the brother was still alive and able to act as trustee, because the trust in that case would not be constituted (no steps were taken to transfer the money to the brother). The trust is valid in this case because the artist intended that both herself and her brother would be trustees.

Question 3

Last month, having taken legal advice that he should start to transfer some of his wealth to lower his potential future inheritance tax bill, a man telephoned an ex-colleague to say, 'I would like you to have my shares in Wright Stuff Limited in case you want to give some for such of my friends that stood by me whilst I was having treatment for my cancer and in such shares as you think is right'. Following the call, the man executed a stock transfer form over his Wright Stuff Limited shares and sent this to his ex-colleague together with his share certificate. The ex-colleague forgot to tell the man during the call that she was about to take her children on a long holiday to Florida, so was not around when the documents arrived at her house.

Last week, the man died. In his will, he appointed a solicitor as his executor and left his estate to the ex-colleague. The ex-colleague cut short her holiday to find the documents relating to Wright Stuff Limited on her doormat.

Do the shares belong absolutely to the ex-colleague?

A Yes, because what the man said over the telephone did not satisfy the test for certainty of intention.

B Yes, because although the man wanted to create a trust, he failed to manifest and prove the declaration of trust in signed writing.

C Yes, because although the man correctly declared a trust, he failed to constitute that trust during his lifetime.

D No, because the man satisfied the every effort test and the shares are therefore held on trust.

E No, because the man clearly intended that the ex-colleague hold the shares on trust for other people.

Answer

You will remember that in order to create a valid trust, the settlor needs to take two steps: declare the trust and put assets into trust. This question is designed to test your knowledge about both aspects.

Option A is correct. Objectively speaking, the man intended to gift the shares to the ex-colleague. The rest of the wording – 'in case you want to give some shares' – is precatory wording only and evidences no intention that the ex-colleague should hold the shares on trust for other people. As there was no lifetime trust, the ex-colleague takes the shares absolutely. (It should be noted that there are also problems with other certainties of subject-matter and objects.)

Option B is wrong. If there were a trust, it would be over shares (personalty). In the case of personalty, the declaration of trust does not need to be manifested and proved in signed writing. This requirement only applies to declarations of trust over land.

Option C is wrong. There was no trust to constitute.

Option D is wrong. Whilst this option correctly applies the every effort test, it fails to take into account the fact that the trust cannot be valid due to the imperfect declaration of trust. (Had the declaration of trust been valid, the man would have satisfied the every effort test. The man executed all the documents that were required and put all documents beyond recall by sending them to the ex-colleague. He had done everything he could to transfer legal title to the shares while he was alive.)

Option E is wrong. The man may have hoped that the ex-colleague might distribute shares to other people, but ultimately there was insufficient intention to create a trust over those shares.

3 Beneficial Entitlement

3.1	Introduction	44
3.2	Capital and income	44
3.3	Fixed interest trusts: vested, contingent and successive interests	45
3.4	Discretionary trusts	47
3.5	The rule in *Saunders v Vautier*	48
3.6	Summary table and flowchart	51

SQE1 syllabus

This chapter will enable you to achieve the SQE1 assessment specification in relation to functioning legal knowledge concerned with the following core principles:

- The classification of beneficial entitlement into fixed, discretionary, vested and contingent interests
- The rule in *Saunders v Vautier* (1841) 4 Beav 115

Note that for SQE1, candidates are not usually required to recall specific case names or cite statutory or regulatory authorities. Cases are provided for illustrative purposes only.

Learning outcomes

By the end of this chapter you will be able to apply relevant core legal principles and rules appropriately and effectively, at the level of a competent newly qualified solicitor in practice, to realistic client-based and ethical problems and situations in the following areas:

- distinguishing between fixed, discretionary, vested and contingent interests;
- understanding what happens to the beneficial interest if someone dies before their interest vests; and
- establishing how beneficiaries can bring a trust to an end early and who has to be involved in that decision.

3.1 Introduction

The nature of a beneficiary's entitlement under a trust varies depending on the terms of the trust. It is important to understand the nature of any beneficial interest in order to be able to advise:

(a) whether the beneficiary's interest is unconditional or conditional and liable to fail if the condition is not satisfied;

(b) when the beneficiary will be able to call for trust property; and

(c) to what the beneficiary is entitled.

This chapter looks at:

- some of the more common types of trusts that can be created;
- the different types of beneficial interests that subsist under such trusts; and
- when the beneficiaries can require the trustees to convey trust property to them, and whether that can happen before the date on which the settlor envisaged the trust would end.

3.2 Capital and income

A trust is a sophisticated instrument that can be used to give different people different types of entitlement. Before we look at different types of trusts and the beneficial interests that subsist under them, we should first briefly address a fundamental distinction between capital and income. A settlor can decide that a particular beneficiary should get both capital and income or just one or the other.

Property is often used to make a return. That return can either be a capital return or an income return (see **Table 3.1** for examples):

Table 3.1 Capital and income returns on common forms of property

Property	Capital	Income
A house	Market value of the house	Rent if the house is let
Shares	Market value of the shares	Dividends (a sum of money paid regularly by a company to its shareholders out of its profits)
Bonds (an 'IOU' instrument issued by a corporate or government borrower)	Market value of the bond	Coupon (a regular repayment on the loan plus interest)
Bank account	The balance on the account	Interest paid (if any)
Antique desk	Market value of the antique	N/A

- A capital return relates to the underlying value of the property in question. A capital gain means that the underlying value of the thing you own has gone up over time.
- An income return is money (or a monetary equivalent) received on a regular basis deriving from property. That income return might be generated regardless of whether the underlying property has made a capital gain.

A beneficiary with an interest in capital is often referred to as having an 'absolute' interest. A beneficiary with an interest in income only is often referred to as having a 'limited' interest.

3.3 Fixed interest trusts: vested, contingent and successive interests

We considered the nature of a fixed interest trust in **Chapter 1**. In a fixed interest trust, the settlor has stipulated upfront who will get what. The interests of beneficiaries under a fixed interest trust are *fixed* by the settlor.

However, the settlor can also decide:

(a) whether a beneficiary should have a *present* entitlement to property, or whether that entitlement should be made conditional on (for instance) the beneficiary attaining a certain age; and

(b) whether and when the beneficiary will get the capital and income generated by the trust, or merely one or the other.

In order to understand who gets what, we need to subdivide *fixed* interests into vested, contingent and successive interests.

3.3.1 Vested interests

A beneficiary has a *vested* interest if that beneficiary exists and does not have to satisfy any conditions imposed by the terms of the trust before becoming entitled to trust property. Their interest is unconditional. If the beneficiary dies before the trust property is paid over to them, the trust property will belong to the beneficiary's estate, ie it will pass as part of the beneficiary's property under their will or intestacy.

⭐ Example

'I give my shares in Aviva plc to my Trustees to hold on trust for my son, Warren.'

Warren does not have to satisfy any conditions before he is entitled to the shares. His interest is therefore vested. Furthermore, Warren is entitled to both the trust capital (the shares themselves) and the trust income (all dividends declared on the shares once the trust is effective). His interest is 'absolute'. This is because my declaration of trust contains no instruction to separate out capital from income – if there is no such instruction, it is assumed that the beneficiary is entitled to both.

If Warren dies before the shares are transferred to him, the shares will be given to his estate and will pass to whoever is entitled under his will or intestacy.

If a beneficiary is a minor (ie under the age of 18 years), the trustees will hold the property on trust for the beneficiary until they reach the age of 18 years. Only once the beneficiary is aged 18 years can the transfer of property to them discharge the trustees from the trust (trust lawyers often call this requirement the need to give 'good receipt').

⭐ Example

Warren (my son from the previous example) is aged 8 years. His beneficial entitlement to the shares is vested – he owns the beneficial title in the shares – but the trustees should not transfer the shares to him for at least another 10 years, when he is aged 18 years.

If Warren were to die under the age of 18 years, the money would form part of his personal estate and would pass to whoever inherits under his intestacy (people under the age of 18 years are too young to make a will).

Once a beneficiary turns 18 years, that does not automatically bring a trust to an end. The trustees will continue to hold the property on trust for the beneficiary until the beneficiary requests that the trust property be transferred to them. Until that happens, the trustees will hold the property on a 'bare trust' (we will consider such trusts later in this chapter).

3.3.2 Contingent interests

A beneficiary has a *contingent* interest if it is conditional upon the happening of some future event that may not happen, or if the beneficiary is not yet in existence (eg a trust for grandchildren and the settlor does not yet have any grandchildren but might in the future). Once the beneficiary satisfies the condition, the beneficial interest vests in them and they have a *vested* interest.

If a beneficiary dies before the happening of the stipulated event, their interest will go back to the settlor unless the settlor has provided that the beneficial interest should pass to someone else.

✪ Example

'I give my shares in Aviva plc to my Trustees to hold on trust for my son, Warren, if he attains the age of 25 years, but if not to Cancer Research UK'. Warren is currently aged 21 years.

Warren's interest is subject to him satisfying a future condition, ie reaching the age of 25 years. His interest is therefore currently conditional. The trustees will hold the shares on trust for him until he at least reaches the age of 25 years. Again, Warren has a conditional interest in both the trust capital (the shares themselves) and the trust income (all dividends declared on the shares). This is because my declaration of trust contains no instruction to separate out capital from income.

I have set out what should happen if the condition is not satisfied (ie if Warren dies before he reaches the age of 25 years). Should this happen, the shares will be transferred to Cancer Research UK. If Warren dies after he reaches the age of 25 years but before the shares are transferred to him, given that his interest at that point is vested, *the shares will belong to his estate and will pass to whoever is entitled under his will or intestacy.*

A trust with a contingent interest is still a *fixed* interest trust, because the settlor has stipulated upfront who gets what (and when) and the trustees have no discretion when it comes to the distribution of trust property.

3.3.3 Successive interests

Trusts can be used to distribute property over successive generations. A common example of such a trust is as follows.

✪ Example

'I give my shares in Aviva plc to my Trustees to hold on trust for my wife, Yara, for life, remainder to my son Adam.'

Under this trust, I have instructed my trustees to separate out capital from income:

- *Yara has a vested, limited interest in trust income during her lifetime. We call Yara the 'life tenant' and her interest is known as the 'life interest'. That interest is said to be 'in possession' – she can enjoy trust income now.*

- *Adam has a vested interest in trust capital. We call Adam the 'remainderman' and his interest is said to be 'in remainder'. Adam's interest is not in possession, but postponed. He cannot enjoy his beneficial interest immediately but has to wait until Yara's right to enjoyment expires.*

When Yara dies, the trustees will transfer trust property to Adam (so long as Adam has reached the age of 18 years). Until that time, whilst Adam has a vested beneficial interest from the day the trust comes into existence, he will not ordinarily receive any trust property until Yara dies. Otherwise, if the trustees could transfer property to Adam during Yara's lifetime, there would be less trust property available to generate income, which might prejudice Yara's interests. Adam's vested interest is therefore postponed until Yara's death. (This does not make Adam's interest contingent. An interest becomes contingent only if the settlor makes that interest conditional on a future event that might not happen. This is not the case here – the life tenant's death is a certainty; indeed, it is inherent in the nature of this kind of trust.)

During their life, the life tenant receives income arising from the trust property. Alternatively, a life tenant can have the 'use and enjoyment' of trust property. This is particularly relevant to trusts over land. For instance, if I put a house on trust for my wife for life, remainder to my son, whilst she is alive my wife can choose to live in the house rent free (ie have the 'use and enjoyment' of the trust property).

In the above example, the interest in remainder is vested. This has important consequences should the remainderman die before the life tenant.

⭐ Example

Should Adam die before Yara, his interest in remainder would not fail. Instead, on Yara's death, the trust property would be transferred to Adam's estate and would pass to whoever inherits his property under his will or intestacy.

However, it is equally possible for the settlor to create a *contingent* interest in remainder.

⭐ Examples

'I give my shares in Aviva plc to my Trustees to hold on trust for my wife, Yara, for life, remainder to my son Adam should he reach the age of 25 years.'

In this example, Adam's interest in remainder is contingent on him reaching the age of 25 years.

If Adam is aged 25 years or over when Yara dies, he will be entitled to call for the trust property to be transferred to him (as above).

However, if Adam dies aged 24 years or under, his interest will fail. As I have not set out what should happen in that situation, the interest in remainder will go back to me (as the settlor) on a resulting trust (see **Chapter 5**).

Trusts that create successive interests are often called 'life interest trusts'. Note that they are still examples of a *fixed* interest trust, because the settlor has stipulated upfront who gets what (and when) and the trustees have no discretion when it comes to the distribution of trust property.

3.4 Discretionary trusts

We considered the nature of discretionary trusts in **Chapter 1**. In a discretionary trust, the settlor typically identifies the *class* of people they would like to benefit but leaves it up to the trustees to decide who amongst that class will in fact benefit and in what amount.

Until the trustees exercise their discretion to distribute property to particular members of the class, no individual member of that class has a beneficial entitlement to the trust fund.

Pending the distribution of trust property by the trustees, the individual members of the class are referred to as the 'objects' of the trust as opposed to beneficiaries (to make it clear that they do not yet have any individual proprietary entitlement). If an individual object is selected by a trustee, at that point they have a (usually) vested right in that part of the trust property that the trustee has decided to transfer to them.

⭐ *Example*

'I give the money in my Barclays Bank plc current account to my Trustees to hold on trust for such of my children and in such shares as they in their discretion see fit'. I have three children: Charles, Danielle and Eduard.

This is a discretionary trust. Until such time as my trustees exercise their discretion, each child is merely an object of the trust and does not have an entitlement to the trust property. All they have is just an expectation or a mere hope that they will get something. If my trustees decide to award all the money to Danielle, she will have a vested interest in that money and (assuming she is aged 18 years or over) can require the trustees to transfer that money to her. In that scenario, neither Charles nor Eduard will have any beneficial interest.

It is possible to combine elements of fixed interest trusts and discretionary trusts.

⭐ *Example*

'I give my shares in Kingfisher plc to my Trustees to hold on trust for my wife, Francesca, for life, remainder to such of my children as survive my wife and in such shares as my Trustees in their discretion see fit'.

In this trust:

- *Francesca has a vested right during her lifetime to the dividends (income) declared on my Kingfisher shares.*

- *My children have no current individual beneficial entitlement (vested or contingent) to those shares. Their beneficial entitlement is subject to them being selected by my trustees after Francesca has died.*

3.5 The rule in *Saunders v Vautier*

We have seen above that a sole, adult beneficiary with a vested beneficial interest can require that trust property be conveyed to them by the trustees, thereby bringing the trust to an end. This seems perfectly logical. Such a beneficiary is the sole owner of the equitable title – which is where the real value of a trust lies – and it seems contrary to reason to preclude that beneficiary from becoming the absolute owner of the property if that is what they want. However, this principle, that a beneficiary can in some situations require the trustees to convey trust property and bring the trust to an end, has been extended beyond a single beneficiary.

We will first address the situation with sole beneficiaries.

3.5.1 Bare trusts

A trust for a sole, adult, mentally capable beneficiary that gives the beneficiary a vested interest is called a 'bare trust'. The beneficiary of a bare trust is often said to be 'absolutely entitled'.

A bare trust is an unusual type of trust because the trustees must handle the trust property as the beneficiary dictates. In particular, the beneficiary can bring the trust to an end at any time by requiring the trustees to convey the whole trust fund to the beneficiary or to other trustees.

Bare trusts are quite common in the investment world. A stockbroker for instance commonly holds the portfolio of shares they are managing on a bare trust for their client. This allows them to take quick decisions on buying and selling shares without needing to always go back to the client, but means that the client can call for the shares to be transferred back to them at any time if they want to end their stockbroker's retainer.

Bare trusts may also arise where a beneficiary who previously had a contingent or remainder interest becomes solely and beneficially entitled to the trust property.

⭐ Example

'I give my shares in Aviva plc to my Trustees to hold on trust for my son, Warren, if he attains the age of 25 years, but if not to Cancer Research UK'. Warren is now aged 25 years.

Now that Warren has turned 25 years, his interest is no longer conditional but vested. He is a sole, adult beneficiary with (presumably) mental capacity. The trust is now a bare trust. Warren can tell the trustees to hand the trust fund over to him.

3.5.2 The extended rule of *Saunders v Vautier*

The above principle has been extended to include trusts that have more than one beneficiary. The beneficiaries can end the trust by calling for a transfer of trust property to themselves or other trustees, so long as *all* the beneficiaries under the trust who could possibly become entitled:

(a) are in existence and ascertained;

(b) are aged 18 years or over and have mental capacity; and

(c) agree to what is being proposed.

'All the beneficiaries under the trust who could possibly become entitled' means that, between them, the people who want to bring the trust to an end must be absolutely entitled, ie there is no other person with a potential interest in the trust fund.

⭐ Examples

(a) *'I give my estate to my Trustees to hold on trust for such of my children now living as reach the age of 21 years and if more than one in equal shares.' There are three children: Gregory (aged 24 years), Harriet (aged 22 years) and Iain (aged 20 years).*

The children can collectively compel the trustees to transfer the trust property to themselves and bring the trust to an end.

In this case, Gregory's and Harriet's interests are vested. Iain's interest is still contingent – he has not satisfied the condition of reaching the age of 21 years. If he died tomorrow, his interest would fail, and it would vest in Gregory and Harriet (my trustees have been directed to hold my estate for such of my children as reach the age of 21 years). Between them, Gregory, Harriet and Iain are absolutely entitled – there is no other potential person with an interest in the trust fund. They are all in existence and over the age of 18 years, so as long as they agree how to bring the trust to an end, the trustees must comply with their directions.

(b) *'I give my estate to my Trustees to hold on trust for my husband, Jack, for life remainder to my daughter, Katherine.' Jack is still alive. Katherine is aged 20 years.*

> *Jack and Katherine can collectively compel the trustees to transfer the trust property to them and bring the trust to an end.*
>
> *In this case, both Jack's and Katherine's interests are vested. Between them, they are absolutely entitled – there is no other potential person with an interest in the trust fund. They are both in existence and over the age of 18 years, so as long as they agree how to bring the trust to an end, the trustees must comply with their directions.*

> (c) *Nicola gave £300,000 to trustees to hold on trust for her cousin, Matt, so long as he reached the age of 30 years. Matt is currently aged 25 years. Nicola died intestate a year ago – her statutory next-of-kin is her estranged husband, Oliver.*
>
> *Matt's interest is contingent – he has not yet satisfied the condition of reaching the age of 30 years. If he died tomorrow, his interest would fail. As Nicola did not set out who in those circumstances would take the interest instead, the beneficial interest would come back to Oliver under a resulting trust (the beneficial interest under a resulting trust usually goes back to the settlor, but as Nicola has died, that interest must go to the beneficiary of her will or intestacy, in this case Oliver). We briefly considered resulting trusts in the **Introduction** and will address them in more detail in **Chapter 5**.*
>
> *Matt therefore cannot bring the trust to an early end by himself. If he wants this to happen, he must get the agreement of Oliver. Between them, Matt and Oliver are absolutely entitled (and presumably meet the other criteria listed for this principle to work). Of course, Oliver might refuse or, more likely, might extract a price for this agreement – for instance he might only agree to bring the trust to an end if Matt is willing to give up his future interest to the entire trust fund in exchange for a 50% share now, with Oliver taking the other 50%.*

The final example above illustrates an important, if surprising, element of this principle. If Matt and Oliver agree a 50/50 split of the trust fund, then they have effectively overridden the terms of the original trust. In one of the other examples, I (the settlor) wanted Jack to have trust income for life, with the trust fund then going to Katherine. But if Jack and Katherine agree to cut a deal whereby the trust comes to an end with Jack getting 20% share of the trust fund and Katherine the rest, then that is their choice and the trustees must comply with that choice. This is a consequence of giving beneficiaries a beneficial entitlement to property – the trust property ultimately belongs to the beneficiaries and they should be entitled to choose who gets it.

Just because you have a group of beneficiaries in agreement with each other does not necessarily mean that the trust will end. You need to analyse the beneficial interests closely to see whether all the beneficiaries in that group are, between them, absolutely entitled.

⭐ Examples

> *'I give my estate to my Trustees to hold on trust for such of my children now living who reach the age of 25 years and if more than one in equal shares'. There are three children: Gregory (aged 22 years), Harriet (aged 20 years) and Iain (aged 18 years).*
>
> *Whilst Gregory, Harriet and Iain are all over the age of 18 years, they are not between them absolutely entitled. If they were to all die before the age of 25 years, then the beneficial interest in the estate will go back to me under a resulting trust, or will pass in accordance with the provisions of my will or on intestacy if I am already dead. As a result, there is someone else with a potential interest in the trust fund and their agreement must be sought before the trust can be brought to an end.*

3.6 Summary table and flowchart

Table 3.2 Summary of beneficial interests

Fixed interest trusts		Nature of beneficial interest		Discretionary trust	Nature of beneficial interest	
		Vested	Contingent		Vested	Contingent
	'trust for A'	A		'to such of [a group of individuals] and in such shares as my trustees see fit'	Neither – no individual beneficial interests unless and until trustees exercise discretion	
Contingent interest trust	'trust for B if 21'	B (if 21+)	B (if 20 or less)			
Life interest trust	'trust for C for life, remainder to D'	C (in income) D (in capital – this interest is postponed whilst C is alive)				
	'trust for E for life, remainder to F if 21'	E (in income) F (if 21+; in capital – this interest is postponed whilst E is alive)	F (if 20 or less; in capital)			

Figure 3.1 The rule in *Saunders v Vautier*

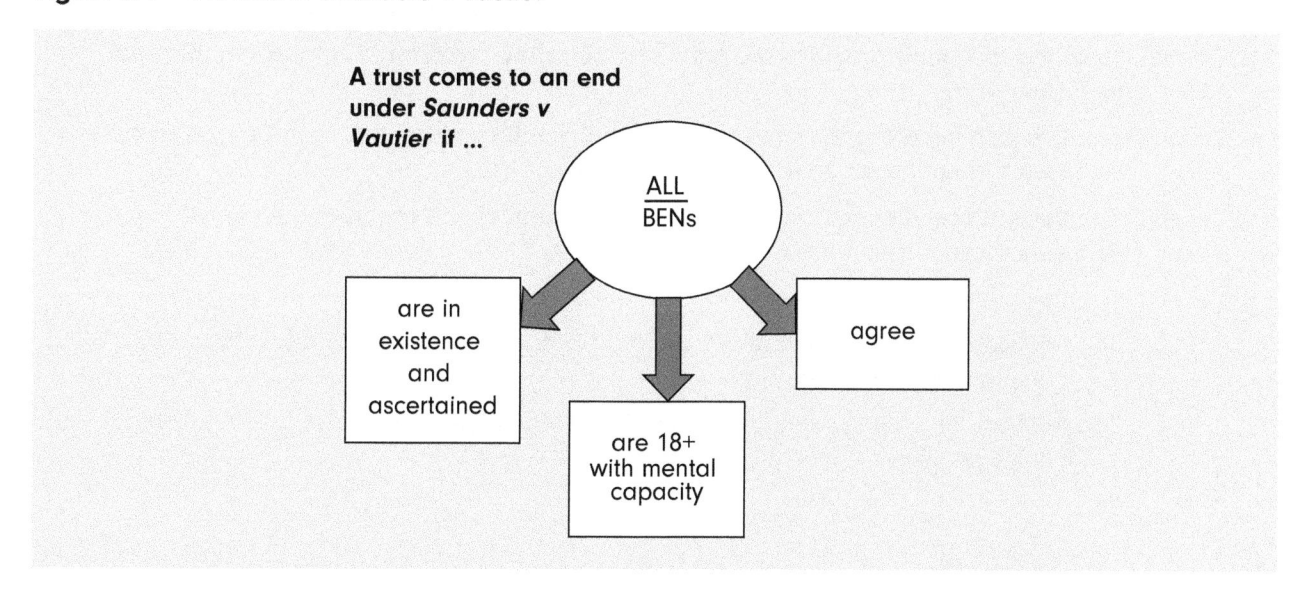

A trust comes to an end under *Saunders v Vautier* if …

ALL BENs
- are in existence and ascertained
- are 18+ with mental capacity
- agree

51

Summary

In this chapter you have considered different types of trusts and the different kinds of beneficial interests that subsist under such trusts:

- *Fixed interest trusts*. In these trusts the beneficial interests have been fixed by the settlor.
- *Classification of beneficial interests*. A beneficiary's interest under a fixed interest trust is either:
    - vested (they have an unconditional entitlement to trust property) or contingent (their entitlement is conditional on a future event that might not happen)
    - absolute (their interest subsists in the trust capital) or limited (their interest subsists in trust income only)
    - in possession (they are entitled to trust capital/income now) or in remainder (their entitlement is postponed until a prior interest expires).
- *Discretionary trusts*. In these trusts the beneficial interests are a matter for the trustees to decide. Until the trustees have exercised their discretion, individual members of the class do not have any beneficial entitlement to trust property.
- *The rule in* Saunders v Vautier. The beneficiary under a bare trust (sole, adult beneficiary) can direct the trustees to transfer trust property to the beneficiary. A group of beneficiaries can do the same, so long as they are between them absolutely entitled to the trust property, are all in existence, aged 18 years or over and in agreement.

Sample questions

Question 1

A dentist died last week. His valid will contained the following provisions:

'Clause 4: My Trustees shall hold £300,000 on trust for such of my children who before the age of 25 years successfully obtain an undergraduate 1st class degree ...

Clause 15: Following the payment of my debts, funeral expenses, all gifts under this will and inheritance tax, whatever remains shall belong to my wife.'

There are two children: a son aged 24 years who graduated two years ago with a 1st class degree, and a daughter aged 17 years who has decided not to go to university. The children have agreed between them to split the £300,000 in equal shares.

Which of the following provides the best advice to the children in relation to the trust under clause 4?

A   The trust can be brought to an end now because the children have agreed between them what should happen to the trust property.

B   The trust can be brought to an end once the daughter has reached the age of 18 years, but not before then.

C   The trust can be brought to an end now, but only if the wife agrees.

D   The trust can be only be brought to an end once the daughter has reached the age of 18 years, but only if the wife agrees.

E   The trust can only be brought to an end if and when the daughter successfully obtains a 1st class degree.

Answer

Option B is correct. At present, the children cannot use the rule in *Saunders v Vautier* to bring the trust to an end because the daughter is under the age of 18 years. Once she reaches the age of 18 years, she and the son will be, between them, absolutely entitled to the trust fund under clause 4. Even if the daughter decides not to go to university and therefore does not satisfy the contingency in clause 4, the trust fund will be paid out to 'such of my children' who satisfy that contingency. As the son has satisfied that contingency, he would in those circumstances be entitled to the trust fund in full. There is no-one else, beyond the son and daughter, who could benefit from the trust fund in clause 4.

Option A is wrong because the daughter is under the age of 18 years and therefore the conditions in the rule of *Saunders v Vautier* have not yet been fully met.

Options C and D are wrong. Whilst it might be good from a family perspective for the wife to agree what happens, her consent is not required. She cannot under any circumstances have a beneficial interest in the trust. Even if the daughter does not go to university, the son will take in full. No trust property will fall into the residuary estate.

Option E is wrong. Whilst the dentist may have wanted both children to go to university, if the son and daughter agree next year to bring the trust to an end, they will be able to do so using the rule in *Saunders v Vautier*.

Question 2

A woman died and was survived by her wife and son who is aged 22 years. Under the terms of her valid will, the woman created a trust fund of her residuary estate in the following terms:

'to be held on trust for my wife for life, remainder to my son if he attains the age of 21 years but otherwise to the Solicitors Benevolent Association'.

The wife is discussing the possibility of bringing the trust to an end with the trustees.

Whose agreement is required to bring the trust to an end now?

A   The wife and the trustees.

B   Only the wife.

C   The wife and son.

D   The wife, son and the Solicitors Benevolent Association.

E   The son and the Solicitors Benevolent Association.

Answer

Option C is correct. The son's beneficial interest was contingent on him reaching the age of 21 years. He has satisfied that contingency and therefore his remainder interest has vested. If the son were to die before the wife, the son's beneficial interest would pass under the terms of his will or intestacy. As at today's date, therefore, the wife and son are, between them, absolutely entitled to the trust fund and can use the rule in *Saunders v Vautier* to bring that trust to an end.

Option A is wrong. The decision as to whether to bring the trust to an end is one for the beneficiaries alone and not the trustees.

Option B is wrong. The wife's interest is limited to income only. She is not, by herself, absolutely entitled to the trust fund.

Options D and E are wrong. As the son has satisfied the contingency, his remainder interest will not fail (even if he dies before the wife). The Solicitors Benevolent Association have no possible beneficial interest under the trust and their consent to bringing the trust to an end is not required.

Question 3

A trust deed contains the following provision:

'My Trustees shall hold my house in Oxford on trust to permit my husband to live in the property for the remainder of his life and after his death to hold the property upon trust for such of my son and daughter who survive my husband and attain the age of 25 years.'

The son is aged 28 years and the daughter is aged 20 years.

Which of the following best describes the beneficial interests in the trust fund?

A   The husband, son and daughter all have vested interests.

B   The husband and the son have vested interests, but the daughter's interest is contingent.

C   The husband has a vested interest, but the son's and daughter's interests are contingent.

D   The husband, son and daughter all have contingent interests.

E   The husband has a contingent interest, but the son's and daughter's interests are vested.

Answer

Option C is correct. The husband has a vested interest. (Ordinarily, the life tenant will receive trust income – in the case of a residential dwelling, this would be any rent generated from letting the dwelling. Instead of receiving rental income, however, the life tenant can instead live in that dwelling rent-free for the rest of his life.) Remainder beneficiaries will have vested (albeit postponed) interests in capital, *unless* the trust makes it clear that their interests are in fact conditional on events that might not happen. In this case, there are two such conditions: (i) the children must reach the age of 25 years; and (ii) they must still be alive when the husband dies (the husband's death is a certainty – the children surviving him is not). The son's and daughter's interests will only vest if they satisfy these two conditions. We do not currently know whether the son and daughter will survive the husband (and can only know that when he dies). Given the specific wording of this trust, their interests are still contingent.

Option A is wrong. The son's and daughter's interests are conditional, not vested.

Option B is wrong. There are two conditions that the son and daughter must satisfy before their interests vest: (i) they have to reach the age of 25 years; and (ii) they have to survive the husband. The son has satisfied the former but not the latter. His interest is therefore still contingent. (This option would have been correct had the wording been 'on trust to permit my husband to live in the property for the remainder of his life and after his death to hold the property upon trust for such of my son and daughter who attain the age of 25 years' – in that case, there is only one condition the children must satisfy, ie reaching the age of 25, which the son has. The wording of the trust must therefore be carefully scrutinised.)

Option D is wrong. The husband has a vested interest – he does not have to satisfy any condition before being able to live rent-free in the house in Oxford.

Option E is wrong. The beneficial interests are the wrong way round.

4 Charitable and Non-Charitable Purpose Trusts

4.1	Introduction	56
4.2	Purpose trusts	56
4.3	Validity rules for the declaration of trust	57
4.4	The beneficiary principle	57
4.5	Rule against perpetuities	58
4.6	Charitable trusts	58
4.7	Valid non-charitable purpose trusts	63
4.8	Summary flowchart	65

SQE1 syllabus

This chapter will enable you to achieve the SQE1 assessment specification in relation to functioning legal knowledge concerned with the following core principles:

- The distinction between charitable trusts and non-charitable purpose trusts

Note that for SQE1, candidates are not usually required to recall specific case names or cite statutory or regulatory authorities. Cases are provided for illustrative purposes only.

Learning outcomes

By the end of this chapter you will be able to apply relevant core legal principles and rules appropriately and effectively, at the level of a competent newly qualified solicitor in practice, to realistic client-based and ethical problems and situations in the following areas:

- distinguishing between trusts for individuals and trusts for purposes;
- recognising the validity issues connected with trusts for purposes;
- advising on how those validity issues are overcome in respect of charitable trusts; and
- advising on how those validity issues are overcome in respect of certain non-charitable purpose trusts.

4.1 Introduction

So far, we have considered trusts that seek to directly benefit individuals.

Settlors may, however, want to use trust property to achieve a purpose or attain an objective or aim, such as the eradication of poverty or to build a gym. These trusts – known as 'purpose trusts' – are a form of express trust. As such, they follow the general rules for creating express trusts, ie:

(a) the settlor must make a valid declaration of trust (see **Chapter 1**); and

(b) property must be put in the trust (see **Chapter 2**).

However, when it comes to considering the declaration of trust, the settlor must be aware of two validity rules that are not generally an issue with trusts for individuals, but which become more problematic for purpose trusts:

(a) the beneficiary principle, which requires that trusts ordinarily directly benefit individuals; and

(b) the rule against perpetuities (in this case, the rule against inalienability of capital), which requires that property should not be locked away in the trust for too long.

This chapter looks at:

- the difference between trusts for individuals and purpose trusts and how you can distinguish between the two;
- the rules relating to valid declarations of trust, with particular reference to the beneficiary principle and the rule against perpetuities;
- why purpose trusts generally offend these rules (especially the beneficiary principle);
- why charitable trusts do not offend these rules and what makes a trust charitable; and
- the types of non-charitable purpose trusts that are still effective.

4.2 Purpose trusts

The trusts we have considered so far – fixed interest trusts and discretionary trusts – are trusts that directly benefit individuals. The ultimate duty of the trustees is to distribute trust property to the individuals designated by the settlor, whether in fixed shares or as a matter of their discretion.

Rather than setting up a trust with the ultimate objective of dividing the trust property between beneficiaries, the settlor may wish to set up a trust to carry out a purpose or advance a cause. Such trusts are known as 'purpose trusts'. The validity of such trusts raises different problems to those raised by trusts for individuals.

Before we address those problems, we will consider the distinction between purpose trusts and trusts for individuals by looking at some examples.

⭐ Examples

(a) 'I give £400,000 on trust to my Trustees for such residents of Bath and in such shares as my Trustees think fit'. In an accompanying letter of wishes, I request my Trustees to distribute money to those residents of Bath who have received public recognition for being good citizens.

This is a trust for individuals. The trustees will distribute trust property to individuals who fall within the class designated by the settlor. They may do so by reference to the criteria set out in the accompanying letter of wishes, but they do not have to.

(b) 'I give £400,000 on trust to my Trustees to promote good citizenship'.

This is a purpose trust. The trustees are not directed to distribute trust property to individuals. Rather, they are directed to achieve the objective, or advance the cause, of good citizenship.

(c) 'I give £400,000 on trust to my Trustees to promote good citizenship amongst my relatives'.

This is a purpose trust. Whilst people are identified in the declaration, they are not to take a sum of cash or a share of trust property. I (the settlor) have specified that the money be used to achieve an objective or advance a cause. It is therefore a type of purpose trust.

4.3 Validity rules for the declaration of trust

The declaration of trust in relation to a purpose trust must in general satisfy the same validity rules that we considered in **Chapter 1**:

(a) Certainty of intention: it must be clear that the person making the declaration intended to create a trust.

(b) Certainty of subject-matter: it must be clear what property is being held on trust.

(c) Certainty of objects: in the case of a purpose trust, the object is the purpose. It must therefore usually be clear what purpose the trustees should be trying to achieve with the trust property. (This does not apply to charitable trusts. Provided the purpose is charitable, it does not matter how vaguely it is expressed. It will fall to the Charity Commission to work out with the trustees exactly what to do with the trust property.)

(d) Beneficiary principle: this principle states that trusts must usually benefit individuals. This clearly creates a problem for purpose trusts.

(e) Perpetuities: property should not be locked away in trusts for too long. Different time-periods are relevant when considering purpose trusts.

(f) Formalities: if the trust property contains land, the declaration of trust must comply with s 53(1)(b) of the LPA 1925.

We will first identify the problems that purpose trusts encounter with the beneficiary principle and the relevant rule against perpetuities, before moving on to consider which types of purpose trusts can overcome these problems.

4.4 The beneficiary principle

When we considered the main building-blocks of a trust (see **Introduction**), we observed that a trust imposes a duty on trustees to look after property for the benefit of others and that this duty can be enforced by the beneficiaries. Generally, trusts are valid only if they have beneficiaries who can, if necessary, go to court to enforce them. This is known as the beneficiary principle.

Purpose trusts potentially offend the beneficiary principle because there is no individual who can go to court to enforce the trust. As a general rule, purpose trusts are void.

In Re Shaw [1957] 1 WLR 51, the court had to consider the validity of a trust created by the author George Bernard Shaw. That trust included undertaking research into how much time would be saved by substituting the present 26-letter alphabet with a 40-letter alphabet. The court observed that for a 'trust to be valid [it] must be for the benefit of individuals ... one cannot have a trust ... for the benefit, not of individuals, but of [purposes]. The reason has often been stated, that the court cannot control the trust'. As this trust did not benefit individuals (and the court could not bring the trust within the permitted exceptions to the beneficiary principle), the trust failed.

4.5 Rule against perpetuities

Property should not be locked away in a trust for too long. As we saw in **Chapter 1**, when it comes to trusts for individuals, the law allows a settlor to lock away trust property for a relatively generous period – up to 125 years.

The rules are not so generous when it comes to purpose trusts. If the purpose trust is not charitable, it will be void if it locks capital away (or, to put it more formally, renders capital inalienable) for a period of more than 21 years. This is known as the 'rule against inalienability of capital'.

Therefore, non-charitable purpose trusts are void for offending the rule against inalienability of capital unless either:

(a) the trust states that it is to last for no more than 21 years (in trust deeds, solicitors will often state that the trust will last 'for as long as the law allows' – this means the same thing); or

(b) the trustees may spend all the trust capital on the purpose and thereby end the trust at any time.

⭐ Examples

(a) *'I give £40,000 to my Trustees so that they may use the income to maintain the changing rooms at Beeston tennis club'.*

This purpose trust will be void as it offends the rule against inalienability of capital. I have directed that the trustees must use income to achieve the specified aim of maintaining the changing rooms. Income is a regular receipt of money derived from property (or capital). In order to generate income, my trustees must therefore lock away the trust capital – if they were to spend trust capital, there would be no underlying property left to generate income. As I have not specified that the trust should come to an end within 21 years, I am effectively telling my trustees to lock away trust capital in perpetuity and maintain the changing rooms forever. This trust will be void.

(b) *'I give £40,000 to my Trustees so that they may build changing rooms at Beeston tennis club'.*

This purpose trust does not offend the rule against inalienability of capital. My trustees can spend the trust capital in one go on building changing rooms and can bring this trust to an end at any time. There is nothing to suggest that this trust should last in perpetuity.

4.6 Charitable trusts

Charitable trusts are exempt from the beneficiary principle *and* the rule against inalienability of capital, and therefore do not encounter the problems that these principles and rules create.

Most charities and charitable trusts are enforced by the Attorney General and regulated by the Charity Commission. To be registered as a charity, the Commission will decide whether the trust satisfies the conditions set out in the Charities Act (CA) 2011:

(a) the trust must be for a charitable purpose;

(b) the trust must have sufficient public benefit; and

(c) the trust must be exclusively charitable.

4.6.1 Charitable purposes

Charitable purposes are listed in s 3(1) of the CA 2011. For the full list, see **Appendix 2**. To be charitable, a trust must seek to promote or attain at least one of these purposes, although charitable trusts often seek to promote or attain more than one.

Thirteen charitable purposes are listed in s 3(1) of the CA 2011. Here we will merely consider the first three:

(a) *The prevention or relief from poverty.* Poverty does not necessarily mean 'destitution' but refers to 'persons who have to go short in the ordinary [meaning] of that term' (*Re Coulthurst* [1951] Ch 661). Charity Commission Guidance states that it is likely to be charitable to relieve the financial hardship of anyone who does not have the resources to provide themselves with the normal things in life that most people take for granted. Trusts under this purpose could include trusts to help the unemployed, to build hostels for asylum seekers or to help people who become impoverished due to famine or natural disaster.

(b) *The advancement of education.* This covers things like the provision of scholarships, the building of educational facilities, the maintenance of museums and libraries, and the payment of teachers and administrative staff. It also covers research so long as that research is useful and the results are published.

(c) *The advancement of religion.* Religion means more than ethical values and philosophical discussions about whether a god exists (although the promotion of such discussions may well fall under the previous head of advancing education). Charitable religious trusts are those which take positive steps to sustain and increase religious belief – 'a belief that there is more to be understood about mankind's nature and relationship to the universe than can be gained from the senses or from science' (*Hodkin v Registrar General of Births, Deaths and Marriages* [2013] UKSC 77). It therefore includes putting money aside to pay for future services, to maintain places of worship or to publish and distribute religious publications.

4.6.2 Public benefit

To be charitable, the purpose being promoted by the trust must have sufficient public benefit. There are two aspects to this test:

(a) the trust purpose must have an identifiable benefit or benefits; and

(b) the benefit must accrue to the public or a sufficiently large section of the public.

4.6.2.1 Identifiable benefits

The benefit of the trust must be clear, and it must relate to the purposes of the charity. Any potential detriments have to be outweighed by the clear primary benefit. A school for pickpockets might be educational but is unlikely to be of benefit.

4.6.2.2 The benefit must be to the public

There is no problem where the benefits of a trust are offered to the whole public, such as trusts to maintain a museum that is open to all. These trusts undoubtedly involve sufficient public benefit even if only a small number take advantage of that benefit and even if the location of the museum means that very few people are likely to walk in.

The position is not so clear-cut if the benefits are only offered to a restricted group. In these cases, what constitutes a sufficient section of the public varies depending on which charitable purpose you are trying to achieve:

(a) *The prevention or relief of poverty.* A trust to relieve poverty amongst named individuals is not charitable. However, a trust to relieve poverty amongst 'my family' or 'my relatives' is charitable. This is generally justified on the ground that the prevention of poverty is such an important objective that anything that seeks to achieve it should be upheld even if the benefit only extends practically to a small number of individuals. This generous rule only applies to trusts for the prevention or relief of poverty.

(b) *The advancement of religion.* Public benefit will be present if either:

   (i) the place of worship is open to all, even if only a small number attend; or

   (ii) whilst the place of worship is not open to all, members of the relevant congregation 'live in this world and mix with their fellow citizens', *Neville Estates v Madden* [1962] Ch 832.

Contemplative religious orders that are cloistered and have no contact with the outside world are not charitable (*Gilmour v Coats* [1949] AC 426).

(c) *The advancement of education and other charitable purposes.* The people who might benefit from these charitable purposes must not be numerically negligible, but also trusts seeking to achieve these purposes have to overcome a number of tests designed to distinguish public from private benefits:

   (i) the 'personal nexus' test. People linked by a personal nexus – ie people linked by a relationship to a particular individual or company – are not a sufficient section of the public. The usual relationships that fall foul of this test are family and common employment.

Examples

'I give £250,000 to my Trustees for the education of the children of employees of Red Anchor Limited'.

This is not charitable because the people who will benefit from education are linked by a personal nexus, ie their parent's employment to a particular company (as was the case in Oppenheim v Tobacco Securities Trust Co Ltd *[1951] AC 297). This is the case even if Red Anchor Limited employs hundreds or thousands of people.*

   (ii) The 'class within a class' test. The class of people who can benefit from a charitable purpose can be limited, so long as those limits are legitimate, proportionate, rational or justifiable given the nature of the charitable trust. For instance, geographical restrictions are often legitimate and rational, particularly when the benefit includes something tangible such as buildings (eg 'I give £350,000 on trust for the building of sheltered accommodation for the elderly residents of Lewisham').

What is not permitted is the imposition of arbitrary restrictions.

In IRC v Baddeley *[1955] AC 572, a gift for the promotion of sports to people resident in West Ham who were or were likely to become Methodists was held not to be charitable. Whilst it was clear that the residents of a particular area were regarded as constituting a sufficient section of the public, the imposition that they must also be Methodists was held to be arbitrary – there was no rationale as to why only Methodists might benefit from sport when the promotion of sport presumably is a matter of general public utility. The class and the benefit did not seem to match up.*

It is sometimes said that if someone attempts to set up a charitable trust with more than one restriction on who can benefit (eg in *IRC v Baddeley* above, the promotion of sport was for the benefit of (a) Methodists in (b) West Ham, ie the gift imposed two restrictions on those who could benefit), that trust must fail because it creates a 'class within a class'. This overstates the issue. At most, all that the 'class within a class' test does is forewarn a settlor that the greater the number of restrictions imposed on accessing the charitable benefit, the greater the care that must be taken to ensure that the restrictions are permissible. The more you attempt to 'slice-and-dice' the section of the public that can benefit, the more careful you have to be to ensure that you have not introduced an arbitrary limitation on eligibility.

(iii) Charitable trusts must not exclude the poor. A charitable institution (such as a school or hospital) can charge fees for the services it provides, so long as any profits are ploughed back into the charitable purpose. However, if an institution charges fees that are so high, they can only be met by richer members of society, this is likely to affect its charitable status.

In Independent Schools Council v Charity Commission *[2012] Ch 214, it was held that fee-charging schools with charitable status must operate in a way that does not exclude the poor if they wished to retain their charitable status. That can include: the provision of scholarships and bursaries, enabling students from local state schools to attend classes or summer schools, and the sharing of teaching or sports facilities. It is up to the trustees (the governors) of the fee-charging school to address how best to meet these obligations, but the level of assistance provided must be more than minimal. Presumably, the higher the fees charged, the more the school will have to do to show a benefit to the wider public.*

4.6.3 Exclusively charitable

To be charitable, the trust must be *exclusively* charitable. A trust with both charitable and non-charitable purposes will not be charitable.

There tend to be two different aspects to this limb of the definition of a charitable trust:

(a) to be charitable, a trust must not have political purposes; and

(b) if a charitable organisation charges fees, the profits from those fees must be ploughed back into the trust rather than be paid over to private individuals (such as the owners of the organisation).

4.6.3.1 Political purposes

Political purposes include:

(a) supporting a political party; and

(b) campaigning for a change in the law (whether here or abroad) or a change in government policy/decisions.

Bodies that have a mixture of charitable and political purposes will not be given charitable status.

In McGovern v Attorney General *[1982] Ch 321, Amnesty International sought charitable status for a trust with purposes that included:*

- *the relief of needy persons within the categories of prisoners of conscience;*
- *attempting to secure the release of prisoners of conscience;*
- *procuring the abolition of torture or inhuman or degrading treatment or punishment;*

- *research into the maintenance and observance of human rights and disseminating that research.*

The trust was denied charitable status because attempting to secure the release of prisoners and procuring the abolition of torture meant that the trust would be campaigning for changes in law and government decisions. These purposes were political.

Charities can engage in political activities that are ancillary or incidental to their main charitable purpose - ie are *a* means of achieving the main charitable purpose - so long as they do not become the dominant means by which the charity carries out its purpose. Oxfam therefore can seek to persuade governments to change policies relating to infrastructure that may help eradicate poverty, as part of its main charitable purpose of preventing poverty.

4.6.3.2 Profits must be ploughed back into the charity

Institutions can retain their charitable status even though they charge fees for their services (so long as the institution does not exclude the poor - see above). If the institution realises a profit, that profit must go back into the charitable purpose.

If an institution is carried on as a commercial venture (eg a private hospital or most residential homes for the elderly) with a view to making profits for individuals, it cannot be charitable.

Let us pull together the three conditions set out in the Charities Act 2011.

⭐ *Examples*

(a) *'I give £50,000 to my Trustees to use the income to relieve poverty among my relatives'.*

This is a charitable trust:

- *The purpose is to relieve poverty, and therefore falls within s 3(1) of the Charities Act 2011.*
- *It exists for the public benefit. Relieving poverty is a clearly identifiable benefit; identifying a class of people who might benefit - even a class as small as 'my relatives' - is sufficient (listing my relatives as named individuals would not be).*
- *It is exclusively charitable.*

The fact that my trustees can only use the income (with the result that the trust is capable of lasting in perpetuity) does not render the charitable trust invalid as such trusts are immune from the rule against inalienability of capital.

(b) *'I give £400,000 to my Trustees to use the income to provide educational scholarships for my children'.*

This is not a charitable trust:

- *The purpose is to advance education, and therefore falls within s 3(1) of the Charities Act 2011.*
- *It is exclusively charitable.*
- *However, it does not exist for the public benefit. Providing scholarships is a clearly identifiable benefit. However, 'my' children are not a sufficient section of the public, because they fail to satisfy the personal nexus test - the people I want to benefit are all connected through family. Note the difference with poverty trusts (above) - the public benefit test can differ from charitable purpose to charitable purpose.*

(c) *'I give £250,000 to my Trustees to campaign for Wales to become an independent sovereign state separate from the United Kingdom'.*

This is not a charitable trust as the main purpose is political - the trust is seeking to change the law.

4.6.4 Summary of charitable trusts

Figure 4.1 Charitable trusts summary diagram (first three charitable purposes)

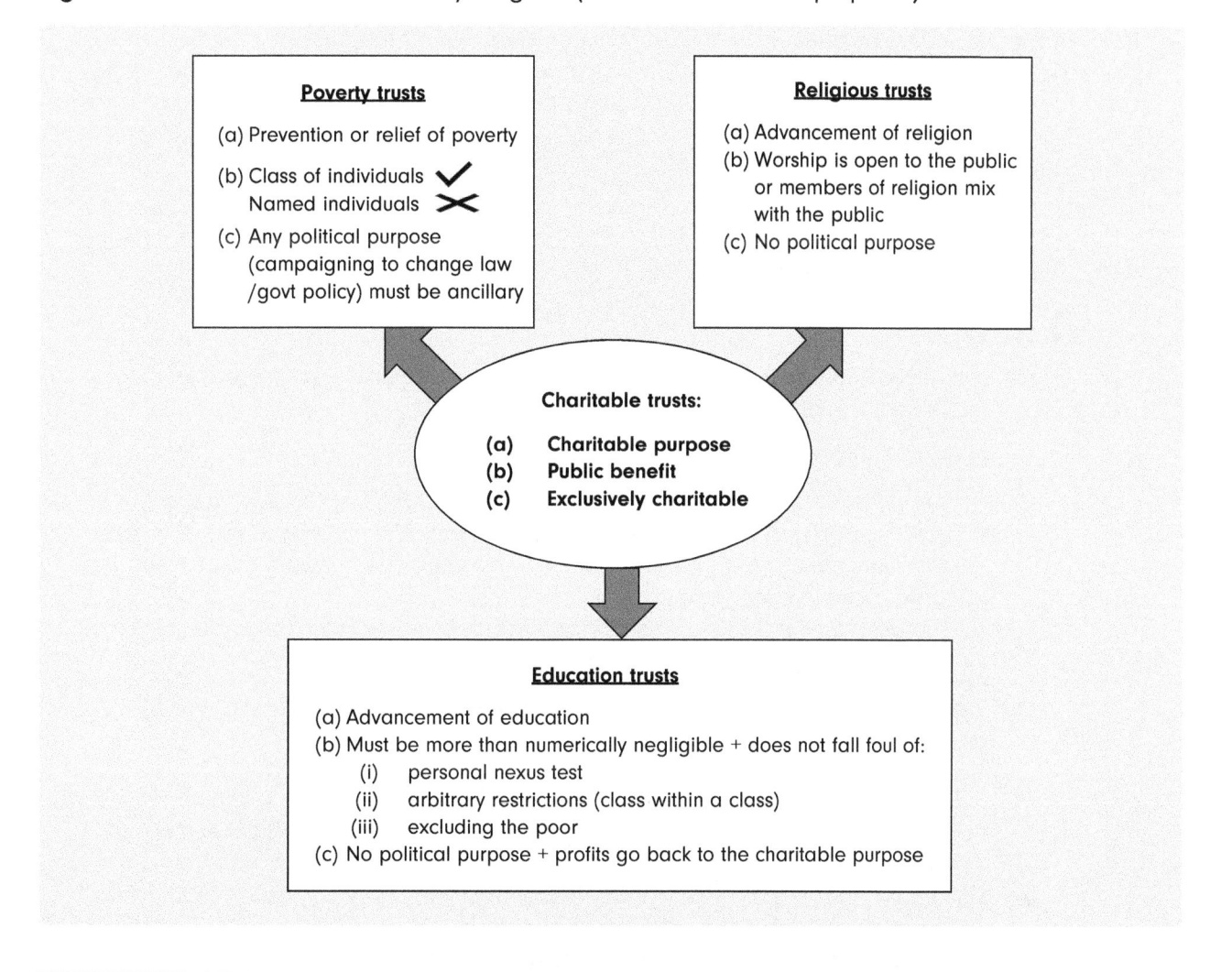

Poverty trusts
(a) Prevention or relief of poverty
(b) Class of individuals ✓
    Named individuals ✗
(c) Any political purpose (campaigning to change law /govt policy) must be ancillary

Religious trusts
(a) Advancement of religion
(b) Worship is open to the public or members of religion mix with the public
(c) No political purpose

Charitable trusts:
(a) Charitable purpose
(b) Public benefit
(c) Exclusively charitable

Education trusts
(a) Advancement of education
(b) Must be more than numerically negligible + does not fall foul of:
    (i) personal nexus test
    (ii) arbitrary restrictions (class within a class)
    (iii) excluding the poor
(c) No political purpose + profits go back to the charitable purpose

4.7 Valid non-charitable purpose trusts

If a purpose trust is not charitable, it will only overcome the beneficiary principle and the rule against inalienability of capital if either:

(a) it is a *Re Denley* trust; or
(b) it is a trust of imperfect obligation.

4.7.1 *Re Denley* trusts

If the declaration of trust identifies the people who will benefit from a particular purpose then problems with the beneficiary principle can be overcome – the people identified in the declaration of trust will be given standing to enforce the trustees' duty to apply trust property to achieve the stated purpose and the court can therefore control the trust.

> *In Re Denley's Trust Deed [1969] 1 Ch 373, a plot of land was transferred to trustees to be maintained and used for a sports and recreation ground for 21 years for the benefit of employees of a named company. Although this was a purpose trust, the court held it was 'outside the mischief of the beneficiary principle'. The purpose was sufficiently clear and tangible to allow the employees to go to court to enforce the trust.*

In order to be a valid *Re Denley* trust:

(a) the purpose of the trust must be sufficiently clear and give rise to a sufficiently tangible benefit;

(b) the persons who stand to benefit from the carrying out of the purpose must be ascertainable. In order to work out who can enforce the purpose trust, it is thought that the description of those persons who stand to benefit must satisfy the given postulant test (see **Chapter 1**). The description of this class of persons must therefore be conceptually certain; and

(c) the trust must not offend the rule against inalienability of capital, ie it must be limited to 21 years in duration or the trustees must be able to spend all the trust capital on the purpose and bring the trust to an end.

⭐ Examples

(a) 'I give £500,000 on trust for building a gymnasium for use by employees of King International Limited.'

This is a valid *Re Denley* trust:

- the purpose of the trust is sufficiently clear and tangible (building a gym);
- the persons who stand to benefit are ascertainable. The employees of King International Limited are a conceptually certain class capable of satisfying the given postulant test; and
- the trust does not offend the rule against inalienability of capital, because the trustees can spend all the capital on building the gym.

(b) 'I give £500,000 on trust for building and maintaining a gymnasium for use by employees of King International Limited'.

This is not a valid *Re Denley* trust:

- the purpose of the trust and the persons who stand to benefit are sufficiently clear; but
- the trust offends the rule against inalienability of capital, because the trustees *must* maintain the gym. Maintenance is an ongoing obligation, for which the trustees will constantly need to lock away capital in order to fund it. As that obligation has not been time-limited to 21 years or less, the trust will be void.

4.7.2 Trusts of imperfect obligation

These trusts include:

(a) trusts to care for specific animals, such as a favourite pet; and

(b) trusts to maintain graves and tombs.

In both cases, there is no human beneficiary who can enforce the trust and they therefore offend the beneficiary principle.

However, as a concession to human weakness, these trusts are valid but unenforceable. For instance, if I leave £225,000 to my trustees to spend it on looking after my dog Bouncer:

- the trust is valid, so if my trustees spend the money on looking after my dog Bouncer, no-one can complain; but
- the trust is unenforceable, so if my trustees do not spend any money on my dog Bouncer, no-one can go to court to compel them to do so. The accepted view in these situations is that the settlor (or, more likely, the residuary beneficiary of the deceased settlor's estate) can go to court to claim the trust property for themselves.

These trusts must comply with the rule against inalienability of capital.

The courts have recognised that these trusts are anomalous and have refused to extend them much further.

⭐ Example

'I give £20,000 to my Trustees to hold on trust to maintain my horse, Max, for as long as the law allows'.

This is a valid trust of imperfect obligation:

- *the purpose is to maintain a specific animal; and*
- *the trust complies with the rule against inalienability of capital because the words 'for as long as the law allows' limit the duration of the trust to the permitted period of 21 years (Re Hooper [1932] 1 Ch 38).*

4.8 Summary flowchart

Figure 4.2 Purpose trusts summary flowchart

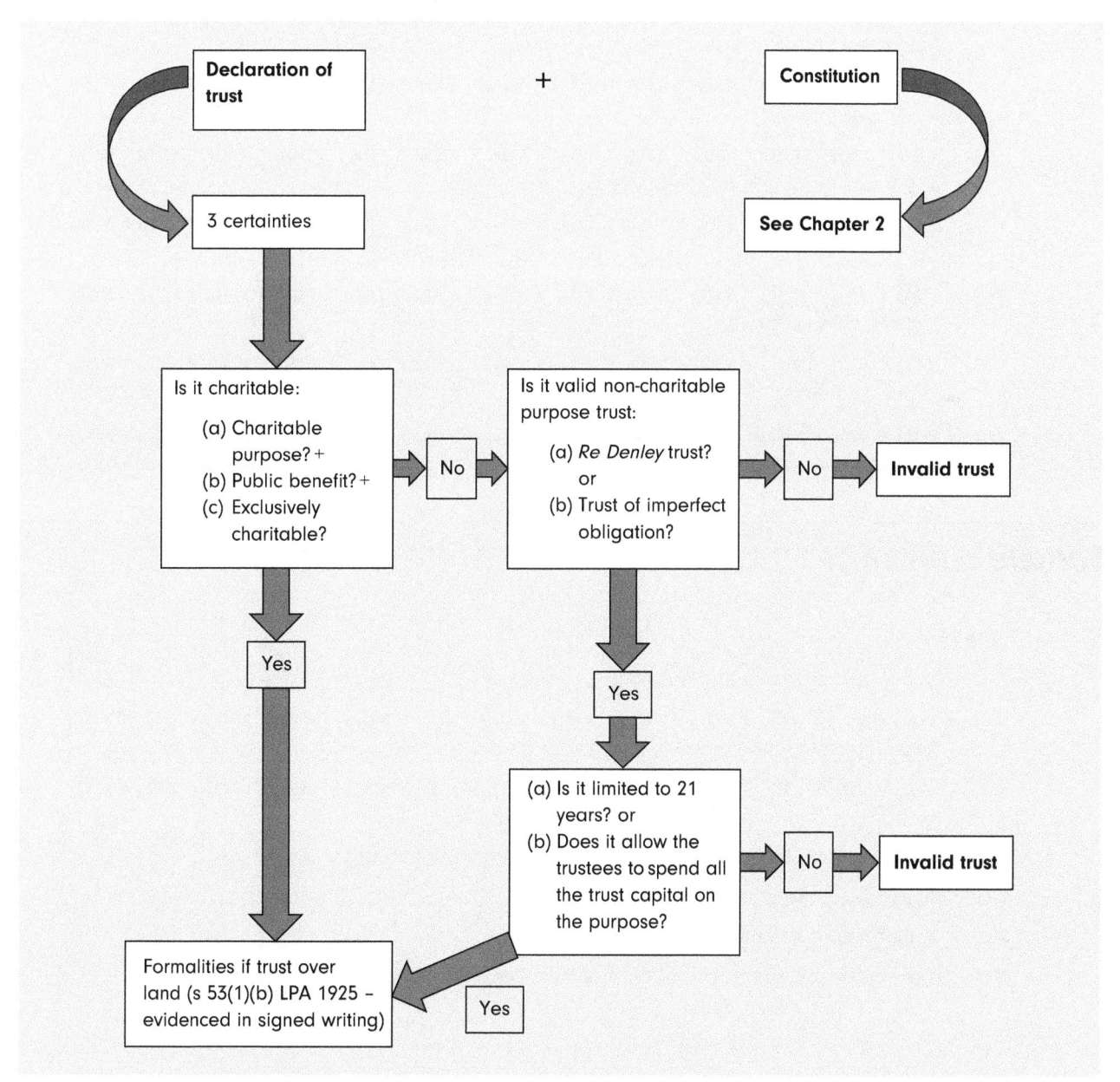

```
Declaration of trust  +  Constitution
       ↓                      ↓
  3 certainties          See Chapter 2
       ↓
Is it charitable:
(a) Charitable purpose? +
(b) Public benefit? +        → No →  Is it valid non-charitable purpose trust:
(c) Exclusively charitable?           (a) Re Denley trust? or
       ↓                              (b) Trust of imperfect obligation?   → No → Invalid trust
      Yes                                    ↓
                                            Yes
                                             ↓
                                    (a) Is it limited to 21 years? or
                                    (b) Does it allow the trustees to spend
                                        all the trust capital on the purpose?  → No → Invalid trust
                                             ↓
                                            Yes
                                             ↓
Formalities if trust over land (s 53(1)(b) LPA 1925 – evidenced in signed writing)
```

Summary

In this chapter you have considered how settlors can create trusts to achieve a purpose or attain an objective and identified how such trusts must overcome problems caused by the beneficiary principle and the relevant rule against perpetuities.

You have considered:

- *How to identify a purpose trust* and how to distinguish these from trusts for individuals.
- *The beneficiary principle.* This principle, which requires that a trust usually benefit individuals (so that, in turn, there are people who can enforce the trust), creates problems unique to purpose trusts. Unless a valid exception to the beneficiary principle can be found, a purpose trust will be void.
- *The rule against inalienability of capital.* This is the rule against perpetuities relevant to purpose trusts. It requires that most purpose trusts must either be time-limited to 21 years or the trustees must be able to spend the trust fund on the specified purpose in one go thereby bringing the trust to an end.
- *Charitable trusts.* Such trusts are exempt from the beneficiary principle and the rule against inalienability of capital. In order to be charitable, the trust must:
    - be for a charitable purpose listed in s 3(1) of the Charities Act 2011;
    - be for the public benefit (the tests for which differ depending on the charitable purpose); and
    - be exclusively charitable (eg political purposes such as campaigning to change the law are generally not permitted).
- *Valid non-charitable purpose trusts.* The following trusts overcome the beneficiary principle but must still comply with the rule against inalienability of capital:
    - *Re Denley* trusts, where the purpose secures a tangible benefit for an ascertainable class of individuals;
    - trusts of imperfect obligation, such as trusts to maintain specific animals, graves or monuments.
- *Creation rules.* Subject to the above, in order to be valid, a purpose trust must follow the rules relating to declarations of trust and the constitution of trusts (**Chapters 1** and **2**).

Sample questions

Question 1

A man's will trust contains the following provisions:

'Clause 8: I give £25,000 to my Trustees to maintain the changing rooms and shower blocks at the Rushcliffe swimming club's site in Nottingham ...

Clause 12: Following the payment of my debts, funeral expenses, all gifts under this will and inheritance tax, whatever remains shall belong to my wife.'

The Rushcliffe swimming club is a non-charitable organisation.

Does clause 8 create a valid trust?

A   Yes, because it satisfies the three certainties.

B   Yes, because the members of the Rushcliffe swimming club can enforce its terms.

C No, because the Trustees are holding the money to achieve a purpose, and all purpose trusts are void.

D No, because the Rushcliffe swimming club is not a charity.

E No, because the trust locks capital away for too long.

Answer

Option E is correct. The testator has tried to create a non-charitable purpose trust. Clause 8 can overcome the beneficiary principle – the trust provides a clear and tangible benefit for an ascertainable group of individuals (the members of the swimming club). However, as the Trustees must maintain the changing rooms and swimming blocks, which is an ongoing obligation, the trust capital might be locked away in perpetuity. The trust is therefore void for offending the rule against inalienability of capital. The trust fund (£25,000) will therefore fall into residue for the benefit of the wife.

Option A is wrong. Whilst this option correctly identifies that clause 8 satisfies the three certainties, that is not by itself sufficient to create a valid trust. As clause 8 is seeking to create a purpose trust, the declaration of trust must overcome the beneficiary principle and the rule against inalienability of capital. It does not overcome the latter.

Option B is wrong. Whilst this option correctly identifies that the trust can overcome the beneficiary principle (as the members of the swimming club can enforce its terms), that is not by itself sufficient to create a valid trust. As this trust is non-charitable, clause 8 must not offend the rule against inalienability of capital. Unfortunately, it does.

Option C is wrong. Not all purpose trusts are void – some are, but many are effective.

Option D is wrong. Just because the club is not a charity does not mean that the trust must be void – some non-charitable purpose trusts can be effective.

Question 2

A woman's valid will contains the following provisions:

'Clause 3: I give £200,000 to my Trustees to educate the young people of Cornwall about the importance of water safety ...

Clause 17: Following the payment of my debts, funeral expenses, all gifts under this will and inheritance tax, whatever remains shall belong to The British Red Cross Society.'

Which of the following statements provides the best advice to the Trustees about clause 3?

A Clause 3 does not create a valid trust because 'the young people of Cornwall' is not conceptually certain.

B Clause 3 does not create a valid trust because the purposes are not exclusively charitable.

C Clause 3 does not create a valid trust because the section of public who will benefit from the purpose are bound by a personal nexus.

D Clause 3 creates a valid trust because the purposes are charitable, and the benefit accrues to a sufficiently large section of the public.

E Clause 3 creates a valid trust as there is a clearly ascertainable class of people who can enforce the trust.

Answer

Option D is correct. Clause 3 creates a valid charitable trust. The purpose (education and/or the saving of lives) falls within the list of charitable purposes under s 3(1) of the Charities Act 2011; the benefit accrues to a sufficiently large section of the public; and the purposes are exclusively charitable. If the Trustees do not know how to apply the money, they could seek further guidance from the Charity Commission.

Option A is wrong. Whilst this option correctly states that the 'young people of Cornwall' is conceptually uncertain, as they are not the object of the trust (the object is the charitable purpose of educating them about water safety), this is irrelevant.

Option B is wrong. The trust is exclusively charitable. There is no suggestion that the woman wanted the Trustees to engage in political activities.

Option C is wrong. The young people in Cornwall are not linked by relationships to a particular individual or company. Therefore, they are not linked by a personal nexus.

Option E is wrong. The 'young people of Cornwall' is not conceptually certain – there will legitimately be different views about when people stop being 'young'. It cannot be said therefore that there is a clearly ascertainable class of people who can enforce the trust. However, option E is also irrelevant given that the trust is charitable.

Question 3

A woman executed a trust deed that contained the following provision:

'I give £200,000 to my Trustees to campaign for legislation to promote better standards of behaviour among those occupying public office.'

The Trustees appointed under the trust deed seek legal advice as to what to do with the £200,000.

Is the trust valid?

A   Yes, because the purpose is charitable.

B   Yes, because there is sufficient public benefit.

C   No, because it is not exclusively charitable.

D   No, because there is no certainty of subject-matter.

E   No, because it fails to satisfy the complete list test.

Answer

Option C is correct. The trust is not exclusively charitable because the settlor is seeking to change the law, which is a political (not charitable) purpose. Furthermore, the trust cannot work as a non-charitable purpose trust because there are no ascertainable beneficiaries who will derive a sufficiently tangible benefit to enforce the trust.

Options A and B are wrong. There may arguably be a charitable purpose (eg the promotion of citizenship) that is of benefit to the public, but that is not sufficient by itself to make the trust valid.

Option D is wrong. There is certainty of subject-matter, being the sum of £200,000.

Option E is wrong. The complete list test is relevant when assessing the validity of fixed interest trusts for individuals. It is not relevant here.

5 Resulting Trusts

5.1	Introduction	70
5.2	Presumptions of resulting trust and advancement	70
5.3	Resulting trusts when the beneficial interest is not completely disposed	75
5.4	Do any formalities attach to a resulting trust?	77

SQE1 syllabus

This chapter will enable you to achieve the SQE1 assessment specification in relation to functioning legal knowledge concerned with the following core principles:

- Resulting trusts and how they arise
- When resulting trusts are (and are not) presumed

Note that for SQE1, candidates are not usually required to recall specific case names or cite statutory or regulatory authorities. Cases are provided for illustrative purposes only.

Learning outcomes

By the end of this chapter you will be able to apply relevant core legal principles and rules appropriately and effectively, at the level of a competent newly qualified solicitor in practice, to realistic client-based and ethical problems and situations in the following areas:

- identifying the presumptions used to determine whether a resulting trust or gift has arisen;
- establishing the evidence needed to rebut those presumptions;
- advising on the operation of resulting trusts when the beneficial interest is uncertain; and
- identifying who takes the beneficial interest under a resulting trust.

5.1 Introduction

So far, we have considered express trusts (trusts that the settlor expressly intends to create). We are now going to consider implied trusts – trusts that are created not because the settlor has directed that there should be a trust, but that are created (or implied) through operation of law. Resulting trusts are implied where a person transfers property to another in circumstances where it is unclear who owns the beneficial interest.

This chapter looks at:

- equitable presumptions that attempt to identify who should take the equitable interest when property is transferred;
- how those presumptions can be rebutted; and
- the use of resulting trusts to identify who holds the beneficial interest when something has gone wrong when trying to create an express trust.

5.2 Presumptions of resulting trust and advancement

A person (A) transfers property to someone else (B). What does that mean legally? Who now owns the property that has been transferred?

In order to work that out, we need more information about the transfer. What did A and B intend? Was it a gift? Did B borrow the property from A promising to give it back? Did B pay for the property? The answers to these questions (and others) will help us work out what the end result should be.

But what if we cannot answer these questions? For instance, it took place a while ago, no-one really knows what happened, and A and B have since died. A's family and B's family are now locked in a bitter dispute. A's family claims that A still owned the property and that they have now inherited it. B's family claims that B became the absolute owner of the property and that the property is now theirs. The law tries to 'second-guess' what the right result should be in the absence of any evidence as to the actual intended result.

Where someone (A) transfers property to another (B), the law applies presumptions in an attempt to work out what the effect of that transfer should be. These presumptions are usually easily rebutted by evidence of A's actual intention in making that transfer.

Different presumptions apply in different circumstances. We will consider, in turn:

(a) situations that might give rise to a presumption of resulting trust;

(b) situations that might give rise to the countervailing presumption of advancement (or gift); and

(c) what kind of evidence might be needed to rebut these underlying presumptions.

We will sometimes refer to the person transferring property (A) as the 'transferor' and the person receiving property (B) as the 'transferee'.

5.2.1 Presumption of resulting trust

5.2.1.1 Voluntary transfer of personalty

'Personalty' is any kind of property other than land. If A transfers personalty they already own to B for free, a presumption of resulting trust will generally arise. Under a resulting trust, B holds the legal title and A gets the equitable interest in the property.

⭐ Example

Sam hands over £100 to his girlfriend, Mary. It is a 'voluntary' transfer because Mary provides no consideration in return.

The presumption is that Mary holds the money on a resulting trust for Sam.

Figure 5.1 A voluntary transfer resulting trust

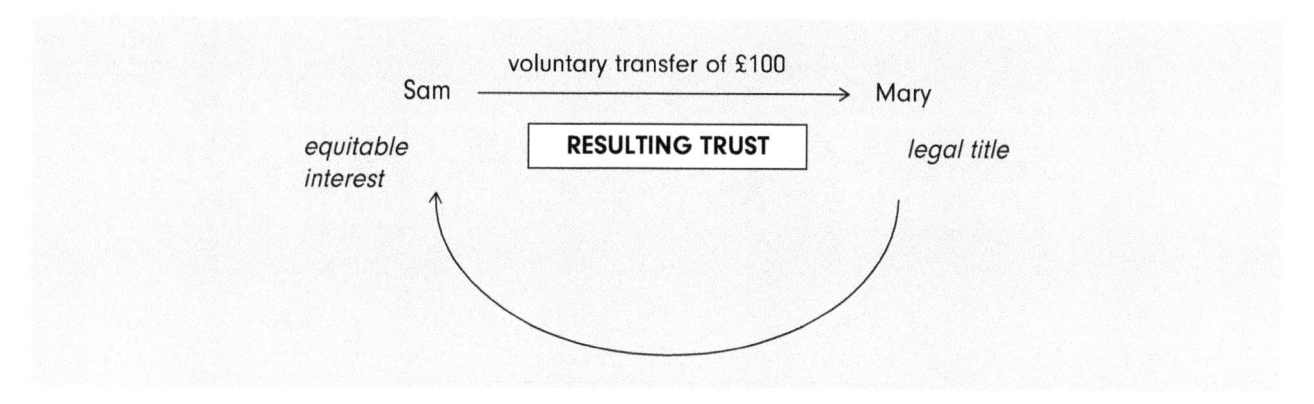

```
                    voluntary transfer of £100
        Sam ─────────────────────────────→ Mary
              equitable   ┌──────────────┐    legal title
              interest    │ RESULTING    │
                   ↑      │   TRUST      │
                    \     └──────────────┘   /
                     _____ ___/
```

You might think the resulting trust is a rather odd result. Surely the more obvious inference is that Sam intended a gift of the money, making Mary the absolute owner. Two things should be borne in mind:

(a) the presumption of resulting trust can be rebutted by evidence of Sam's actual intention. If the occasion was Mary's birthday and the money was contained in a birthday card, the natural inference to raise would be that Sam intended to gift that money to Mary and make her the absolute owner of £100. Alternatively, if Sam said, 'here is your birthday present', it would be clear that a gift was intended. We generally therefore only apply this underlying presumption of resulting trust when there is no evidence (whether through words or conduct) of the giving party's intention when making the transfer;

(b) as we shall see later on in this chapter, a different presumption (of advancement) might apply to family members who might be expected to make gifts to each other.

5.2.1.2 Voluntary transfers of land

This presumption of resulting trust is less likely to apply if the property being transferred is land (or 'realty'). Section 60(3) of the LPA 1925 provides that '[i]n a voluntary conveyance a resulting trust for the grantor shall not be implied merely by reason that the property is not expressed to be conveyed for the use or benefit of the grantee'. In some cases, this provision has been taken to mean that there should be no presumption of resulting trust arising out of a voluntary transfer of land (*Ali v Khan* [2002] EWCA Civ 974). If this is correct – and this is not free from doubt – it is still *possible* for a resulting trust to arise out of a voluntary transfer of land, but the court would need some evidence or additional factor (eg that the transferor and transferee are strangers) to arrive at that conclusion. It cannot simply be presumed in the absence of evidence.

5.2.1.3 Purchase money cases

X purchases property from a seller. However, rather than becoming the owner of that property, X arranges for the property to be put in the name of Y. Y will become the owner holding legal title to the property. However, there may be a presumption that X intended Y to hold that property on a resulting trust for X. Under this resulting trust, X will own all of the equitable interest in that property.

Trusts

Figure 5.2 A purchase money resulting trust

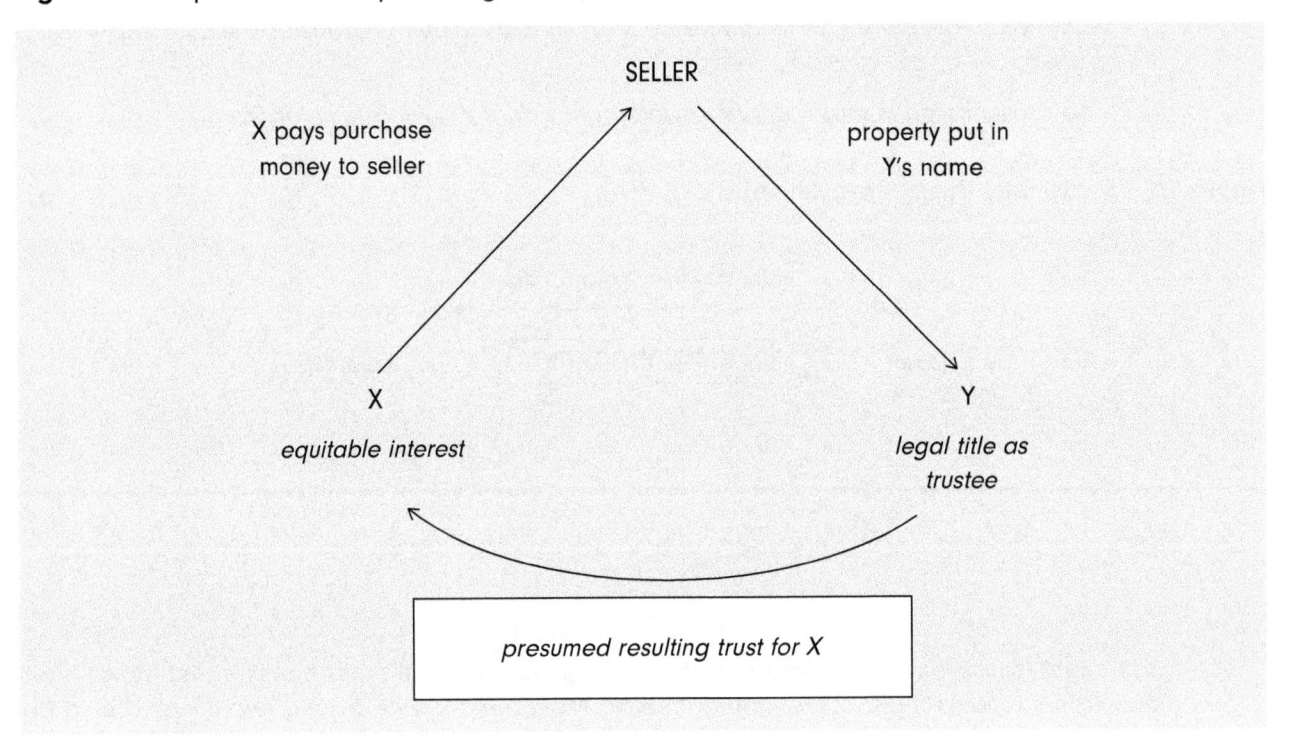

[Diagram: SELLER at top. X pays purchase money to seller (arrow from X up to Seller). Property put in Y's name (arrow from Seller down to Y). X has equitable interest. Y has legal title as trustee. Curved arrow from Y back to X labelled: presumed resulting trust for X]

Similarly, if X contributes towards the purchase price of property in the name of Y (the balance being paid by Y), there may be a presumption that X intended Y to hold that property on a resulting trust for X and Y – the size of X's and Y's beneficial interest under this resulting trust will be proportionate to the size of their respective contributions.

⭐ Example

Tess and her daughter, Maggie, decide to buy a house to let to tenants. Tess contributes £40,000 and Maggie pays the remaining £360,000 of the purchase price. The house is conveyed into Maggie's sole name (so she alone holds the legal title).

Figure 5.3 An example of a purchase money resulting trust

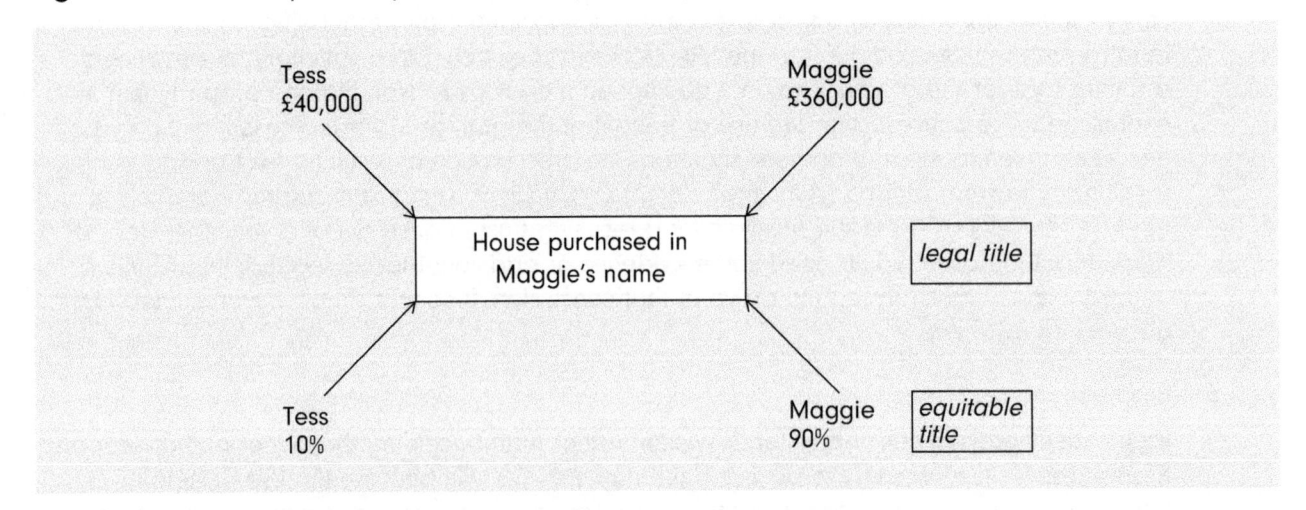

[Diagram: Tess £40,000 and Maggie £360,000 contribute to House purchased in Maggie's name. Maggie has legal title. Tess 10% and Maggie 90% equitable title.]

72

The presumption is that Maggie holds the house on a resulting trust for herself and Tess. As Tess paid 10% of the purchase price, she gets an equitable interest under the resulting trust of 10% of the house. If Maggie were to later sell the house for £500,000, Tess would be entitled to 10% of that sale price, ie £50,000.

The presumption of a resulting trust in favour of a contributor of the purchase price of property applies to both personalty and realty. However, for a contribution to give rise to a presumption of resulting trust, that contribution must be:

(a) contemporaneous with the purchase – it does not count if someone tries to make a 'contribution' after the event; and

(b) directed towards the actual purchase price itself – if X pays the price tag and Y pays the lawyers' fees in relation to their advice on the purchase, only X's contribution counts.

(As we shall see in **Chapter 6**, a couple's beneficial interests in the family home tend to be fixed using different rules that try to achieve 'fairness' between the couple by looking at factors other than merely who has contributed what money. If a house has been purchased as a form of investment by two people who are not a couple – as was the case in the above example when mother and daughter bought a house to let to tenants – then the presumption of resulting trust still has a role to play.)

5.2.2 Presumption of advancement

In some voluntary transfer and purchase money cases, a different presumption applies. This is known as the presumption of advancement (or presumption of gift). When the presumption of advancement applies, there is no resulting trust and the transferor is presumed to be gifting property to the transferee.

The presumption of advancement applies when equity regards the transferor as being under a moral obligation to provide for the transferee (or, rather, regarded the transferor as being under such an obligation back in the 19th century). It applies in cases of voluntary transfers and provision of purchase money:

(a) from father to child (the child here can be either a minor or an adult);

(b) from person *in loco parentis* to child. A person *in loco parentis* is effectively a guardian who has taken on the responsibility to provide financially for a child. This responsibility generally finishes when the child reaches the age of 18 years;

(c) by husband to wife; and

(d) by fiancé (male) to fiancée (female), so long as the couple subsequently marry.

Note that the presumption of advancement does not apply if the roles are reversed. The presumption of advancement does not apply if a wife voluntarily transfers property to her husband or adult children voluntarily transfer property to their father. In both of these situations, the presumption of resulting trust will apply, unless rebutted by contrary evidence.

⭐ Examples

(a) Richard purchases a house in the name of his wife, Sienna. In the absence of any evidence to the contrary, the presumption of advancement applies. It is presumed that Richard has gifted that house to his wife.

(b) Sienna purchases a house in the name of her husband, Richard. In the absence of any evidence to the contrary, the presumption of resulting trust applies. It is presumed that Sienna retains the beneficial interest in the house.

The presumption of advancement has long been considered sexist. Section 199 of the Equality Act 2010 will abolish the presumption of advancement, but it has not yet been brought into force.

5.2.3 Rebutting the presumptions

It is important to remember that the presumptions of resulting trust and advancement are merely *presumptions*. They can be rebutted. Indeed, their main role is to allocate the evidential burden of proof, identifying who has to prove what. They are a starting point for the court. The presumptions hold good only pending facts to the contrary.

⭐ *Example*

Victoria bought shares in the name of her partner, Willow. There is an initial presumption that Victoria intended Willow to hold the shares on a resulting trust for her. Victoria dies, giving all her estate on her death to Xavier. Xavier claims that the equitable interest in the shares belong to him.

Xavier does not need to prove anything initially. There is a presumption of resulting trust, and if there is no evidence of Victoria's intention, Xavier will inherit her equitable interest. The burden of proof will fall on Willow to show that the shares belong absolutely to her, rebutting the presumption. She will have to produce evidence in court that Victoria intended to make a gift to her.

If there is evidence that something else was intended, these presumptions are readily rebutted.

However, the evidence to rebut an underlying presumption must be of the transferor's intention before or at the time of transfer. Any evidence of your intention after the transfer can only be used against you – you cannot rely on evidence of your own acts or declarations occurring after the transfer that help your case because that would mean you could win your case by making up evidence after the event.

⭐ *Example*

Allen purchased a house in the name of his daughter, Beatrice. Allen retained the title deeds until his death five years later and his wife clearly recalls that Allen always intended his son-in-law, Carlton, to repay the purchase price. Shortly before his death, Allen signed a document that gave directions that the house would be divided between his three children.

In this example, you would start with the presumption of advancement – a father is purchasing property in the name of his child. You would initially presume therefore that Allen intended to make a gift of the house to Beatrice.

However, when we look at the evidence contemporaneous with the purchase, the fact that Allen retained the title deeds (which suggests that he intended to assert some kind of ownership right over the house) and the clear evidence of his widow that Allen wanted Carlton to pay him back should be sufficient to rebut the presumption of advancement and replace it with a resulting trust (see Warren v Gurney *[1944] 2 All ER 472).*

The document subsequently signed by Allen purporting to divide the house between his three children would not be admissible in support of the case that Allen retained an equitable interest in the house, because an act or declaration subsequent to the transfer can only be admitted against the person who made that act or declaration and not in his favour.

5.2.4 Summary flowchart

Figure 5.4 Presumptions of resulting trust and advancement flowchart

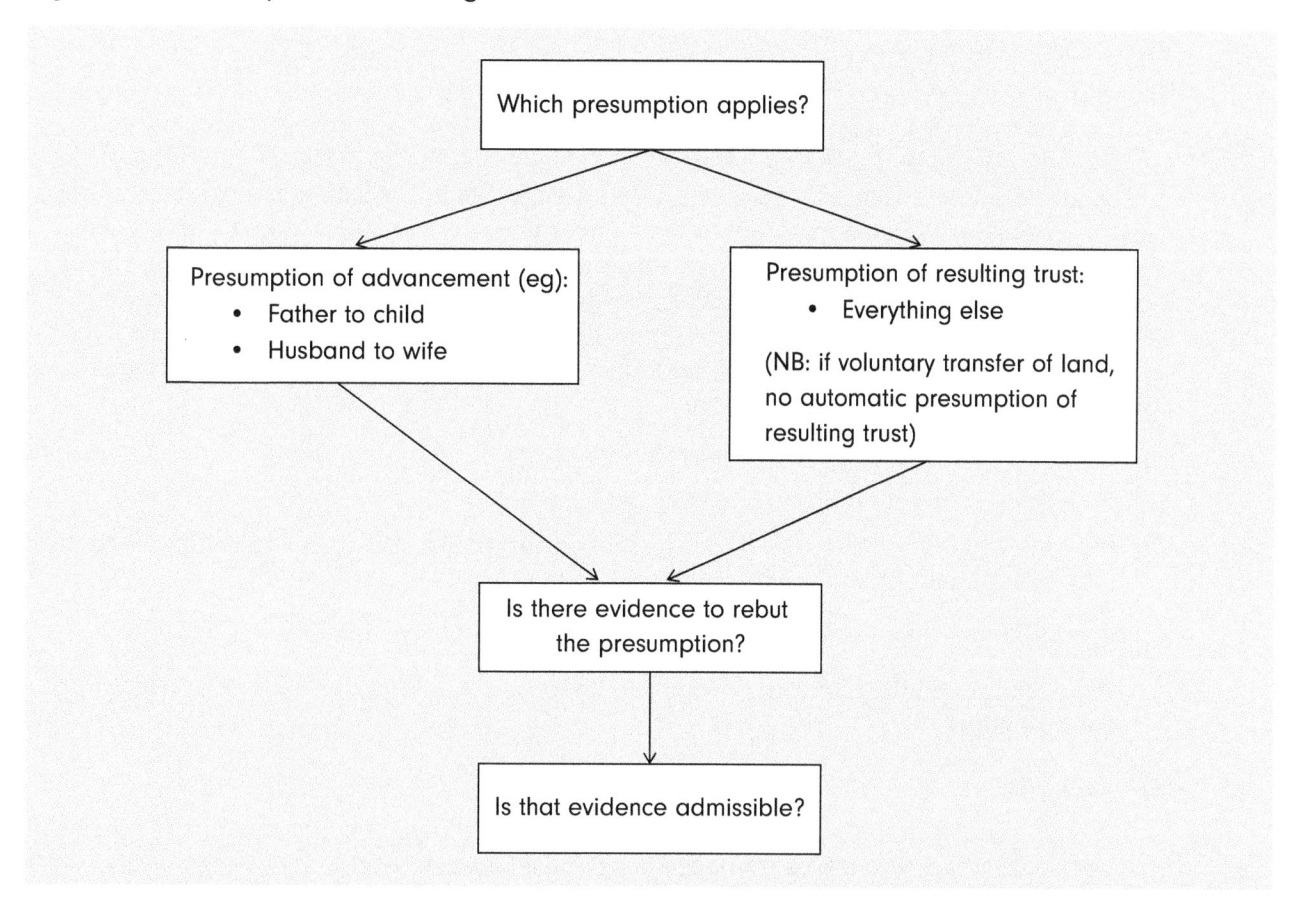

```
                    Which presumption applies?
                    /                        \
                   /                          \
  Presumption of advancement (eg):      Presumption of resulting trust:
    • Father to child                     • Everything else
    • Husband to wife                   
                                        (NB: if voluntary transfer of land,
                                        no automatic presumption of
                                        resulting trust)
                   \                          /
                    \                        /
                    Is there evidence to rebut
                         the presumption?
                               |
                               v
                    Is that evidence admissible?
```

5.3 Resulting trusts when the beneficial interest is not completely disposed

We have already seen in the **Introduction** that when property is transferred to a third party with the intention that an express trust be created, but something goes wrong that prevents the express trust taking effect, then a resulting trust is implied in favour of the settlor. The resulting trust vests the beneficial title back into the name of the settlor. These resulting trusts are sometimes called 'automatic resulting trusts' to distinguish them from the resulting trusts that arise by operation of the presumptions considered earlier.

Figure 5.5 Resulting trust when express trust fails

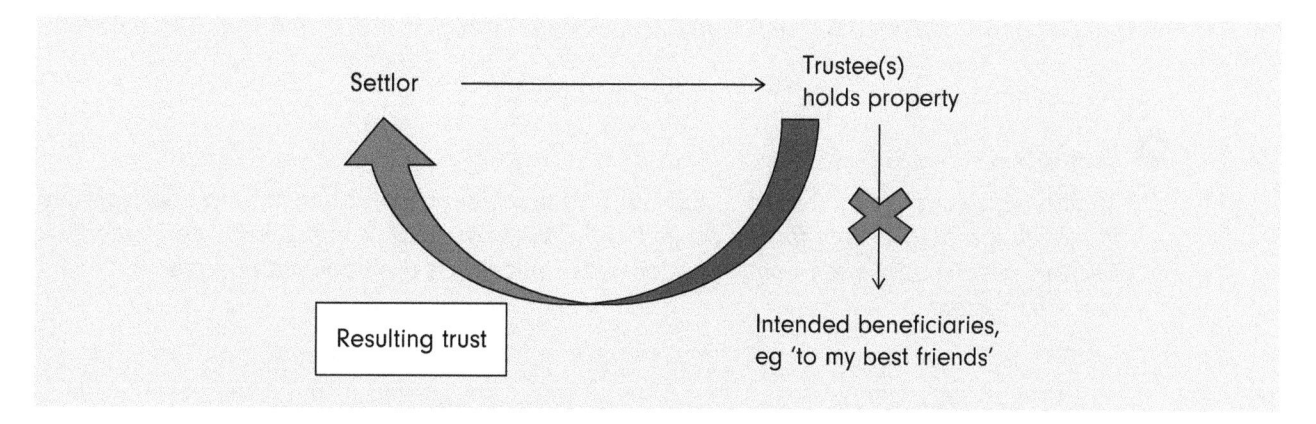

```
   Settlor  ————————————>  Trustee(s)
      ^                    holds property
      |                         |
      |                         ✗
      |                         |
      |                         v
  Resulting trust        Intended beneficiaries,
                         eg 'to my best friends'
```

In **Figure 5.5**, the settlor has attempted to create an express trust 'to my best friends'. We know that trusts require certainty of objects and that express trusts require (at least) conceptual certainty. 'To my best friends' is not conceptually certain because different people will take different views as to what constitutes 'friendship' and against what criteria a 'best' friend should be measured. The express trust fails.

That leaves the trustees holding legal title to property without anyone apparently holding the equitable title. The trustees clearly cannot have the equitable title, because then they would be absolute owners and that would defeat the settlor's intention to create a trust. It is said that 'equity abhors a vacuum' – someone must hold the equitable title. In the absence of any contrary intention, it is presumed that, if the express trust were to fail, the settlor would want the property back. The equitable title results – or jumps – back to the settlor (or, if the settlor has died, the equitable title results back to the beneficiary of the settlor's residuary estate or the statutory next-of-kin on intestacy). The trustees will hold the trust property on bare trust for the settlor – the settlor can then direct that the trust property be conveyed back to them, using the rule in *Saunders v Vautier*.

An automatic resulting trust therefore arises where:

(a) the settlor transfers property to trustees on trust; but
(b) the anticipated trust does not dispose of all or part of the equitable interest, because the declared trust is void or does not exhaust the trust fund.

An attempted trust might not dispose of the equitable interest where:

(a) there is a gap in the beneficial ownership because there is no beneficiary who attains a vested interest;

⭐ Example

James appoints Kamila a trustee of £250,000 for the benefit of Laura should she reach the age of 25 years. Laura dies when she is aged 22 years.

As Laura did not satisfy the condition of reaching the age of 25 years, her beneficial interest never vested. The beneficial interest must vest in someone, so a resulting trust arises by operation of law to vest the beneficial interest back in the name of James (the settlor).

(b) the attempted trust lacks certainty of objects (such as a trust for 'my best friends');
(c) the attempted trust does not define the beneficial interests with sufficient certainty;

⭐ Example

Paul appoints Quentin a trustee of £250,000 to give 'a decent amount to Ruby and the rest to Sylvia'.

This attempted trust does not define the beneficial interests with sufficient certainty. What is meant by a 'decent amount'? The attempted trust therefore fails for lack of certain subject-matter, and the equitable title results back to Paul.

(d) the attempted trust offends the rules against perpetuity;

⭐ Example

Michael appoints Neil a trustee of £250,000 'to use the income to maintain a sportsground in the village of Bramcote for the benefit of the employees of Marsh Consulting Limited'. Michael died shortly after, naming Oxfam International as the beneficiary of his residuary estate.

Michael attempted to create a purpose trust, but it offends the rule against inalienability of capital. As the trust is not charitable (due to the personal nexus involved – the benefit accrues to people who share a common employment), the trust can only be valid if the trustees can spend capital in one go or the duration of the trust is limited to 21 years. As neither applies here, the trust is void.

Equitable title to the £250,000 results back to Michael's estate, and the money will ultimately be paid over to Oxfam International as Michael's residuary beneficiary.

(e) the attempted trust offends the beneficiary principle.

5.4 Do any formalities attach to a resulting trust?

Whilst you need written evidence of an *express* trust over land in order to comply with s 53(1)(b) of the LPA 1925, the same is not true of an *implied* trust (such as a resulting trust). Section 53(2) of the LPA 1925 makes it clear that an implied trust can be created without any formality.

Summary

In this chapter, you have considered how the law uses resulting trusts to work out where the beneficial interest in property should go when that is unclear, either because there is no evidence of what the transferor intended to do with the beneficial interest or because what the transferor intended to do with the beneficial interest has not worked for some reason.

You have considered:

- *Which situations give rise to an underlying presumption of resulting trust.* If a transferor voluntarily transfers property they own to another or purchases property for another, in most situations this gives rise to a rebuttable presumption that the transferor intended to keep all or some of the beneficial interest in that property.

- *Which situations give rise to an underlying presumption of advancement.* However, in very specific situations where the relationship between transferor and transferee is one that conveys a financial responsibility on the transferor to look after the transferee (or, at least, a sense of financial responsibility viewed through the spectacles of Victorian morality), then the voluntary transfer of property or the purchase of property for another gives rise to a rebuttable presumption of advancement or gift. The transferor is presumed to transfer the legal *and* equitable title and the transferee takes the property free of any interests that the transferor used to have.

- *How those presumptions can be rebutted.* It is always important to remember that these presumptions are *just* presumptions. They can be rebutted if there is admissible evidence that indicates what the transferor intended at the time. Indeed, the presumptions can usually be easily rebutted by contrary evidence. To be admissible, such evidence must usually either be before or contemporaneous with the transfer. Any words or conduct subsequent to the transfer can only be admitted as evidence of what was intended against the party who said the words or engaged in that conduct.

- *The use of resulting trusts to plug an equitable vacuum.* If the settlor intended to create an express trust and has transferred legal title in property to the intended trustees, but the trust fails (because the settlor has failed to follow the rules relating to the declaration of trust that we have considered in Chapter 1), it is presumed that those trustees will hold that property on a resulting trust back to the settlor.

Sample questions

Question 1

A man bought shares in a company. His son's name was listed as the owner of the shares in the company's register of members. The son was aged 25 years. On the same day as the purchase took place, the son emailed the man to say, 'Hi Dad. When I get the share documents, I will send these over to you as agreed. As we also agreed, if any dividends are paid on these shares, I will forward those on to you as well.'

A year later, the man instructed a solicitor to draw up a will for him. He said that the value of the shares had doubled over the last year and that he wanted to leave them to his wife.

Does the man have a beneficial interest in the shares?

A   Yes, because he paid for the shares.

B   Yes, because the email from the son a year ago is sufficient to rebut the presumption of advancement that would have otherwise applied.

C   Yes, because the fact that he instructed a solicitor to draft a will leaving the shares to the wife is sufficient to rebut the presumption of advancement that would have otherwise applied.

D   No, because the presumption of advancement applies and can never be rebutted.

E   No, because his name is not listed in the company's register of members.

Answer

Option B is correct. The man has purchased shares in the name of his son. Whilst the presumption of advancement applies where a father transfers property to, or purchases property for, his child, here there is likely to be sufficient evidence to rebut that presumption. That evidence is the email contemporaneous with the purchase recording an agreement that the man would hold the share certificate (which indicates an intention that the man should continue to have some kind of interest in the shares) and that future dividends would be paid to the man (which indicates some kind of entitlement to the shares). It is likely therefore that the man has retained a beneficial interest in the shares.

Option A is not the best answer. Just because the man paid for the shares does not necessarily mean that he will retain an interest in them.

Option C is wrong. Whilst the presumption of advancement initially arose on the purchase of the shares, this cannot be rebutted by the instructions the man gave to the solicitor. The man would want to use those instructions as evidence that he retained an interest in the shares. However, evidence of words and conduct after the purchase had taken place would only be admissible against the man's case and could not be used in support of his case. As a result, the instructions to the solicitor are not sufficient by themselves to rebut the presumption of advancement.

Option D is wrong. Whilst it is correct to say that the presumption of advancement initially arose on the purchase of the shares, it is not correct to say that this presumption can never be rebutted. The presumptions of resulting trust and advancement are just presumptions and are often readily rebutted in the light of contrary evidence.

Option E is wrong. Whilst the man does not own legal title to the shares given that his name is not listed in the register of members, he can still own the beneficial interest in the shares.

Question 2

Three years ago, an estate agent sent a letter, enclosing a cheque for £10,000, to a paramedic that said, 'As agreed, cash this cheque and give most of it to your daughter and then the rest to your son when they reach the age of 21 years'. The daughter was then aged 18 years and the son was aged 12 years. The paramedic cashed the cheque.

The daughter has now reached the age of 21 years and has found the letter. She wants the paramedic to transfer at least a half share of the money to her (she has not discussed this with her brother). The estate agent has recently fallen out with the paramedic and has written to the paramedic demanding that she return the money to him.

Must the paramedic return the money to the estate agent?

A   Yes, because whilst the estate agent tried to create a trust in favour of the paramedic's children, that trust failed due to uncertain intention.

B   Yes, because whilst the estate agent tried to create a trust in favour of the paramedic's children, that trust failed due to uncertain subject-matter.

C   Yes, because whilst the estate agent tried to create a trust in favour of the paramedic's children, the trust offended the relevant perpetuity rules.

D   No, because the daughter has reached the age of 21 years and her entitlement to the money has vested.

E   No, because the estate agent created a valid trust. Given that the declaration of trust did not specify the shares that each child would get, the law presumes that each child gets an equal share.

Answer

Option B is correct. The estate agent tried to create an express trust. The reason that trust is ineffective is due to the beneficial interests being uncertain (which is an aspect of the second certainty – certainty of subject-matter). The paramedic does not know how to separate the trust property between the daughter and son. All she knows is that she must give the daughter more than the son, but beyond that the distribution between the two is unclear. The paramedic therefore holds the legal title in the money on resulting trust for the estate agent. As that resulting trust is a bare trust and the estate agent is absolutely entitled, he can call for that money back.

Option A is wrong. There is certainty of intention – it is clear that the paramedic had to hold the money on trust for other people.

Option C is wrong. Had the trust been valid, the contingent interests were clearly capable of vesting within the perpetuity period of 125 years (being the perpetuity period relevant to trusts for individuals).

Option D is wrong. As the express trust fails, the daughter has no beneficial interest in the money, whether she reaches the age of 21 years or not.

Option E is wrong. This is not a case where the law can presume that each person should get an equal share as this runs counter to the estate agent's intention in setting up the trust (the only thing we know for certain is that he wanted the daughter to get more than the son).

Question 3

A son owned a house. His father came to live with him four years ago. Two years ago, the son and his wife separated. The son was worried that his wife might divorce him and was worried about what that might mean for the house. He therefore transferred the house into the father's sole name. No money exchanged hands between father and son. The son and wife have now reconciled and no divorce proceedings are ongoing.

Throughout the past four years, the father and son welcomed paying lodgers into the house. The money from these lodgers was only ever paid to the son.

The father has recently died and, in his valid will, left the house to his daughter.

Which of the following statements best describes why the son has a beneficial interest in the house?

- A The son has a beneficial interest because he continued to live in the house.
- B The son has a beneficial interest because a presumption of resulting trust arose in the son's favour that has not been rebutted on the facts.
- C The son has a beneficial interest because a presumption of advancement arose in the son's favour that has not been rebutted on the facts.
- D The son has a beneficial interest because a resulting trust can be inferred on the facts.
- E The son has a beneficial interest because a presumption of advancement arose in the father's favour but this has been rebutted on the facts.

Answer

Option D is correct. When the son transferred the house into the father's sole name, he was making a voluntary transfer of realty. In most cases, when a son voluntarily transfers property to a father, a presumption of resulting trust will apply. However, the position seems to be different for realty (land) – in these cases, it seems that no presumption of resulting trust will apply simply because one party has voluntarily transferred land to another. Having said that, a resulting trust is likely to be inferred in this case, given that the son continued to profit from the income being generated from the house. This additional evidence indicates an intention that the son retained a beneficial ownership in the house even when he transferred the legal interest to his father.

Option A is wrong. The mere fact that you live in a house does not by itself give you a beneficial interest in that house.

Option B is wrong. Whilst there is some doubt, the effect of s 60(3) of the LPA 1925 appears to prevent a presumption of resulting trust arising merely by the fact that one person has voluntarily transferred land to another. This option therefore is not the best description of why the son has a beneficial interest in the house.

Option C is wrong. Whilst a presumption of advancement would have arisen had the father voluntarily transferred land to his son, no similar presumption arises when a son voluntarily transfers land to his father. The transfer is the wrong way round.

Option E is wrong. A father can never benefit from the presumption of advancement. Victorian morality dictates that a father is financially responsible for his children. In the right situations, the presumption of advancement may benefit his children, but never him.

6 Trusts of the Family Home

6.1	Introduction	82
6.2	Ownership of the family home	82
6.3	Express trusts of the family home	83
6.4	Resulting trusts of the family home	84
6.5	Common intention constructive trusts of the family home	84
6.6	Proprietary estoppel	89

SQE1 syllabus

This chapter will enable you to achieve the SQE1 assessment specification in relation to functioning legal knowledge concerned with the following core principles:

- The establishment of a common intention constructive trust
- The rules that apply when legal title in the family home is held in the name of both parties and when legal title is held in the name of a sole party
- How the law treats express declarations or agreements as to the equitable ownership over the family home
- How the law treats direct and indirect contributions towards the family home
- The requirements to establish proprietary estoppel

Note that for SQE1, candidates are not usually required to recall specific case names or cite statutory or regulatory authorities. Cases are provided for illustrative purposes only.

Learning outcomes

By the end of this chapter you will be able to apply relevant core legal principles and rules appropriately and effectively, at the level of a competent newly qualified solicitor in practice, to realistic client-based and ethical problems and situations in the following areas:

- recognising express trusts over the family home;
- recognising resulting trusts over the family home;
- recognising common intention constructive trusts over the family home, in particular how such trusts are established and how the beneficial shares under such a trust are quantified; and
- advising on proprietary estoppel as a separate equitable mechanism to establish an interest in the family home.

6.1 Introduction

For a large number of people, the family home will be their most important and most valuable asset. However, not everyone will pay sufficient attention as to how that asset is owned and how their interests in that asset are protected. Often, the first time they start to seriously consider these issues is when the family relationship starts to break down.

When a married couple divorce, statute helps work out who is entitled to what share of the family home. When unmarried couples separate, equity does this job and has developed a number of different mechanisms to try and reach a fair result, the two most important being the common intention constructive trust and proprietary estoppel.

This chapter looks at:

- briefly how legal title to the family home can be held (a much more detailed review of this can be found in the **Land Manual**);
- the practical deficiencies in using express trusts and resulting trusts to work out the beneficial shares in the family home;
- the establishment of a common intention constructive trust in cases either where the family home is owned jointly or where the family home is owned solely by one person;
- the quantification of each person's beneficial interest in the family home under a common intention constructive trust; and
- the use of proprietary estoppel as an alternative mechanism for establishing interests in the family home.

Trusts are often used to establish ownership rights in the family home as between unmarried couples. When looking at different trusts in this chapter, unless otherwise stated, the family unit living in the family home will be comprised of one unmarried couple, and each individual will be referred to as a 'partner'. Proprietary estoppel, by contrast, has a much wider scope, and whilst it can be used to establish ownership rights between couples, it is also used to establish ownership rights in the family home between generations.

6.2 Ownership of the family home

6.2.1 Joint ownership

When two or more people own land, the land is held on trust. Generally, in the case of a family home, the legal and beneficial owners of the home will be the same. A husband and wife, for instance, who buy a house together will usually be both the legal owners and the beneficial owners.

The legal title in the family home must be held by the couple as 'joint tenants'. As most land is registered, the couple are often referred to as registered co-proprietors.

The equitable title may be held by the couple as joint tenants or tenants in common:

(a) Joint tenants are equally entitled to the family home. As a result, when one partner dies, the other partner becomes entitled to the family home automatically.

(b) Tenants in common have distinct beneficial interests or shares in the family home. The size of those shares can generally be in whatever proportion the couple wants – equal or unequal. As tenants in common are not entitled to the entire family home – just their defined share in the home – they are not entitled to the whole family home on the death of their partner. Instead, when one partner dies, their beneficial interest in the home passes under the terms of their will or under intestacy.

When a couple purchases their family home and have decided whether they want to hold the equitable estate in the home as joint tenants or tenants in common, they should then evidence that decision in signed writing. You will recall from **Chapter 1** that if a settlor wishes to create an express trust over land, the settlor must evidence the declaration of trust in signed writing in order to comply with s 53(1)(b) of the LPA 1925.

When purchasing a house in joint names, a couple can finalise a valid declaration of trust by completing the relevant section of TR1, the transfer form (deed) used to transfer legal title in registered land. Whilst it is invariably completed, the relevant section is not in fact compulsory, and so it is possible for a couple to purchase their family home in their joint names without creating an express trust. The law then needs to work out (or quantify) the beneficial interests or shares each partner has in the home. This often becomes most relevant when the partners split up and need to separate assets between them, including the family home that they previously lived in together.

6.2.2 Sole ownership

Alternatively, one partner might be the sole registered proprietor of the family home. In this case, that partner owns the legal title to the home, but might still hold it on trust for themselves and their partner. Again, if the couple decides on the beneficial interests each of them have in the house, they should ideally evidence that decision in signed writing to create an enforceable express trust. However, most couples are unlikely to think of this or realise that it is a good idea.

If there is no express trust, the law still has a role to play in working out (or quantifying) the beneficial interests each partner has in the home. Once again, this often becomes most relevant when the partners split up and need to separate the family home between them.

6.2.3 Regimes dealing with separating couples

If couples split up, how the family home is dealt with depends on whether they were married / in a civil partnership (on the one hand) or unmarried (on the other):

(a) If the couple were married or in a civil partnership and subsequently divorce (or seek to have a civil partnership dissolved), the family courts are given wide redistributive powers under the Matrimonial Causes Act (MCA) 1973 to determine who gets what out of the divorce. These wide powers can be used to quantify the beneficial interests in the family home and apply whether or not the couple created an express trust over the home when they purchased it.

(b) If the couple were not married, engaged or in a civil partnership (ie they were cohabiting), then their affairs are governed by the ordinary principles of trusts law. A common myth about people who cohabit is that their relationship amounts to 'common law marriage' and that they therefore acquire the same rights as married couples after a period of cohabitation. This is not the case – there is no statutory regime equivalent to the MCA 1973 that applies to cohabitees. If they split up and want to sell the family home, then their beneficial interests in that home (and therefore the amount of money they will get on its sale) will be quantified using trusts.

The rest of this chapter considers the position of cohabiting couples.

6.3 Express trusts of the family home

If the couple have created an express trust over the family home, then their beneficial interests in the family home are set out in their declaration of trust. The express trust will usually determine who gets what. To be enforceable, the declaration of trust must be evidenced in signed writing in order to comply with s 53(1)(b) of the LPA 1925.

If the couple become registered co-proprietors of the family home, then often (but not always) they will have also created an express trust that deals with the beneficial interests in the home. An express trust over the family home is much less likely when only one partner is the registered proprietor.

If an express trust has not been created, we need to consider whether an *implied* trust over the land has arisen by operation of law. You will recall from **Chapter 5** that implied trusts do not need to be evidenced in signed writing (LPA 1925, s 53(2)) and therefore can potentially arise whether or not the partners have given any thought to how the family home will be owned.

6.4 Resulting trusts of the family home

We saw in **Chapter 5** that if someone contributes money to purchase property in the name of another, a resulting trust will often be presumed that gives that party a beneficial interest commensurate with the amount of their contribution.

However, a resulting trust only focuses on contributions to the purchase price that are made contemporaneous with the purchase itself. This has a number of important consequences when it comes to purchasing family homes:

(a) Only contributions towards the purchase price count. The payment of ancillary items – such as conveyancing fees, stamp duty or other bills – does not give rise to a resulting trust.

(b) Only contributions made at the time of purchase count. A cash payment towards the deposit (on exchange of contracts) or the completion price gives rise to a resulting trust. However, generally speaking, most of the purchase price of a family home is funded by a mortgage, which is repaid through subsequent monthly instalments. If the mortgage is not in your name, but you nevertheless pay off that mortgage *after* the date of purchase, that will not give rise to a resulting trust.

(c) Most importantly, a resulting trust only recognises *monetary* contributions. If a couple agrees to divide their labour, with one partner (A) buying the house and the other partner (B) looking after the children (for instance), a resulting trust would completely ignore B's non-financial contribution to the family.

⭐ Example

Jarred and Linda want to move in together. They put in an offer of £500,000 for a house, which is accepted. Jarred pays a 10% deposit on the house sale and gets a mortgage to cover the rest of the purchase price. He forgets to budget for conveyancing fees and stamp duty land tax and asks Linda to pay for these, which she does.

Once they have moved in, Linda takes over responsibility for paying off the mortgage.

Linda would not be entitled to any beneficial interest in the home under a resulting trust, because she has not contributed to the purchase price at the time of purchase. This seems rather unfair given that she has paid off the mortgage for the house and therefore has in reality paid much more for the house than Jarred.

Given these difficulties, in the absence of an express trust, the beneficial interests in the family home are now generally determined using a common intention constructive trust.

6.5 Common intention constructive trusts of the family home

6.5.1 Home is jointly owned

If both partners are registered as co-proprietors, they hold the legal title to that home jointly and equally. If the couple have not created an express trust that addresses the beneficial interests in the home, it is presumed that each partner's beneficial interest in the home is also joint and equal. It is often said that 'equity follows the law'. The partners are presumed to hold the house on trust for themselves in equal shares.

It should be noted that the partners are not holding the house on an express trust – they have not *expressly* intended to create this trust. Instead, the trust is *implied* to prevent unfairness between the partners. The law is trying, in the interests of fairness, to work out what the partners would have intended had they given the matter any thought. The partners are therefore said to hold the house on a 'common intention constructive trust'.

If a claiming partner wants to persuade the court they should be entitled to a larger beneficial share, not only must they evidence an agreement or common intention to that effect, but also that they relied on that agreement/intention to their detriment. For instance:

(a) If the partners came to a clear agreement as to how the family home would be owned on which the claiming partner relied to their detriment, the beneficial interests will be that which the partners have agreed.

(b) If an agreement or common intention as to the shares of the family home have changed over time, that change must be supported by detrimental reliance. For instance, if one partner finances the construction of an extension or major improvement to the family home (being an example of detrimental reliance), it might have been intended that, going forwards, that partner would have a greater interest in the property than at the time of acquisition.

(c) In the absence of any clear agreement as to each partner's share of the family home, the court will require evidence that the parties intended to share the house unequally and so acted to their detriment, before it will survey the whole course of dealing between the partners relevant to their ownership and occupation of the property to ascertain what is fair having regard to that course of dealing. The 'whole course of dealing' enables the court to quantify the size of each partner's share in the family home, but the detrimental reliance triggers that quantification exercise.

Factors that the court may take into account when surveying the whole course of dealing between the partners include:

(a) advice or discussions at the time of purchase;

(b) the reasons why the home was transferred into their joint names;

(c) the nature of the partners' relationship;

(d) whether they had children for whom they had a responsibility to provide a home;

(e) how the purchase was financed, both initially and subsequently;

(f) how the partners arranged their finances; and

(g) how they discharged the outgoings on the home and other household expenses.

However, the courts have been keen to stress that it will be a very unusual case where partners will be taken to have intended that their beneficial interests should be anything other than equal. For instance, merely contributing unequally to the initial purchase price is unlikely to displace the general rule. What will usually be needed is evidence that the couple intended throughout their relationship to keep their financial affairs separate.

6.5.2 Home is solely owned

If only one partner is the registered proprietor of the family home, then in the absence of an express trust, the other partner may be able to secure a beneficial interest in the home if a common intention constructive trust can be established. It is important to note here that there is no presumption of joint beneficial ownership (as would be the case if the house had been registered in the names of both partners). Instead, the partner whose name is not on the legal title has the burden of establishing that they are entitled to a beneficial interest in the first place.

In this section, we shall refer to the partner who is the registered proprietor as the 'legal owner' and the partner who is not the registered proprietor as the 'claiming partner'.

There are two stages that must be followed in cases where the family home is solely owned:

- Stage 1 – the common intention constructive trust must be established (where the home is jointly owned, this is presumed); and
- Stage 2 – the beneficial interests under the trust must be determined or quantified.

6.5.2.1 Stage 1: Establishing the trust

The law on Stage 1 was set out in the case of *Lloyds Bank plc v Rosset* [1991] 1 AC 107. Whilst this case has been criticised academically and judicially, it is still a leading case in this area.

A claiming partner can only obtain an interest in the family home under a common intention constructive trust if it can be shown that:

(a) there was a common intention between the partners that both were to have an interest; and that

(b) the claiming partner acted to their detriment in reliance on that common intention.

The recent case of *Hudson v Hathway* [2022] EWCA Civ 1648 confirms that if a claiming partner wants to establish:

- (where the home is solely owned) a constructive trust of the family home; or
- (where the home is jointly owned) that they have the greater beneficial share of the family home;

then 'detrimental reliance' must always be proven.

Although the detrimental reliance need not consist of expenditure of money or other quantifiable financial detriment, it does have to be substantial.

There are two methods of establishing these elements:

(a) In method 1, the common intention is express.

(b) In method 2, the common intention is inferred from conduct.

6.5.2.2 Method 1: Express common intention + detrimental reliance

Under this method, you generally need to find a (typically oral) agreement or understanding between the couple that the home is to be shared beneficially, ie that both parties would have an interest in the home.

⭐ Examples

(a) Victoria owns a house in her sole name. She has been going out with Yosef and, when the relationship starts to get serious, tells him, 'there is no point in us living apart. I want you to think of this house as much yours as mine'. This statement suggests that both parties are to have a beneficial interest in the property.

(b) Adam owns a house in his sole name. His girlfriend, Bethan, is renting a flat but is finding it difficult to keep up with the rent. Adam tells her 'the last thing I want is for you to be homeless, so why don't you finish the lease and move into my house'. This statement does not really address issues of property ownership or that Adam intends to share the ownership of his house with Bethan. It may be that all Adam meant was to ensure that Bethan had a roof over her head. It is unlikely therefore that this kind of statement would be enough, by itself, to demonstrate an express common agreement or understanding that Bethan was to have a beneficial interest in the home.

(c) Cyril owns a house in his own name. His boyfriend, Dylan, is currently getting a divorce from his estranged husband. Cyril wanted to put the house into their joint names, but on taking legal advice, he was told this was not advisable at the time because it might prejudice Dylan's divorce. Nevertheless, it is likely that Dylan can establish a common intention that he would have an interest in the home (but for the divorce, Cyril would have put Dylan's name on the title; see Grant v Edwards [1986] 1 Ch 638).

If an express common intention can be established, then it is necessary for the claiming partner to show that they acted to their detriment or significantly altered their position in reliance on the agreement. Financial contributions towards the house (eg paying off some of the mortgage or paying for improvements/alterations to the home) and/or substantial payments of housekeeping expenses certainly suffice. Non-monetary, 'domestic' contributions (such as giving up a job to look after children) may well suffice, but the position here is less clear-cut.

6.5.2.3 Method 2: Inferred common intention + detrimental reliance

If there is no express common agreement or understanding about how the family home is to be owned (which will often be the case), the court has to look at the couple's conduct and see whether it can infer a common intention that both partners were to have an interest. A common intention can generally only be inferred from:

(a) a direct contribution to the purchase price; or

(b) a significant contribution to mortgage payments falling due after the purchase.

> *It is possible, in very defined circumstances, that indirect payments to the purchase of the family home might be sufficient to enable a court to infer a common intention. In Le Foe v Le Foe [2002] 1 FCR 107, the court had to use the law of trusts to establish whether a married wife had beneficial shares in the family home. (This was not a divorce case, and therefore the MCA 1973 did not apply. Instead, the case was brought against the backdrop of a building society trying to repossess a home for failure to pay off the mortgage.) Mrs Le Foe paid for the household expenses, which enabled Mr Le Foe to make payments towards the mortgage (even if not, ultimately, enough). The court felt able to infer a common intention that Mrs Le Foe should have a beneficial interest in the family home because her substantial financial contributions enabled Mr Le Foe to make those payments: 'it was an arbitrary allocation of responsibility that [Mr Le Foe] paid the mortgage, service charge, and outgoings, whereas [Mrs Le Foe] paid for day to day domestic expenditure. I have clearly concluded that [Mrs Le Foe] contributed indirectly to the mortgage repayments'. It would therefore appear that when payment of household expenses by one partner enables the other partner to pay the mortgage, these financial contributions might be taken into account.*

Strictly speaking, a partner seeking to establish a common intention constructive trust using *inferred* common intention must still show that they acted to their detriment or significantly altered their position. However, the fact that you can only generally infer a common intention from financial contributions means that those contributions perform the twofold function of establishing both the common intention *and* showing that the claiming partner has acted upon it. For instance, if a claiming partner has made significant contributions towards the mortgage, this enables the court to both infer the necessary common intention *and* demonstrate that the claiming partner acted to their detriment in reliance on that common intention.

Despite *Hudson v Hathway* being part of the continuing judicial trend in the case of Method 1 (express common intention) that the accompanying detrimental reliance can be non-monetary and domestic (so long as it is substantial), *Hudson v Hathway* does not change the position in Method 2 (inferred common intention) that the only way of inferring common intention is through direct (and possibly indirect) financial contributions.

⭐ Example

> *Eve was going out with Frank when (with the benefit of a mortgage) she purchased a house in her sole name. She asked Frank to pay the stamp duty land tax and conveyancing legal fees, telling him that she would pay him back (although she never did). Frank moved in to live with her shortly after.*
>
> *For the next 10 years, Eve was responsible for paying off the mortgage, although Frank agreed to pay off the mortgage for six months while Eve was between jobs. Frank paid for a new bathroom and for a patio to be laid in the back garden.*

The relationship then started to cool and Frank moved out. Eve has put the house on the market and Frank claims that he should be entitled to a share of the sale proceeds.

In the absence of any express discussion about how the home would be owned when Frank moved in, can a common intention that Frank was to have a beneficial interest in the home be inferred from conduct?

It cannot be inferred from Frank paying the stamp duty land tax and conveyancing fees as this was intended to be a loan, so it was not a contribution to the purchase price. Furthermore, the payment of costs ancillary to the purchase is generally not regarded as a contribution to the purchase price itself.

It cannot be inferred from Frank paying to refurbish the home as this is not a contribution to the purchase price or mortgage.

However, Frank is on much stronger ground to claim a beneficial interest when we address the six months of mortgage instalments he paid. So long as the court considers that this constitutes a significant enough contribution to the mortgage, then a common intention constructive trust will have arisen.

6.5.2.4 Stage 2: Quantifying the beneficial shares

Once a common intention constructive trust has been established (under either method), the next stage is to quantify the size of the partners' respective beneficial interests or shares in the family home. By contrast to homes in joint names, there is no presumption of joint beneficial ownership.

If the partners came to an agreement as to the size of their respective beneficial interests, then that agreement will be respected. However, it is much more likely that there will be no evidence of what shares were intended. In this case, the court will award such shares as it considers fair having regard to the whole course of dealing between the partners in relation to the property. The list of factors will broadly be the same as those listed at **6.5.1**.

⭐ *Example*

Georgina owns a house in her sole name. Her partner, Hattie, moves in and pays a third of the monthly mortgage instalments. Georgina and Hattie have a joint expenses account that pays for household utilities (electricity, gas etc). Georgina pays £150 of her own money every month into the joint account, and Hattie pays £350. Hattie stays at home to look after their two children and is responsible for the weekly grocery shop. Georgina and Hattie have never discussed whether and how the family home should be shared between them.

In order to get a beneficial share in the family home, Hattie has to establish a common intention constructive trust. There was no agreement or understanding as to how the family home should be owned, so Hattie can only establish such a trust if there is a course of conduct from which a common intention can be inferred. She is paying off a third of the mortgage. This can be used both to infer the necessary common intention and demonstrate the required detrimental reliance.

That does not necessarily mean that she will get a third share in the family home. When it comes to quantifying Hattie's beneficial interest in the home, the court will consider what is fair having regard to the whole course of dealing between her and Georgina. This will include the fact that Hattie is responsible for bringing up the children and her greater contribution towards the running costs of the home. It is likely therefore that Hattie's beneficial share will be greater than a third.

6.5.3 Summary flowchart

Figure 6.1 Common intention constructive trusts summary flowchart

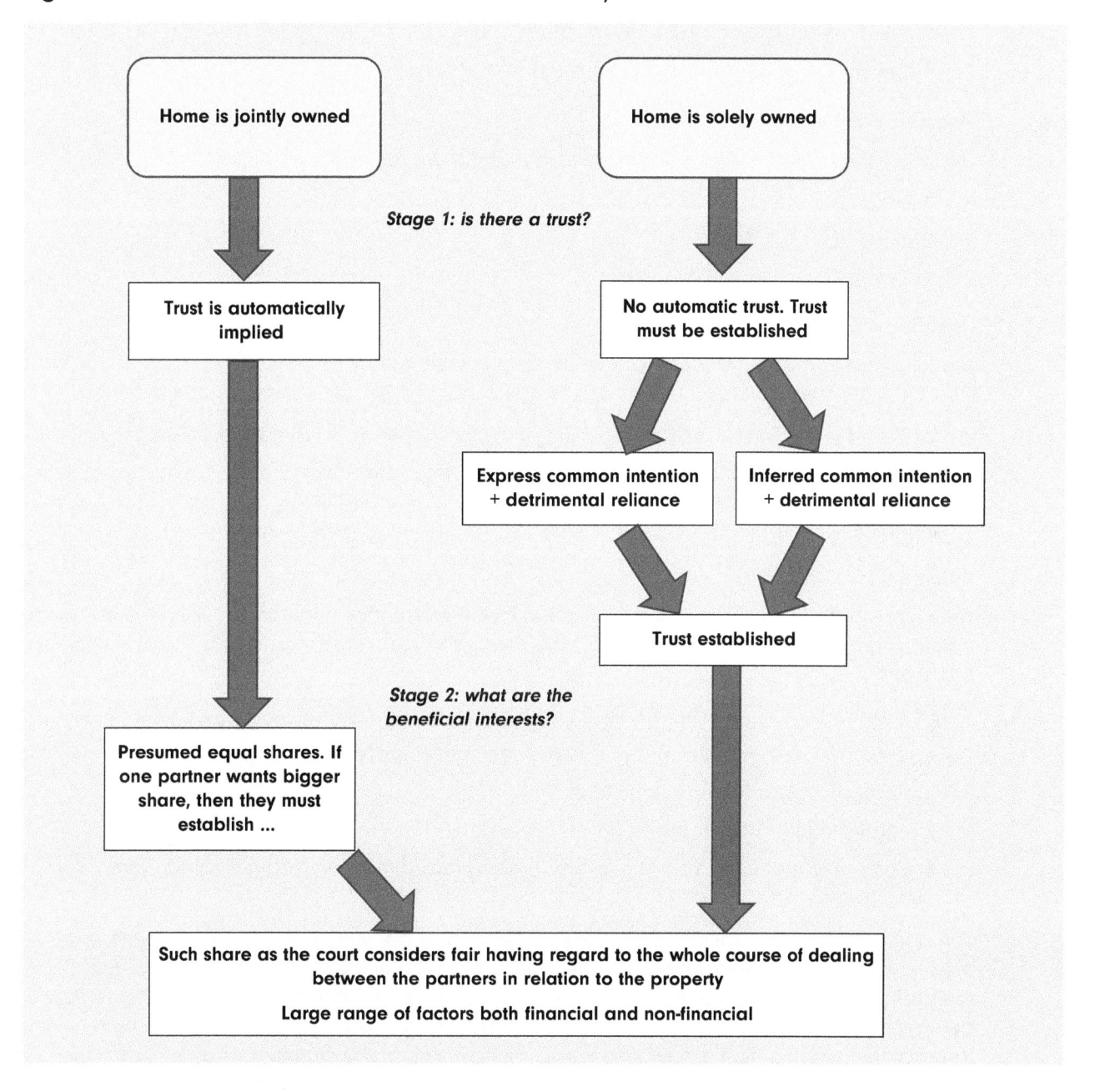

```
Home is jointly owned                    Home is solely owned

        │         Stage 1: is there a trust?        │
        ▼                                            ▼
Trust is automatically              No automatic trust. Trust
implied                             must be established
                                           │              │
                                           ▼              ▼
                              Express common intention   Inferred common intention
                              + detrimental reliance     + detrimental reliance
                                           │              │
                                           ▼              ▼
                                      Trust established
        │                                    │
        │    Stage 2: what are the           │
        │    beneficial interests?           │
        ▼                                    │
Presumed equal shares. If                    │
one partner wants bigger                     │
share, then they must                        │
establish ...                                │
        │                                    │
        ▼                                    ▼
Such share as the court considers fair having regard to the whole course of dealing
between the partners in relation to the property
Large range of factors both financial and non-financial
```

6.6 Proprietary estoppel

Proprietary estoppel is another method by which a partner may become entitled to an interest in the family home. However, it extends much further than this.

Proprietary estoppel prevents someone from going back on their word in relation to property, when it would be unfair to do so. It asks whether 'it would be unconscionable [unfair] for a party to be permitted to deny that which, knowingly or unknowingly, he has allowed or encouraged another to assume to his detriment' (*Taylor Fashions Ltd v Liverpool Victoria Trustees Co Ltd* [1982] QB 133). If the answer is yes, it will provide some form of relief to the party that has suffered detriment. It is commonly relied on when a relative or friend has been assured by the legal owner of the family home that the home 'will be yours when I die', only to find that the legal owner has subsequently left the home to someone else in their will.

When talking about proprietary estoppel, we shall refer to the relevant parties as the 'claiming party' and the 'legal owner'.

Like common intention constructive trusts, there are two stages involved in proprietary estoppel:

- Stage 1 – the estoppel must be established; and
- Stage 2 – the estoppel must be satisfied (remedies).

6.6.1 Stage 1: Establishing the equity

There are three key elements to establishing a claim in proprietary estoppel:

(a) Assurance

(b) Detriment

(c) Reliance

6.6.1.1 Assurance

The legal owner must have made a representation or created or encouraged an expectation that the claiming party would become entitled to an interest in land. The assurance can either be:

(a) active – the legal owner tells the claiming party that they have or will have an interest in land; or

(b) passive – there is conduct on the part of the claiming party that clearly suggests that they think they have a right to property. The legal owner knows this (or must have known it) but remains silent and fails to disabuse the claiming party of their belief.

6.6.1.2 Detriment

The claiming party must show that they acted to their detriment in reliance upon the assurance made. The detriment need not consist of the expenditure of money, so long as it is something substantial.

Things that have been held to amount to detriment include:

(a) spending money on refurbishing a home or improving property;

(b) working without adequate remuneration;

(c) giving up a job and moving to a new area; and

(d) looking after someone who is gravely ill (especially if that involved giving up more remunerative employment).

The detriment that the claiming party has received must be weighed against any benefits they have obtained. For instance, if someone is assured a future interest in property, quits their tenancy and lives rent-free in the property in which they hope to acquire an interest, the detriment of moving to a new area must be balanced against the benefit of obtaining rent-free accommodation. In those circumstances, it may be that the claiming party has not on balance suffered any detriment with the result that a claim in proprietary estoppel must fail (*Watts v Storey* (1983) 134 NLJ 631).

6.6.1.3 Reliance

The assurance and detriment must be connected to each other. The assurance must cause the claiming party to act to their detriment.

The assurances relied on do not have to be the sole reason for the claiming party's conduct. However, a claim in proprietary estoppel will fail if it can be shown that the claiming party acted for reasons other than the assurance. For instance, a claiming party is asked to look after an elderly relative and is promised that the house owned by the relative will be left to the claiming party on the relative's death. The claiming party gives up their job and home and moves in with the elderly relative, looking after them without payment. This is a form of detriment. However, when the elderly relative dies and leaves their house to someone else, the new legal owner may argue that the claiming party's conduct arose out of 'natural love and affection' for the elderly relative, rather than proprietary self-interest, and that any claim in proprietary estoppel should fail.

⭐ Example

Idris is the sole owner of a large house with considerable grounds in Devon. When he gets older, he starts to worry that he can no longer look after the house and grounds properly. He therefore invites his niece, Janet, and her husband, Keith, to move in and share the house with him. Janet and Keith live in Sheffield and have two young children. They are initially reluctant about having to move so far away, but Keith recently lost his job and is attracted by a new start and they also think the house and grounds would be a great place for the kids to grow up. To try and clinch the deal, Idris tells Janet that he would leave the house and grounds to them in his will if they wanted. Janet and Keith agree. They spend around £20,000 renovating the house when they arrive. They live there rent-free. Subsequently, when Idris starts to become frail, Janet spends most of her time looking after him (for which she is not remunerated). When Idris dies, Janet and Keith find out that Idris has left the house and grounds to his estranged son, Lionel.

Janet and Keith can probably assert a claim in proprietary estoppel. Idris made an active assurance that his home would be theirs on his death. Janet and Keith have suffered a number of different forms of detriment (such as moving to a new area, improving the property, looking after Idris for no remuneration), although the fact that they have received the benefit of rent-free accommodation should be balanced against these detriments. It is likely that Janet and Keith acted in this way because they thought Idris would leave his home to them (although Lionel may argue that they had their own reasons for moving, such as wanting a new start).

6.6.2 Stage 2: Satisfying the equity (remedies)

Once the elements of proprietary estoppel have been made out, the court has a discretion over whether a remedy should be awarded and, if so, which type.

The remedies that the court can grant include:

(a) transfer of the legal ownership in land;

(b) grant of a lease;

(c) some right of occupancy (eg the right to live in a house rent-free for life);

(d) financial compensation; or

(e) a beneficial share in the home.

In exercising its discretion, the court will usually adopt the following 5-step approach:

- Step 1: Is the legal owner's repudiation of their assurance unconscionable, given the claiming party's detrimental reliance? If the estoppel has been established (stage 1 above), then the answer will ordinarily be yes.

- Step 2: If so, the court will ordinarily hold the legal owner to their assurance. If the legal owner promised to transfer property, the court should ordinarily enforce that promise by transferring the property to the claiming party.

- Step 3: The burden is on the legal owner to prove that enforcing the assurance (step 2) would be out of all proportion to the detriment sustained by the claiming party. If established, the court may be constrained to limit the remedy granted. For instance, if the legal owner promised to leave a generous inheritance to the claiming party if the claiming party cared for the legal owner for the rest of their life, the court may limit the remedy granted if the legal owner unexpectedly died two months later. Where the full nature of the assurance is unclear, it may be easier for the legal owner to persuade the court to depart from full enforcement.

- Step 4: If the assurance involved the transfer of property on the legal owner's death, it might be possible for the court to order the transfer of that property whilst the legal owner is still alive, but the court should generally require a discount for accelerated receipt.

- Step 5: The court should consider any remedy 'in the round', asking itself whether the remedy would do 'justice between the parties, and whether it would cause injustice to third parties'.

It can be noted at this point that there may be some overlap between the common intention constructive trust and proprietary estoppel, particularly when it comes to cohabiting couples and trying to work out whether a claiming partner has an interest in the family home. The main difference between these two mechanisms is that the common intention constructive trust, if established, guarantees the claiming partner a beneficial share in the home; whereas proprietary estoppel gives the court a discretion over the remedy that the claiming partner will be awarded (which might be much more than a beneficial share – such as a transfer of the entire freehold – or much less).

Finally, a claiming party under proprietary estoppel may find themselves barred from obtaining a remedy:

(a) If the claiming party's conduct is inequitable or unconscionable (eg they have acted deviously, dishonestly or deceitfully), then they may be denied the relief to which they would have otherwise been entitled. As we saw in the Introduction, 'he who comes to equity must come with clean hands'.

(b) An unreasonable delay in bringing a claim in proprietary estoppel may defeat the claim. Equity does not assist a party who has failed to assert their rights within a reasonable time – 'delay defeats equity'.

6.6.3 Summary flowchart

Figure 6.2 Proprietary estoppel summary flowchart

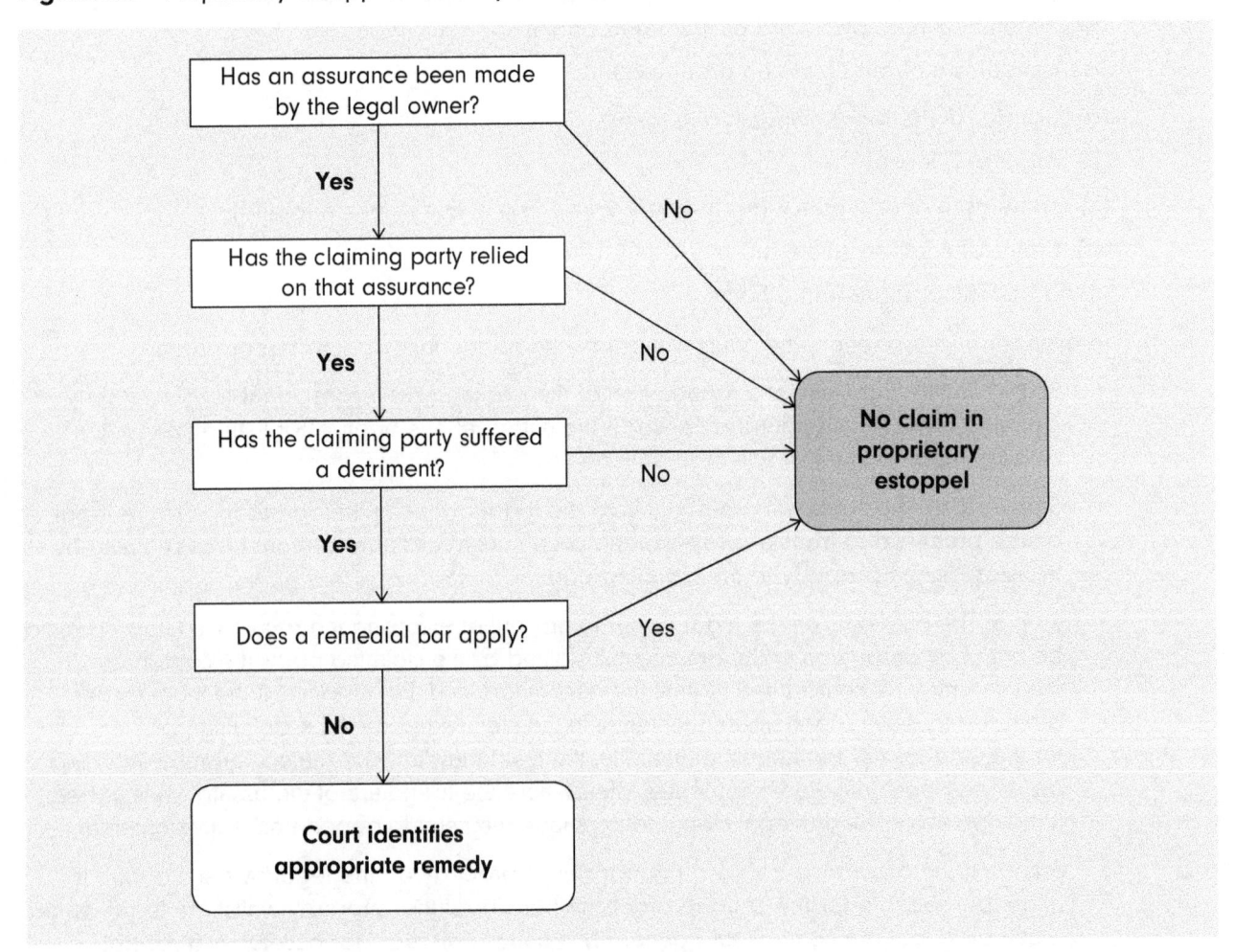

```
Has an assurance been made by the legal owner?
    │ Yes                           \ No
    ▼                                \
Has the claiming party relied on that assurance?
    │ Yes                    No ──→
    ▼                                 ──→  No claim in
Has the claiming party suffered                proprietary
a detriment?                                   estoppel
    │ Yes                    No ──→
    ▼                                 ──→
Does a remedial bar apply?      Yes ──→
    │ No
    ▼
Court identifies appropriate remedy
```

Summary

In this chapter, you have considered how the law uses common intention constructive trusts and proprietary estoppel to identify who might be entitled to interests in the family home and safeguard those interests, even when the family members themselves did not think about their entitlements or take any steps to protect them.

You have considered:

- *How the family home might be owned legally and beneficially.* If a couple has purchased the family home in their joint names, then usually they will take steps to create an enforceable express trust over the home (although this is not guaranteed). If one partner owns the family home in their sole name, it is still possible for the other partner to own a beneficial share in the home, but this is less likely to arise under an express trust, because the couple might not give the need for an express trust any thought.

- *Why resulting trusts might not be appropriate in dealing with the family home.* A resulting trust only gives you a beneficial interest in land if you contributed towards the purchase price at the time of purchase – if so, your beneficial interest is commensurate with the value of your financial contribution. This might give rise to results that are considered unfair. As a result, the law now largely quantifies the beneficial interests of each partner using a common intention constructive trust.

- *How the beneficial shares are quantified when the family home is jointly owned.* In the absence of an express trust, equity will generally follow the law, meaning that the partners own the beneficial interest in the house jointly and equally. If one partner wants a bigger share, they will have the onus of persuading the court to depart from this presumption.

- *How the beneficial shares are established and quantified when the family home is solely owned.* In the absence of an express trust, the party who does not own the legal title (ie is not a registered proprietor) must establish a common intention constructive trust. This requires them to demonstrate a common intention that they would have a beneficial interest in the home (either through an express understanding or inferred from conduct) and that they have relied on that intention to their detriment. The court will then assess what beneficial shares would be fair given the whole course of dealing between the partners.

- *How proprietary estoppel can be used to give people interests in the family home.* If the legal owner assures another party that they will have an interest in the home, and that other party acts to their detriment in reliance on that assurance, the legal owner may be estopped (prevented) from denying them that interest. However, whether that means the party claiming an interest will get a beneficial share in the home is ultimately a matter for the court's discretion.

Sample questions

Question 1

A man started to go out with a woman who lived in the same town. The woman was about to buy a house. She paid most of the deposit on the house but needed some help from the man. He agreed to lend her some money, which she repaid the following month. The mortgage was taken out in her sole name.

The man's tenancy came to an end around the same time and he lost his job. He moved into the house. The woman told the man that although the house was in her name, he should consider the house as much his as it was hers. The man looked for work but could not find a job. The man was therefore unable to make any contribution to the mortgage repayments, the running of the house or any renovations to the house.

Trusts

The relationship has now come to an end. The man did not marry the woman and there were no children. The woman has put the house on the market.

Does the man have a beneficial interest in the house?

A Yes, because he was the beneficiary under an enforceable express trust.

B Yes, because there was an express agreement to that effect.

C Yes, because he lent the woman money to pay the deposit without which she could not have bought the house in the first place.

D No, because no declaration of trust was manifested and proved in signed writing.

E No, because the house was in her sole name, which automatically prevents him taking a beneficial interest.

Answer

Option D is correct. In order to work out why, we shall first consider why the other options are wrong.

Option A is wrong. The woman's statement to the man that he should consider the house as much his as hers might demonstrate an intention to create an express trust, but as that express trust was to be over land, to be effective it must have been evidenced in signed writing. This has not happened.

Option B is wrong. Whilst there was an express common understanding that the man was to take a beneficial interest in the house, that would only give rise to a common intention constructive trust (or a claim for proprietary estoppel) if he had acted on that understanding to his detriment. There does not appear to be anything on the facts that would constitute detrimental reliance.

Option C is wrong. Whilst a contribution to the deposit can create beneficial interests under an implied trust, lending the money for a deposit does not constitute a 'contribution' for these purposes.

Option E is wrong. Just because the legal title to a home is in the sole name of one partner does not automatically prevent the other partner from getting a beneficial interest in the home.

Option D is therefore the best answer. For the reasons set out above, the man cannot assert an interest under an implied trust (resulting or constructive) or proprietary estoppel, nor can he assert a beneficial interest by way of an express trust. In order to be enforceable an express trust must comply with s 53(1)(b) of the LPA 1925, ie it must be evidenced in signed writing. This has not happened.

Question 2

Five years ago, a man and his girlfriend were looking for a house that they could move into and call their family home. They found a house they both liked. The man told his girlfriend that he would pay the deposit but asked whether she could pay the conveyancing fees for him because he had forgotten to budget for this. She did so. When they first went to see their solicitor on the purchase of the house, they agreed that the house should be put in their joint names. However, after discussions with the bank to get a mortgage, the bank advised it would be better for the house and mortgage to be in the man's sole name, because his girlfriend had a low credit rating that might make it difficult for them to get mortgage finance. The girlfriend agreed to this.

Over the next five years, the man paid the monthly mortgage instalments. His girlfriend got a job three years ago, and since then has paid for the expensive work that was done to put in a new bathroom and kitchen.

The relationship between the man and his girlfriend has now broken down. She has moved out and the man is looking to sell the house.

Does the girlfriend have an interest in the house?

A   Yes, because paying the conveyancing fees gives her an interest in the house under a resulting trust.

B   Yes, because there was an express understanding that she was to have an interest on which she relied.

C   Yes, because whilst there was no express understanding that she was to have an interest, the fact that she paid to install a new bathroom and kitchen means that she will get an interest under a common intention constructive trust.

D   No, because no trust was manifested and proved in signed writing.

E   No, because she did not make any payment towards the deposit or the subsequent mortgage instalments.

Answer

Option B is correct. The evidence suggests that but for the bank's advice to keep the house in the man's sole name, it would have been registered in the joint name of him and his girlfriend. That can constitute an express common intention that his girlfriend was to have an interest in the home. She has also suffered detrimental reliance in the substantial payments she has made to household improvements and expenses.

Option A is wrong. To give rise to a resulting trust, any contribution must be to the purchase price itself, not to ancillary items such as legal fees.

Option C is wrong. There was an express common understanding that ownership of the house would be shared. In any event, in the absence of such an express understanding, it is unlikely that the payments the girlfriend did make would be sufficient to enable a common intention of ownership to be inferred. There is no suggestion that she made any significant payment towards the purchase price or mortgage.

Option D is wrong. Whilst it is correct to say that there can be no express trust, because such a trust over land would have to be evidenced in signed writing, it is not correct to say that there cannot therefore be any trust, and a common intention constructive trust will have arisen on the facts. Such implied trusts do not need to be evidenced in signed writing.

Option E is wrong. Given that there was an express common understanding that the house be shared, the court can take a wider view as to what constitutes detrimental reliance beyond those items listed in this option.

Question 3

An elderly aunt asks her niece to move in and look after her. The niece loves her aunt but expresses reservations about whether such a move would be possible. She has a child who goes to school near to where she lives; she works full-time and there is talk that she might get a promotion. In order to persuade the niece to change her mind, the aunt promises that when she dies, she will leave the house to the niece. The niece agrees to move in. She provides her aunt with round-the-clock care for no pay (other than the aunt meeting all her living expenses), quits her job and takes her child out of school, home-schooling him whenever there is a free moment.

Eight years later, the aunt dies. The niece finds out that the aunt has left her house to a friend.

Which of the following statements best describes why the niece might have an interest in the house?

A The niece should have an interest under a common intention constructive trust arising out of the express understanding that she was to have an interest in the house.

B The niece should have an interest under a common intention constructive trust arising out of an inferred understanding that she was to have an interest in the house.

C The niece should have an interest because she can establish proprietary estoppel arising out of an active assurance, which automatically guarantees her an interest in the house.

D The niece should have an interest because she can establish proprietary estoppel arising out of an active assurance, which means it is likely that she will get an interest in the house.

E The niece should have an interest because she can establish proprietary estoppel arising out of a passive assurance, which means it is likely that she will get an interest in the house.

Answer

Option D is correct. The aunt actively assured the niece that the house would belong to her and the niece appears to have relied on that assurance to her detriment. Whilst the court has a discretion about what remedy to award, it is likely that the court will award the niece an interest in the house. (Indeed, on the facts, it is likely that that interest would be an absolute ownership right to the entire house. The court would therefore transfer the house to her.)

Options A and B are wrong. Common intention constructive trusts are used to establish present interests in property (ie when two partners share a house together). They are not used to establish future interests in property, as in this scenario. The niece will need to assert proprietary estoppel. Proprietary estoppel prevents the aunt from backtracking on her assurance that in the future the house will belong to the niece.

Option C is wrong. Whilst proprietary estoppel can be established in this case, that does not automatically guarantee the niece a proprietary interest in the house. The remedy is ultimately within the discretion of the court.

Option E is wrong. The assurance in this case was active not passive. This is not a case where the aunt stood back and allowed the niece to think that she was getting some kind of proprietary interest – the aunt had actively suggested this.

PART 2
ADMINISTRATION OF TRUSTS

7 Trustees: Appointment, Removal and Retirement

7.1	Introduction	100
7.2	Who can be a trustee	100
7.3	Minimum and maximum number of trustees	100
7.4	Appointment, removal and retirement of trustees by express power	100
7.5	Retirement of trustees	101
7.6	Removal of trustees	102
7.7	Appointment of additional trustees	103
7.8	Death of a trustee	104
7.9	Appointment of an attorney	104

SQE1 syllabus

This chapter will enable you to achieve the SQE1 assessment specification in relation to functioning legal knowledge concerned with the following core principles:

- Who can be a trustee
- The appointment of trustees
- The removal of trustees
- The retirement of trustees

Note that for SQE1, candidates are not usually required to recall specific case names or cite statutory or regulatory authorities. Cases are provided for illustrative purposes only.

Learning outcomes

By the end of this chapter you will be able to apply relevant core legal principles and rules appropriately and effectively, at the level of a competent newly qualified solicitor in practice, to realistic client-based and ethical problems and situations in the following areas:

- identifying who can be a trustee;
- establishing the changing identity of trustees over the life of the trust; and
- advising on the ability to appoint an attorney (a deputy) to exercise trustee functions when the appointed trustee is unavailable.

7.1 Introduction

The settlor's most important decision when setting up a trust is whom to appoint as the trustee(s). The trustee is under a duty to look after (and invest) property for the benefit of others. Particularly where the trust is to last for any significant period of time, the settlor must consider carefully who best can discharge this duty: is it a family member who is close to the beneficiaries and therefore can be trusted to look after their interests; is it an independent professional who understands how a trust works and the relevant duties with which a trustee must comply; or is it best to appoint a mixture of both?

The trust might continue for some time. Once the settlor makes their decision and names the trustees they want to appoint in the declaration of trust, what happens if a trustee is no longer able to continue their role, whether through illness, death or simply lack of interest?

This chapter looks at:

- who can be a trustee;
- how trustees are appointed, the circumstances in which they can retire and the circumstances in which other people can compel trustees to step down; and
- whether trustees can appoint a 'deputy' to stand in for them should they need to take a short break.

We will consider these issues in the context of express trusts.

7.2 Who can be a trustee

Most adults with mental capacity can be appointed to act as a trustee (there are certain statutory disqualifications in relation to more specialised trusts, such as charity trusts and pension trusts, but these are outside the scope of this manual).

A company can also act as a trustee (whether alone or in conjunction with human trustees) so long as it is authorised to do so by its constitutional documents. 'Trust corporations' are corporate trustees that carry out trust business for profit.

7.3 Minimum and maximum number of trustees

Trusts over land should have at least two human trustees or a sole trust corporation. This is to ensure that, should the trustees need to sell the land, a buyer can purchase it safe in the knowledge that any beneficial interests have been overreached (see the **Land Manual** for further detail).

Trusts of personalty can have a sole trustee, although as a practical matter it is generally better to appoint more than one to ensure that each trustee can supervise what the other is doing.

Trusts over land cannot have more than four trustees. Trusts of personalty can have more than four trustees (although this is unlikely to be either practical or cost-efficient for many trusts).

As express trusts can involve a mixture of both land and personalty, it is best practice to ensure that there are always between two and four trustees in office at any one time.

7.4 Appointment, removal and retirement of trustees by express power

The declaration of trust may contain express powers for trustees to be appointed, replaced or removed. However, statute provides wide powers in this regard, and it is accordingly relatively rare for trust documents to contain additional powers.

We shall therefore move on to consider the relevant statutory powers that allow trustees to be appointed, to be removed or to retire. The powers that trustees can exercise are set out in the Trustee Act (TA) 1925, and the powers that beneficiaries can exercise are set out in the Trusts of Land and Appointment of Trustees Act (TLATA) 1996.

7.5 Retirement of trustees

This can take place as follows:

Retirement of a trustee

A trustee who wishes to retire must use one of the following provisions:

(1) **The trust instrument** may contain an express power for trustees to retire but this is unusual.

(3) **Section 36(1) of the TA 1925**

- The retiring trustee must be replaced by the appointment of a new trustee.
- Who appoints the new trustee?
    (a) the person nominated in the trust instrument to exercise the s 36 power, but if none
    (b) the continuing trustee(s) (which includes the retiring trustee if they are willing to join in the appointment).
- s 36 states that the appointment must be in writing. Why is it advantageous to use a deed? (See TA 1925, s 40)
    Under s 40, a deed automatically vests the trust property (apart from company shares and some other limited forms of property) in the continuing and new trustee.

(2) **Section 39 of the TA 1925** allows a trustee to retire without being replaced. Conditions:

(a) there will be two trustees or a trust corporation left
(b) the trustee retires by deed
(c) the other trustees consent by deed.

Is a trustee who has retired liable for breaches of trust?

A retiring trustee remains liable for their own breaches but will not be liable for future breaches unless they retired to facilitate the breaches.

⭐ Example

Erin and Flavia were appointed as trustees. Erin now wants to retire.

She cannot retire under s 39 of the TA 1925, as that would only leave Flavia as a trustee, and s 39 does not enable an existing trustee to retire where there would be fewer than two remaining (human) trustees. Erin or Flavia would therefore have to find a replacement trustee who can be appointed upon Erin's retirement, pursuant to s 36(1) of the TA 1925 (see above).

7.6 Removal of trustees

This can take place as follows:

Removal and/or replacement of a trustee

Trustees or the beneficiaries may want to remove and/or replace a trustee (sometimes against the trustee's will). They need to use one of the following provisions.

(1) **The trust instrument** may contain an express power to remove and/or replace trustees but this is unusual.

(2) **Section 36(1) of the TA 1925**
- Grounds for replacing a trustee:
  (a) the trustee is dead
  (b) remains outside the UK for more than 12 months
  (c) desires to be discharged (retire)
  (d) refuses to act (disclaims)
  (e) is unfit to act
  (f) is incapable of acting (eg mental or physical incapacity)
  (g) is a minor.
- Who effects the replacement?
  (a) the person nominated in the trust instrument to exercise the s 36 power, but if none:
  (b) the continuing trustee(s) including a retiring trustee if they are willing to join in the appointment;
  (c) if all trustees have died, the PRs of the last surviving trustee.
- Section 36 states that the appointment must be in writing. Why is it advantageous to use a deed? (See TA 1925, s 40)
  Under s 40, a deed automatically vests the trust property (apart from eg company shares) in the continuing and new trustee.

(3) **Section 41 of the TA 1925**
- Grounds? The court will *replace* a trustee if it is expedient to do so and it is otherwise inexpedient, difficult or impractical to appoint without the court's assistance.
- The court makes the appointment following an application by the trustees or the beneficiaries.
- The court will only replace a trustee if it is not in the best interests of the trust for them to continue. Mere dislike of a trustee is generally insufficient.

(4) **Section 19 of the TLATA 1996** allows beneficiaries to serve a written direction on a trustee or trustees to retire and appoint the person (if any) specified in the direction.
- s 19 does not apply if the trust instrument:
  ○ excludes it, or
  ○ the trust instrument nominates someone to appoint new trustees.
- s 19 applies only if the beneficiaries are of full age and capacity and taken together are absolutely entitled to the trust property.
- Following a valid written direction, the trustee must retire by deed if:
  (a) reasonable arrangements have been made to protect their rights;
  (b) after their retirement there will be two trustees or a trust corporation left; and
  (c) another person is appointed to replace them or the continuing trustees consent by deed to their retirement.

⭐ Example

Two years ago, Abigail appointed Ben and Ciara to act as trustees when she first set up the trust. For the first six months, everything seemed to work. However, Ciara then left the UK to live in Spain, has been there ever since and has not helped Ben run the trust for some time. There is no express provision in the declaration of trust that deals with the appointment or retirement of trustees. Ben wants to appoint David to help run the trust in Ciara's place.

David can be appointed as a new trustee under s 36(1) of the TA 1925. Ciara has been out of the country for more than 12 months. Given that there is no person nominated for the purpose of appointing new trustees in the trust instrument, Ben should appoint David as a new trustee. This appointment should be made by deed, so as to take advantage of the automatic vesting provision of s 40 of the TA 1925.

⭐ Example

In my will, I appointed George and Harriet to act as trustees for 'such of my children who attain the age of 25 years'. The beneficiaries under this trust are Ivan (aged 28 years), Juliette (aged 23 years), and Kevin (aged 19 years). The beneficiaries have fallen out with George and would like to force him to retire.

Ivan, Juliette and Kevin are (taken together) absolutely entitled to the trust property. The trust property is to be divided between 'such of my children' who attain the age of 25 years, and as Ivan has satisfied this contingency, no-one outside my children can become entitled (if Juliette and Kevin were to die tomorrow without satisfying this condition, then all of the trust property would vest solely in Ivan). As the children are all over the age of 18 (and assuming they have capacity), the three of them can consider exercising their rights under s 19 of the TLATA 1996.

However, the beneficiaries cannot simply demand that George retire because then there would only be one remaining trustee in office (Harriet). The beneficiaries would therefore also have to direct that someone else be appointed as trustee in George's place.

7.7 Appointment of additional trustees

This can take place as follows:

Appointment of additional trustees

Trustees or beneficiaries may not want any of the existing trustees to step down but may want to appoint an additional trustee. They should use one of the following provisions.

(1) **The trust instrument** may contain an express power to appoint new trustees but this is unusual.

(2) **Section 36(6) of the TA 1925**
- Who makes the appointment?
  The person nominated in the trust instrument or, if none, the continuing trustee(s).
  There can be no more than four trustees once the additional appointments are made.
- s 36 states that the appointment must be in writing. Why is it advantageous to use a deed? (See TA 1925, s 40) Automatic vesting of trust property as above.

(3) **Section 41 of the TA 1925**
- Grounds?
  As above. The court will appoint a new trustee if it is expedient to do so and it is otherwise inexpedient, difficult or impractical to appoint without the court's assistance.
  The court makes the appointment following an application by the trustees or the beneficiaries.

(4) **Section 19 of the TLATA 1996** allows beneficiaries to serve a written direction on the current trustees requiring the appointment of an additional trustee. For conditions see above.

⭐ Example

Andrew and Tara were selected to be trustees of a discretionary trust, with a trust fund worth £4 million. Andrew is a primary school teacher and Tara is a GP receptionist. They are feeling out of their depth and would like to appoint some professionals to act alongside them as trustees. There is no provision in the trust document for the appointment of new trustees.

They are friends with Charles (a private client solicitor), Daniel (a barrister) and Esther (a financial adviser). They would like to appoint all three of them to act as co-trustees.

However, Andrew and Tara can only appoint two further trustees. They therefore need to decide which two of the three possible candidates are best-placed to act as additional trustees and then Andrew, Tara and the two selected trustees should execute a deed for that purpose.

7.8 Death of a trustee

If two or more trustees are appointed, they will hold legal title to trust property as joint tenants, with the result that if one dies, the legal title will devolve to the surviving trustees (TA 1925, s 18). If there is only one surviving trustee left, that trustee should be advised to appoint a replacement trustee under s 36(1) of the TA 1925 to ensure the continuity of trust administration.

7.9 Appointment of an attorney

If a trustee is concerned that they might not be able to perform their functions in running the trust for a period of time, they should consider delegating those functions to a 'deputy' called an attorney.

The delegation should be made by deed in the form prescribed under s 25 of the TA 1925. The delegation can run for a period of up to 12 months. Written notice about the delegation must be given to all other trustees and any other person with the power to appoint new trustees within seven days of delegation.

The delegating trustee will be automatically liable for the acts or defaults of the attorney as if they were the acts or defaults of the trustee.

As well as one trustee individually delegating their functions to an attorney, the trustees collectively can delegate decisions on how best to invest trust property to an independent financial adviser. This collective delegation will be addressed in **Chapter 10**.

Summary

In this chapter, you have considered who can be appointed to act as a trustee and how the identity of the trustees can change over the lifetime of a trust.

You have considered:

- *How many trustees there should be*. Generally, a trust should have between two and four trustees in office at any one time.
- *How trustees can retire from their trusteeship*. In the absence of any express provision in the declaration of trust, trustees will commonly retire pursuant to the provisions of the TA 1925. If there will be less than two trustees left in office once the outgoing trustee retires, a replacement trustee must be appointed.

- *How trustees can be removed from their trusteeship.* In the absence of any express provision in the declaration of trust, trustees can be removed by the trustees, the beneficiaries or the court. Different conditions attach to each of these methods of removal.

- *How additional trustees can be appointed.* In the absence of any express provision in the declaration of trust, additional trustees can be appointed by the trustees, the beneficiaries or the court. Different conditions attach to each of these methods of appointment.

- *How trustees can delegate their functions to an attorney.* If a trustee knows they will not be able to exercise their functions for a certain period of time, they should delegate those functions to an attorney. However, they should choose their attorney with care, because they will remain liable for the acts of that attorney.

Sample questions

Question 1

In his valid will, a man created a trust over his residuary estate for such of his children surviving his death and, if more than one, in equal shares. Two trustees were appointed to manage the trust. The will contained no express provisions dealing with the appointment or retirement of trustees.

The man was survived by three children who are currently aged 22, 19 and 16 years respectively. The beneficiaries are unhappy with the way that the trustees have managed the trust since the man's death.

Which of the following best describes whether the beneficiaries can remove the trustees?

A   The beneficiaries have no power to remove trustees, as the removal, retirement and appointment of trustees is a matter for the trustees alone.

B   The beneficiaries cannot direct that the trustees should retire because they are not of full age and capacity to make such a direction.

C   The beneficiaries cannot apply to the court to remove the trustees because any application to the court for removal of a trustee must be made by the trustees themselves.

D   The beneficiaries can direct that the trustees should retire because taken together they are absolutely entitled to the trust fund.

E   The beneficiaries can direct that the trustees should retire but only if they appoint replacement trustees in their place.

Answer

Option B is correct. Beneficiaries can direct that trustees must retire, but only if they satisfy the conditions set out in s 19 of the Trusts of Land and Appointment of Trustees Act 1996. Beneficiaries can only use this statutory provision if they are all of full age and capacity. This is not the case here because one of the beneficiaries is under the age of 18 years.

Options A and C are wrong in stating that the matter of the appointment, removal and retirement of trustees is a matter for trustees alone and that only trustees can apply to court to assist with such matters. The appointment and removal of trustees can be directed by the beneficiaries so long as they satisfy the statutory conditions of s 19 of the TLATA 1996, and beneficiaries can apply to the court to replace trustees if it is expedient to do so and it is otherwise inexpedient, difficult or impractical to replace trustees without the court's assistance.

Trusts

Option D is wrong. Whilst it is correct to say that the children are, taken together, absolutely entitled to the trust fund, this is only one of the statutory conditions that must be satisfied in order for beneficiaries to take advantage of s 19 of the TLATA 1996 – they must also be of full age and capacity. This is not the case here.

Option E is wrong. The option correctly reminds us that if the beneficiaries were able to use s 19 of the TLATA 1996 to direct that the current trustees must retire, they would also need to appoint replacement trustees – when using s 19 of the TLATA 1996 there must be at least two trustees (or a trust corporation) in office after those trustees directed to retire have done so. However, option E overlooks the fact that the beneficiaries cannot use s 19 of the TLATA 1996 in the first place given that they are not all of full age.

Question 2

Three trustees were appointed by the settlor to hold property on trust for the testator's four nieces, all of whom are currently under the age of 18 years. The trust deed contained no express provisions dealing with the appointment or retirement of trustees.

Shortly after their appointment, one trustee decided that he did not want to take part in the running of the trust and went abroad to live in his second home in the south of France. Fifteen months later, the two remaining trustees want to tell their co-trustee that they have removed him from office.

Which of the following best describes whether the two trustees can remove their co-trustee living in France?

A The two trustees can remove their co-trustee in writing and continue to run the trust themselves.

B The two trustees can remove their co-trustee by informing him orally and continue to run the trust themselves.

C The co-trustee cannot be removed under any circumstances as he was originally appointed by the settlor.

D The two trustees cannot remove their co-trustee without also appointing a replacement co-trustee.

E The two trustees cannot remove their co-trustee and replace him with someone else without making an application to the court.

Answer

Option D is correct. The two trustees could remove their co-trustee on the grounds that he has been outside the UK for more than 12 months (see TA 1925, s 36(1)). However, they can only remove the co-trustee on this ground if they appoint a replacement trustee in his place.

Option A is wrong. The two trustees have no power themselves to remove their co-trustee without appointing a replacement trustee.

Option B is wrong. Not only will the trustees be unable to remove their co-trustee without replacing him, if the trustees want to exercise statutory powers to remove co-trustees, they will have to notify the removed trustee in writing – orally confirming this to the outgoing trustee is insufficient.

Option C is wrong. The statutory powers to remove trustees can apply to those trustees originally appointed by the settlor.

Option E is wrong. The two trustees can remove and replace their co-trustee without making an application to the court.

Question 3

A woman is about to undergo surgery and has been advised that she will need to take at least six months off work in order to recover. The woman is a trustee and is worried about being able to perform her functions as trustee while she is recovering from the surgery. There is nothing in the trust deed that says anything about appointing someone else to step into her role.

Which of the following best describes whether she can appoint someone else to step into her role while she is unable to perform her functions?

A   She can appoint an attorney by telephone and should take care about who she appoints.

B   She can appoint an attorney by deed and should take care about who she appoints.

C   She can appoint an attorney by deed and does not need to worry about who she appoints.

D   She cannot appoint an attorney as she was personally chosen by the settlor to be a trustee.

E   She cannot appoint an attorney as there is nothing in the trust deed that allows this.

Answer

Option B is correct. The trustee can (and should) appoint an attorney to carry on her role while she is indisposed. That appointment must be made by deed. As the trustee will be automatically (vicariously) liable for any defaults of the attorney, she should take great care in selecting someone she thinks will do a good job.

Option A is wrong. The appointment of an attorney must be made by deed (TA 1925, s 25) and cannot take place over the telephone.

Option C is wrong. The trustee will be automatically (vicariously) liable for any defaults of the attorney she appoints, so she must take care when making her selection.

Option D is wrong. The fact that she is an original trustee, chosen personally by the settlor, does not prevent her from appointing an attorney.

Option E is wrong. A trustee can use the power granted under s 25 of the TA 1925 to appoint an attorney regardless of whether or not the trust deed contains any express provision on the matter.

8 Trustee Powers: Maintenance and Advancement

8.1	Introduction	110
8.2	Express powers in the declaration of trust	110
8.3	Power to apply income for beneficiaries who are minors	110
8.4	Duty to pay income to certain beneficiaries	112
8.5	Power to pay capital to or for beneficiaries	112
8.6	Summary flowchart	115

SQE1 syllabus

This chapter will enable you to achieve the SQE1 assessment specification in relation to functioning legal knowledge concerned with the following core principles:

- Trustees' statutory powers of maintenance
- Trustees' statutory powers of advancement

Note that for SQE1, candidates are not usually required to recall specific case names or cite statutory or regulatory authorities. Cases are provided for illustrative purposes only.

Learning outcomes

By the end of this chapter you will be able to apply relevant core legal principles and rules appropriately and effectively, at the level of a competent newly qualified solicitor in practice, to realistic client-based and ethical problems and situations in the following areas:

- establishing when trustees can apply income to maintain beneficiaries who are minors;
- establishing when trustees must distribute income to adult beneficiaries; and
- establishing when trustees can advance capital to beneficiaries.

8.1 Introduction

I have been appointed a trustee in my friend's will. Property has been left on trust for the testator's son, Charles, if he attains the age of 25 years. Charles is 18 years old and is about to go to university. His mother has been short of money since the testator's death and will not be able to pay Charles' tuition fees and living expenses when he leaves home. The trust has more than enough money in it to help Charles. Can I, the trustee, give Charles some money from the trust now, even though he is not strictly entitled to it until he reaches the age of 25 years?

The situation of beneficiaries might change after a trust has been created. The trustees may need some flexibility to adapt to those changing circumstances, particularly where a beneficiary might need trust property early and especially if the trustees think that is what the settlor would have wanted.

This chapter looks at:

- powers available to trustees to give beneficiaries trust income early;
- circumstances in which trustees must pay trust income over to beneficiaries even where their rights have not yet vested; and
- powers available to trustees to give beneficiaries trust capital early.

We have already considered income and capital returns that might be generated by property in **Chapter 3**. You are advised to take a look back at this chapter to refresh your memory of the differences between the two and which types of beneficiaries are entitled to what kind of return.

8.2 Express powers in the declaration of trust

A settlor may expressly provide in the declaration of trust that trustees can, in the future, pay income or capital to beneficiaries before they become strictly entitled to trust property. If they do so, those express provisions must be followed.

In the absence of any express provision in the declaration of trust, the TA 1925 gives trustees various powers to pay income or capital early to beneficiaries. The settlor can modify or exclude these statutory powers as much as they wish.

For the most part, we will assume that the settlor has not made any express provision for the early payment of income or capital to beneficiaries and has not modified or excluded the statutory powers in any way.

8.3 Power to apply income for beneficiaries who are minors

Income is a return paid on a regular basis generated from capital. Common examples of income returns include:

(a) dividends paid on shares;

(b) interest paid on bank accounts; and

(c) rent paid for the occupation of land.

It is likely therefore that a trust will include forms of property that are regularly producing income returns.

Pursuant to s 31 of the TA 1925, trustees have the power to use income to pay for the maintenance, education and benefit of a beneficiary under the age of 18 years (an 'infant beneficiary' or a minor) so long as the following conditions are satisfied:

(a) there is no contrary provision in the declaration of trust; and

(b) the trustees can only exercise this power in favour of minor beneficiaries who have some kind of interest in income, whether vested or contingent, but not where there are any 'prior interests' to income.

Trustees cannot use s 31 of the TA 1925 to apply income for a beneficiary where someone else is the life tenant. In life interest trusts – eg a trust for my husband for life, remainder to my son – the trustees must pay income to the life tenant (my husband). During his lifetime, my husband has a prior interest to income, which must be respected.

⭐ Example

I create a trust for my husband, Rajesh, for life, remainder to my son, Saleem. Saleem is currently aged 8 years.

While he is alive, Rajesh is the only person interested in income. My trustees cannot use the statutory powers under s 31 of the TA 1925 to apply income for Saleem's benefit while Rajesh is still alive.

If Rajesh were to die two years later, there would be no interest in income prior to Saleem's interest and Saleem would therefore become the type of beneficiary in favour of whom the trustees can exercise their statutory powers under s 31 of the TA 1925.

If the trustees wish to apply income for a minor beneficiary's maintenance, education or benefit, the trustees should not pay income directly to the beneficiary. For very young beneficiaries that would make no practical sense, and it makes no legal sense because minors cannot give their trustees good receipt. Therefore, instead, the beneficiaries should pay the income direct to the beneficiary's parent or guardian, or alternatively directly to the maintenance, education or benefit provider. For instance, if the beneficiary is going to a fee-paying school, the trustees can use income generated by the trust to pay the school directly.

Section 31 of the TA 1925 gives the trustees the *power* to apply trust income for the maintenance, education or benefit of a beneficiary under 18 years of age. However, they are not *obliged* to use the trust income in this way. The trustees cannot be compelled to exercise this power under s 31 of the TA 1925. Whether or not they exercise the power is a matter for their discretion.

⭐ Example

Trustees are holding trust property for the benefit of Tessa. Tessa is aged 12 years. Tessa's father has telephoned the trustees to demand that they use some of the trust income to pay for Tessa's martial arts lessons. There are no provisions for the early release of income or capital in the declaration of trust.

The trustees can apply income for Tessa's maintenance, education or benefit. She has a vested right to trust income, and martial arts lessons are likely to be for her education or benefit. The trustees can therefore apply income for these purposes, although they would be best advised paying that income direct to the father or the person running the lessons (trustees should not pay income directly to beneficiaries under the age of 18 years).

However, whilst the trustees have the power *to apply trust income for this purpose, they cannot be compelled to do so, and they would be entitled to reject the father's demands. If they decide not to apply the income at this stage, they should accumulate that income – ie invest it for Tessa's future benefit – and then transfer that accumulated income with the trust capital to Tessa when she calls for the trust property on or after her 18th birthday.*

8.4 Duty to pay income to certain beneficiaries

Section 31 of the TA 1925 contains a slight twist when addressing the position of adult contingent beneficiaries. Adult contingent beneficiaries are entitled to trust income as it arises and trustees *must* pay that income to them, pending the vesting of their beneficial interests.

⭐ Example

I create a trust for Ulrika if she attains the age of 25. Ulrika is now aged 15 years. Ulrika's interests are currently contingent – she must satisfy the condition of reaching the age of 25 years before her interests in the trust property vest.

Until Ulrika reaches the age of 18 years, the trustees have a discretionary power to apply trust income for her maintenance, education or benefit (and a duty to accumulate any income not so used).

When Ulrika reaches the age of 18 years, but before her interest vests, the trustee discretion to apply income for her maintenance, education or benefit ceases. That discretionary power is replaced with a duty to pay trust income to Ulrika as it arises until she reaches the age of 25 years.

Once Ulrika reaches the age of 25 years and obtains a vested interest in the trust property, she can call for the trust property to be conveyed to her, at which point the trust capital and any accumulated trust income (from when she was a minor) will be paid to her.

If an adult contingent beneficiary dies before the condition is satisfied (eg if Ulrika in the above example dies before reaching the age of 25 years), their estate will receive nothing – no capital and no accumulated income. No-one else will have the right to reclaim any income properly paid to the adult contingent beneficiary before their death.

8.5 Power to pay capital to or for beneficiaries

Capital refers to the underlying trust property itself. Under s 32 of the TA 1925, trustees have the power to pay or apply trust capital early for a beneficiary's advancement or benefit so long as the conditions in **Table 8.1** are satisfied.

If the beneficiary seeking trust capital is under the age of 18 years, the trustees should apply that capital for the beneficiary by paying monies directly to the third party who will improve the material situation of the beneficiary. A trustee would be ill-advised to pay capital direct to a beneficiary under the age of 18 years because that beneficiary cannot give good receipt.

It should be remembered that s 32 of the TA 1925 gives the trustees the *power* to advance trust capital to a beneficiary (if the statutory conditions are met). However, they are not *obliged* to advance capital. The trustees cannot be compelled to exercise this power under s 32 of the TA 1925. Whether or not they exercise the power is a matter for their discretion.

Let us consider an example to bring together the various conditions in s 32 of the TA 1925.

⭐ Example

Trustees are holding property worth £400,000 on trust for such of the settlor's children as attain the age of 25 years. The settlor has two children: Fabien (aged 18 years) and Gabriella (aged 15 years). The trust document, dated 11 March 2018, contains no express provisions dealing with the early payment of income or capital.

Table 8.1 Statutory conditions on advancing capital

	Condition	Example
(a)	There is no contrary provision in the declaration of trust.	
(b)	The beneficiary has an interest in capital. Such beneficiaries include: (i) beneficiaries with a vested interest in trust capital (whether in possession or in remainder); and (ii) beneficiaries with a contingent interest in trust capital.	I create a trust for my husband, Rajesh, for life, remainder to my son, Saleem. Saleem is currently aged 8 years. Under this life interest trust, Saleem is the only person interested in capital. As the life tenant, Rajesh is only interested in income, with the result that my trustees cannot pay capital to him. (If my trustees wish to apply trust capital for the early benefit of Saleem, they must first obtain the written consent of Rajesh – see condition (e).)
(c)	The payment must be for the beneficiary's advancement or benefit. This includes any use of money that will improve the material situation of the beneficiary. This is broad in application – most things will improve the material situation of the beneficiary, save perhaps for money that will be used for pleasure, leisure or hobbies. The trustees have to be careful to ensure that the capital being advanced will benefit the beneficiary in some way and will not solely benefit someone else. However, if the advancement is made to or for the benefit of the beneficiary, it does not matter that there is an incidental benefit to other people.	A trust has been created for the benefit of two grandchildren. Their mother requests the trustees to advance capital while the grandchildren are under the age of 18 years. The trustees know that the reason for this request is that the mother wants to use the capital to pay off her overdrafts. If the trustees advance capital for this reason, they will be in breach of trust (*Re Pauling's Settlement Trusts* [1964] 1 Ch 303).
(d)	For trusts created after 1 October 2014, the advance payment must not exceed the beneficiary's entitlement. For trusts created on or before 1 October 2014, the trustees can only advance up to half the beneficiary's entitlement.	In my will dated 27 November 2008, I made provision for a trust for each of my children in equal shares. When I died on 16 March 2016, I had two children – Wesley (aged 10 years) and Yvonne (aged 8 years). Four years later, Yvonne's guardian wants the trustees to apply the sum of £40,000 out of the trust fund for Yvonne's benefit. The total trust fund is valued at £60,000. The trustees can only apply up to £30,000 for Yvonne's benefit, being the total amount of her beneficial entitlement (ie representing her half share in the trust). It should be noted that whilst I executed my will before October 2014, the will only became effective on my death in 2016. The trust within the will is therefore deemed to have been created on death.

	Condition	Example
(e)	The payment is taken into account when the beneficiary becomes entitled to trust capital.	I create a trust for Adam and Britney if they reach the age of 21 years. Britney (then aged 19 years) is given an advancement of £15,000. When Britney reaches the age of 21 years and calls for her share of the trust property, she will receive a half share in the trust capital *minus* the £15,000 advancement already paid. If Britney were to die before reaching the age of 21 years, her estate would not have to pay back the advancement. (These accounting rules are sometimes referred to as the 'hotchpot rules'.)
(f)	If there is a beneficiary with a prior interest, an advancement to another beneficiary can only take place if the prior interest-holder is an adult and has given written consent to the advancement. The most common example of a beneficiary with a prior interest is the life tenant.	I create a trust for Catrina for life, remainder to Dianne (currently aged 25 years) and Elma (currently aged 20 years) if they obtain the age of 30 years. Elma requests that the trustees advance capital to her. Elma has an interest in capital. However, if the trustees were to advance capital to her, this might prejudicially affect Catrina, because there would be less capital available to generate the trust income to which she is entitled. To safeguard her interests, the trustees can only advance capital to Elma if Catrina gives her fully informed consent in writing. Note that the trustees do not need to get written consent from Dianne. Dianne's interests do not rank *prior* to the interests of Elma (even though Dianne's interest will vest first). Rather, their interests rank equal to each other. The advancement of capital to Elma is unlikely to prejudice Dianne because any advancement to Elma is limited to her beneficial share.

Fabien has demanded that the trustees use the trust fund to pay his university fees. Gabriella has said that if the trustees pay for Fabien's university fees, then they must buy her a jet ski.

The trustees can make an advance of anything up to £200,000 to Fabien. (This is a trust created after 1 October 2014. The trustees can therefore advance anything up to the value of his presumptive share in the trust fund.) Fabien has an interest in capital and the advancement to pay his university fees should improve his material situation. However, s 32 of the TA 1925 gives trustees the power *to advance capital – they are not obliged to do so. Fabien cannot compel the trustees to pay for his university fees if they decide not to.*

The trustees cannot buy Gabriella a jet ski under s 32 of the TA 1925 because it is not for her advancement or benefit (hobby items are unlikely to improve someone's material situation in life).

Finally, note that the trustees can advance capital to Fabien without having to discuss this with Gabriella or seek her consent. Gabriella's consent is not required because she does not have a prior interest.

8.6 Summary flowchart

Figure 8.1 Advancement and maintenance summary flowchart

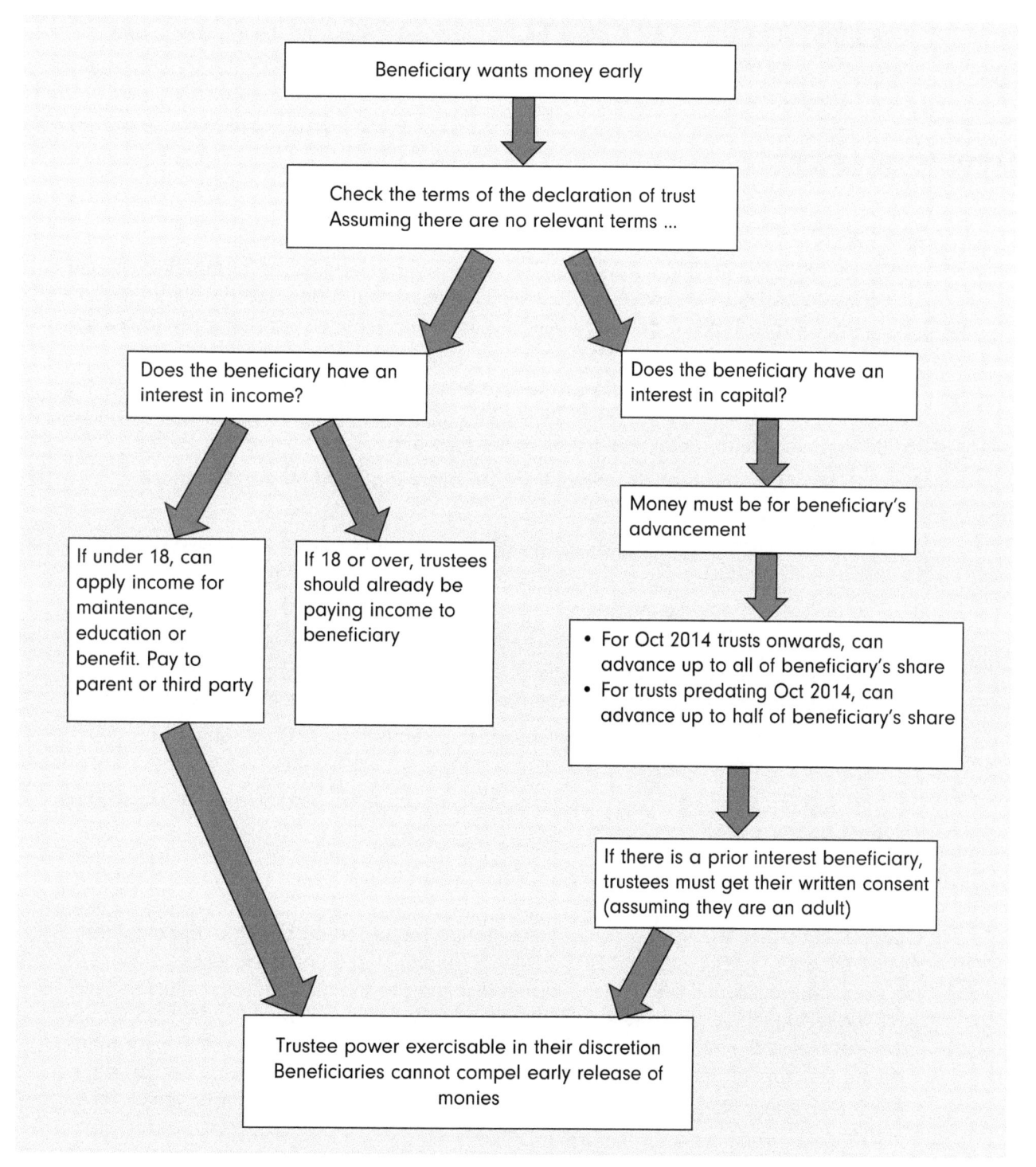

```
                    Beneficiary wants money early
                                │
                                ▼
                    Check the terms of the declaration of trust
                    Assuming there are no relevant terms ...
                           │              │
                    ┌──────┘              └──────┐
                    ▼                            ▼
       Does the beneficiary have an    Does the beneficiary have an
            interest in income?              interest in capital?
                  │                                  │
          ┌───────┴────────┐                         ▼
          ▼                ▼              Money must be for beneficiary's
    If under 18, can   If 18 or over,              advancement
    apply income for   trustees should                 │
    maintenance,       already be                      ▼
    education or       paying income       • For Oct 2014 trusts onwards, can
    benefit. Pay to    to beneficiary        advance up to all of beneficiary's share
    parent or third                        • For trusts predating Oct 2014, can
    party                                    advance up to half of beneficiary's share
          │                                           │
          │                                           ▼
          │                              If there is a prior interest beneficiary,
          │                              trustees must get their written consent
          │                                    (assuming they are an adult)
          │                                           │
          └──────────────┐          ┌────────────────┘
                         ▼          ▼
                Trustee power exercisable in their discretion
                Beneficiaries cannot compel early release of
                                  monies
```

Summary

In this chapter you have considered statutory powers available to trustees to pay monies early to or for beneficiaries:

- *Statutory powers of maintenance.* Trustees can apply income for the maintenance, education or benefit of a beneficiary under the age of 18 years so long as they have a beneficial interest in income. Trustees *must* pay income to adult contingent beneficiaries with an interest in income.

- *Statutory powers of advancement.* Trustees can apply or pay capital to beneficiaries interested in capital for their advancement or benefit. Various conditions must be satisfied before capital can be applied early.

- *Powers not duties.* It is important to remember that these are powers that trustees can exercise in their discretion. Trustees are not obliged to exercise these powers and beneficiaries cannot compel them to do so.

Sample questions

Question 1

A woman was appointed to act as a trustee under a trust deed dated 16 March 2009 and is holding property currently valued at £200,000 on behalf of a boy aged 17 years and a girl aged 15 years. The boy and girl have equal shares in the trust property. There are no administrative provisions in the trust deed.

The boy wants to start his own car garage and has asked the trustee to use £80,000 of the trust fund to buy spare parts for his business. The girl's parent has asked the trustee for £5,000 to pay for some additional tuition to help the girl pass her upcoming exams.

Which of the following best describes how the trustees should respond to these requests?

A   The trustee must pay the monies requested because the boy and girl have vested interests in the trust.

B   The trustee can pay the monies requested but does not have to – whether or not the monies are paid is within the trustee's discretion.

C   The trustee can pay the monies requested on behalf of the boy but not the girl, because the request must come from the beneficiary and not the beneficiary's parent.

D   The trustee can pay the monies requested on behalf of the girl but not the boy, because the boy is asking for too much money.

E   The trustee cannot pay the monies requested because the beneficiaries are both under the age of 18 years.

Answer

Option D is correct. The trustee can pay the monies requested on behalf of the girl if the trustee chooses, because the girl is interested in capital, the amount requested is within the permitted statutory limits, and the money will improve the girl's material situation. The girl's request meets all of the relevant statutory criteria listed in s 32 of the TA 1925 for the advancement of the monies sought. This is not true of the boy's request, which is for more than the statutory maximum permitted. As this trust was created before October 2014, the trustees can only exercise their discretion up to half of his presumptive share, in this case £50,000.

Trustee Powers: Maintenance and Advancement

Option A is wrong. The trustee is not obliged to satisfy monetary requests from beneficiaries under the age of 18 years, even if the interests of those beneficiaries are vested.

Option B is wrong. Whilst it is correct to say that s 32 of the TA 1925 confers a discretionary power on the trustee to advance capital, that power is not completely unfettered. Any advance must satisfy the statutory criteria listed in s 32 of the TA 1925. The sum requested by the boy does not.

Option C is wrong. Any capital advanced must be for the beneficiary's benefit – it must improve that beneficiary's material situation in life. The request for capital to pay for the girl's extra tuition will satisfy this requirement, even if the request for the money came from her parent.

Option E is wrong. The trustee can use her power under s 32 of the TA 1925 to advance capital on behalf of a beneficiary under the age of 18 years, so long as the statutory criteria listed in that section are met.

Question 2

A barrister executed a trust deed that contained the following provision:

'The Trustees shall distribute the Trust Fund to my daughter should she reach the age of 25 years, but if not to my brother.'

There are no relevant administrative provisions in the trust deed.

The daughter is currently aged 21 years and complains that the trustees have not paid her any money since the trust was created. She claims that she has repeatedly asked the trustees for money to help pay her living expenses while she was at university. The brother, who did not go to university himself, was always against the trustees helping the daughter out with her living expenses.

Which of the following best describes whether the daughter was entitled to any money?

A The daughter should have been paid money because she is the only beneficiary under the terms of the trust.

B The daughter should have been paid capital from the trust as that would have been a proper advancement.

C The daughter should have been paid income generated from the trust over the last three years.

D The daughter should not have been paid any money because until her interests vest, the trustees can only pay money with the consent of the brother.

E The daughter should not have been paid any money because her interests are currently contingent.

Answer

Option C is correct. The daughter is an adult, contingent beneficiary. As such, under s 31 of the TA 1925, she is entitled to income as and when it arises, and the trustees were under a duty to pay her income from when she became 18 years old.

Option A is irrelevant. If there were two or more adult, contingent beneficiaries, then they would all be paid their share of income as and when it arose.

Option B is wrong. Whilst the trustees had the discretionary power to advance capital to the daughter, they were not under a duty to do so.

Option D is wrong. Whilst the views of the brother would be relevant if the daughter was thinking of bringing the trust to an end (as his consent would be required to engage the rule in *Saunders v Vautier*), his views do not change the trustees' duty to pay income to the daughter now that she is an adult.

Option E is wrong (certainly as it relates to income). Whilst the daughter's interest is contingent, now that she is an adult s 31 of the TA 1925 entitles her to be paid income as and when it arises.

Question 3

A woman executed a lifetime trust on 16 March 2018 that contained the following provision:

'My Trustees shall hold the Trust Fund [currently valued at £200,000] for my sister for life, and for my son and daughter in remainder'.

There are no relevant administrative provisions in the trust deed.

The daughter is aged 16 years. The daughter recently secured good GSCE grades and has been selected to attend a fee-paying school for her A-levels (which will take her two years to complete). The school charges £10,000 for each term of tuition.

Which of the following best describes whether the trustees can help the daughter in paying the school fees?

A   The trustees must advance money to the daughter because the daughter has an interest in trust capital.

B   The trustees can advance money to the daughter because the payment would be for the daughter's advancement or benefit.

C   The trustees can advance money to pay the school because the payment should be within the limits of what the trustees can advance.

D   The trustees must advance money to the daughter so long as the sister agrees in writing.

E   The trustees can advance money to pay the school so long as the sister agrees in writing.

Answer

Option E is correct. The daughter's request for money meets most of the statutory criteria set out in s 32 of the TA 1925 for the advancement of trust capital, but the trustees can only exercise their power to advance that capital if the sister agrees in writing. This is because the sister, as life tenant, has a prior interest. Also note that the daughter is still a minor and therefore cannot give good receipt. The trustees would be ill-advised to pay any money directly to the daughter. It would be better if they pay that money to the school.

Options A and D are wrong. The trustees are under no duty to advance money to the daughter. Section 32 of the TA 1925 merely confers a power on the trustees, which they may exercise in their discretion.

Option B is wrong. Whilst the money would be for the daughter's advancement or benefit, the trustees should not advance any money directly to her as she cannot give good receipt for that money. (Option D contains the same problem.)

Option C is not the best option. As the trust was created after 1 October 2014, the trustees can advance up to the limit of the daughter's presumptive share, ie up to £100,000. Assuming that her A-levels take two years to complete, the total fees will fall under this limit. However, this is not the only statutory criteria that the trustees must consider. The main issue in this scenario is that the trustees must secure the sister's prior written consent. Without that consent, the trustees cannot advance anything to the daughter.

9 Trustees' Duties When Running a Trust

9.1	Introduction	120
9.2	Differences between powers and duties	120
9.3	Express provisions in the declaration of trust	121
9.4	Duty of care	121
9.5	Duties when starting out as trustee	121
9.6	Duty to act impartially between beneficiaries	122
9.7	Duty to act personally and unanimously	122
9.8	Duty to exercise discretions properly	123
9.9	Reasons for the exercise of a power	124
9.10	Disclosure of information	124
9.11	Summary flowchart	125

SQE1 syllabus

This chapter will enable you to achieve the SQE1 assessment specification in relation to functioning legal knowledge concerned with the following core principles:

- Trustees' duty of care

Note that for SQE1, candidates are not usually required to recall specific case names or cite statutory or regulatory authorities. Cases are provided for illustrative purposes only.

Learning outcomes

By the end of this chapter you will be able to apply relevant core legal principles and rules appropriately and effectively, at the level of a competent newly qualified solicitor in practice, to realistic client-based and ethical problems and situations in the following areas:

- establishing the duty of care that trustees owe when running a trust;
- identifying the steps that trustees must take when they are newly appointed;
- identifying the principles that trustees must abide by when taking decisions on behalf of the trust; and
- advising on the disclosure of information on the running of the trust by trustees to beneficiaries and whether there is a duty to give reasons for decisions taken.

9.1 Introduction

The trustees are the managers of the trust. They are under a duty to observe the terms of the trust and act in the best interests of the beneficiaries, who can complain to the court if the trustees commit a breach of trust.

The management role of trustees and the enforcement role of beneficiaries can create conflict. Often a reason for the settlor setting up a trust is that they believe that the trustee is better placed to manage property than the beneficiaries. It would be wrong if the law gave the trustees complete autonomy; they have to be answerable to the beneficiaries whose property they are managing. However, it would be equally unacceptable if the beneficiaries were allowed to dictate how the trustees managed every aspect of the trust. A balance between these two extremes needs to be struck.

This chapter looks at:

- the difference between duties (which the beneficiaries can compel) and powers (which are largely a matter for the trustees);
- the standard of care trustees must adopt when running the trust;
- the steps that trustees must take when starting as a trustee;
- how trustees take decisions and exercise powers when running a trust; and
- whether trustees must give reasons for their decisions or disclose information about the trust to beneficiaries.

A key element of running the trust is maintaining (and increasing) the value of the trust fund for the benefit of beneficiaries. Trustees must regularly review the trust fund and assess whether they should sell certain trust investments and buy others. We shall consider the specific statutory regime that applies to investments in **Chapter 10**.

As well as exercising the proper level of care when running the trust, trustees must also ensure they do not put themselves into positions where their own self-interest conflicts or competes with the interests of the trust. The trustees must remain loyal to the trust at all times and are dissuaded from exploiting the trust for their own ends by the imposition of fiduciary duties. We shall consider these separate duties in **Chapter 11**.

9.2 Differences between powers and duties

Beneficiaries can compel trustees to perform duties. For example, in a fixed interest trust, trustees are under a duty to distribute trust property at the right time to the right beneficiaries. Should the trustees refuse to do so, the beneficiaries can enforce the duty by obtaining a court order.

Beneficiaries have very little control over the exercise of powers. We have considered two important statutory powers in the running of a trust in **Chapter 8** – the powers that enable trustees to give money early to certain beneficiaries. We saw that trustees are under no duty to exercise these powers and the beneficiaries cannot force them to do so.

Most decisions that trustees take in the running of a trust involve the exercise of powers. When it comes to these powers:

(a) trustees must consider from time-to-time whether to exercise them; and

(b) if they do decide to exercise them, they must ensure that they do so properly (see **section 9.8** below).

However, so long as the trustees meet these requirements, beneficiaries have no rights of complaint.

9.3 Express provisions in the declaration of trust

Before we look at some examples of what might amount to a breach of trust on the part of a trustee, please note that all these examples are subject to the express provisions of the declaration of trust. The settlor is, in the trust document, generally free to exclude, modify or amplify the general law. In particular, settlors may consider limiting or excluding the trustees' liability for any breach of trust.

We shall assume for the rest of this chapter that there are no express provisions in the trust document that seek to amend the general law.

9.4 Duty of care

When running a trust, a trustee must take 'all those precautions which an ordinary prudent man of business would take in managing similar affairs of his own' (*Speight v Gaunt* (1883) 9 App Cas 1). This is an objective standard, although the standard can be higher for paid, professional trustees. Solicitors, for instance, who are paid to act as trustees are expected to exercise that care and skill which could reasonably be expected of solicitors acting as experts in their own particular field.

⭐ Example

Gerald, a beneficiary, alleges that the trust fund is worth less than it should be because the trustees handled the tax affairs of the trust negligently.

The trustees must act as reasonably prudent business-people. Such people would take necessary precautions to ensure that their affairs are handled in a tax-efficient manner, such as taking professional tax advice. If the trustees failed to do the same in relation to the trust, they would breach their duty of care.

As we shall see in **Chapter 10**, a similar duty of care applies in the context of investment decisions.

9.5 Duties when starting out as trustee

A trustee newly appointed to office (whether at the start of a trust or part-way through its life) must:

(a) ensure that they have been properly appointed;

(b) ascertain what the trust property consists of and take all reasonable and proper measures to obtain control of the trust property – if the transfer of trust property to the new trustee is outstanding, the new trustee must press for that transfer to take place;

(c) review the trust document and associated paperwork to familiarise themselves with the trust and how it works – the other trustees must produce papers relating to the administration of the trust;

(d) enquire into the past business of the trust to ensure that there have been no past breaches of trust, and to take appropriate action to remedy any breaches; and

(e) where there are chattels held on trust, ensure that a proper inventory is drawn up.

⭐ Example

Henry has recently been appointed trustee over a trust for company shares because the beneficiaries were dissatisfied with two previous trustees: Imogen and Imelda. Henry has not asked to see any trust documents and the company shares remain registered in the joint names of Imogen, Imelda and Jane (the other trustee who remains in office).

Henry has failed to take steps to become familiar with the terms of the trust or enquire into why Imogen and Imelda were removed from office (they may have committed previous breaches of trust). Henry and Jane have failed to take steps to put the shares in their joint names. If his inactivity causes any loss to the trust, Henry may be liable.

9.6 Duty to act impartially between beneficiaries

When exercising their powers, a trustee may be faced with a choice between two beneficiaries, whose interests appear to conflict with each other. Faced with such a situation, the trustee must act impartially in the interests of each beneficiary. This does not necessarily mean that beneficiaries must be given equal treatment, nor does it mean that trustees must consult either or both beneficiaries, nor give either side a 'fair hearing'. However, a trustee must not benefit one beneficiary at the expense of another and may find themselves in breach of trust if they continually prefer the interests of one beneficiary over the other.

9.7 Duty to act personally and unanimously

As we saw in **Chapter 7**, it is best practice to have between two and four trustees running a trust at any one time. We have also seen that each co-trustee is under a duty to take all reasonable and proper measures to take control of trust property, preferably by ensuring that property is vested in the name of all the trustees.

Co-trustees must generally take decisions unanimously (unless the trust document provides otherwise). This is an important safeguard – it limits the opportunities for one trustee to abuse their legal powers.

⭐ Example

Arthur, James and Wilfred are appointed trustees. Arthur and James are interested in purchasing an undeveloped parcel of land for which a planning application to build student accommodation is being sought. Wilfred has spoken to a local developer who believes that the application is likely to fail given the number of student residences that have already been built in the neighbourhood. Wilfred therefore opposes the purchase of the site.

Arthur and James cannot outvote Wilfred and go ahead with the purchase, nor will they be able to secure court approval for the purchase (Wilfred has properly and soundly exercised his discretion not to invest in the land). The site cannot be purchased on behalf of the trust.

Trustees must act personally – they must be personally active in the running of a trust. Outside of statutory powers to delegate decision-making to others (such as the appointment of an attorney under s 25 of the TA 1925 that we briefly considered in **Chapter 7**), trustees cannot sit back and allow others to take decisions on their behalf. If a trustee:

(a) leaves matters in the hands of a co-trustee without enquiry;

(b) allows trust funds to remain in the sole control of a co-trustee;

(c) fails to watch over and, if necessary, correct the conduct of their co-trustees; or

(d) fails to take action knowing that a co-trustee was committing, or about to commit, a breach of trust;

this passive trustee may be liable to make good any loss that the beneficiaries suffer.

Finally, whilst trustees can take advice from experts – legal, financial or otherwise – they cannot allow the experts to take decisions for them.

⭐ Example

John sets up a trust for his children and grandchildren, and gives the trustees express powers to pay capital or income out of the trust fund early to all or any of the beneficiaries. The trustees – Lionel, Henry and Janet – have no experience or understanding of trusts. Various monies are paid to beneficiaries in purported exercise of the express powers given, but in fact the trustees are simply doing whatever John tells them to.

Lionel, Henry and Janet will be in breach of trust for failing to act personally in the management of the trust. They are under a personal duty to consider the appropriateness of any early payments, but in allowing themselves to be dictated to by John, they have failed to do so.

9.8 Duty to exercise discretions properly

Whilst beneficiaries cannot compel trustees to exercise discretionary powers in a particular way, they can intervene if the trustees exercise those powers improperly. Having decided to exercise a power, trustees must exercise that power:

(a) in good faith;

(b) rationally;

(c) for the purpose for which it was created;

(d) with regard to relevant material matters and without regard to irrelevant ones;

(e) with regard to all relevant facts; and

(f) with regard to any legitimate expectation that a beneficiary might have that the power be exercised in a particular way (see **section 9.9** below).

⭐ Example

A discretionary trust exists for the settlor's children and grandchildren. The trustees decide to distribute trust property only to those with red hair who have their birthday in March.

The court may well intervene to prevent such distributions because the exercise of the discretion appears irrational, perverse or based on irrelevant matters.

9.9 Reasons for the exercise of a power

Trustees do not generally need to give reasons for their decisions (but if they do decide to give reasons, the beneficiaries and the court can enquire into their soundness). However, where a particular beneficiary has a legitimate expectation that a discretion will be exercised in their favour, the trustees may be obliged to give reasons and advance warning if they are thinking of exercising their discretion differently.

⭐ Example

The trustees have over the past 10 years exercised their discretion annually to give Ada a capital advance. The trustees cannot simply discontinue these payments without warning Ada and giving her the opportunity to persuade the trustees to continue with the payments.

9.10 Disclosure of information

Beneficiaries are entitled to see the following documents:

(a) the trust document or will that created the trust;

(b) the trust accounts; and

(c) a schedule of trust investments or other documents that show how trust property is invested.

Beneficiaries are not allowed to demand documents that record trustees' deliberations on a discretion or power. Trustees are not obliged to give reasons for their decisions and beneficiaries cannot circumvent this by demanding documents in which decisions are recorded. Trust diaries and minutes of trust meetings that record why trustees took particular decisions are therefore unlikely to be handed over by trustees.

For similar reasons, beneficiaries cannot demand sight of letters of wishes from settlors. When creating a discretionary trust, the settlor may furnish the trustees with a non-binding letter of wishes that sets out how the settlor would like the trustees to exercise their discretion in distributing trust property. Since the letter of wishes exists to facilitate the confidential exercise of a trustee's discretion, a trustee is not required to disclose the letter of wishes to beneficiaries.

If the beneficiaries want to see documents that record the reasons trustees took for exercising or not exercising a power in a particular way then they can apply to the court for disclosure. The court will consider that application under its inherent jurisdiction to supervise the administration of the trust. In considering whether to order disclosure, the court will usually start with the presumption that such documents should not be disclosed, unless such disclosure is in the interest of the sound administration of the trust (eg where there is good evidence that trustees might have committed a breach of trust). The court may refuse disclosure where it would cause family members to fall out, or if it were to reveal confidential information about the finances or state of health of individual beneficiaries.

9.11 Summary flowchart

Figure 9.1 Trustees' duties summary chart

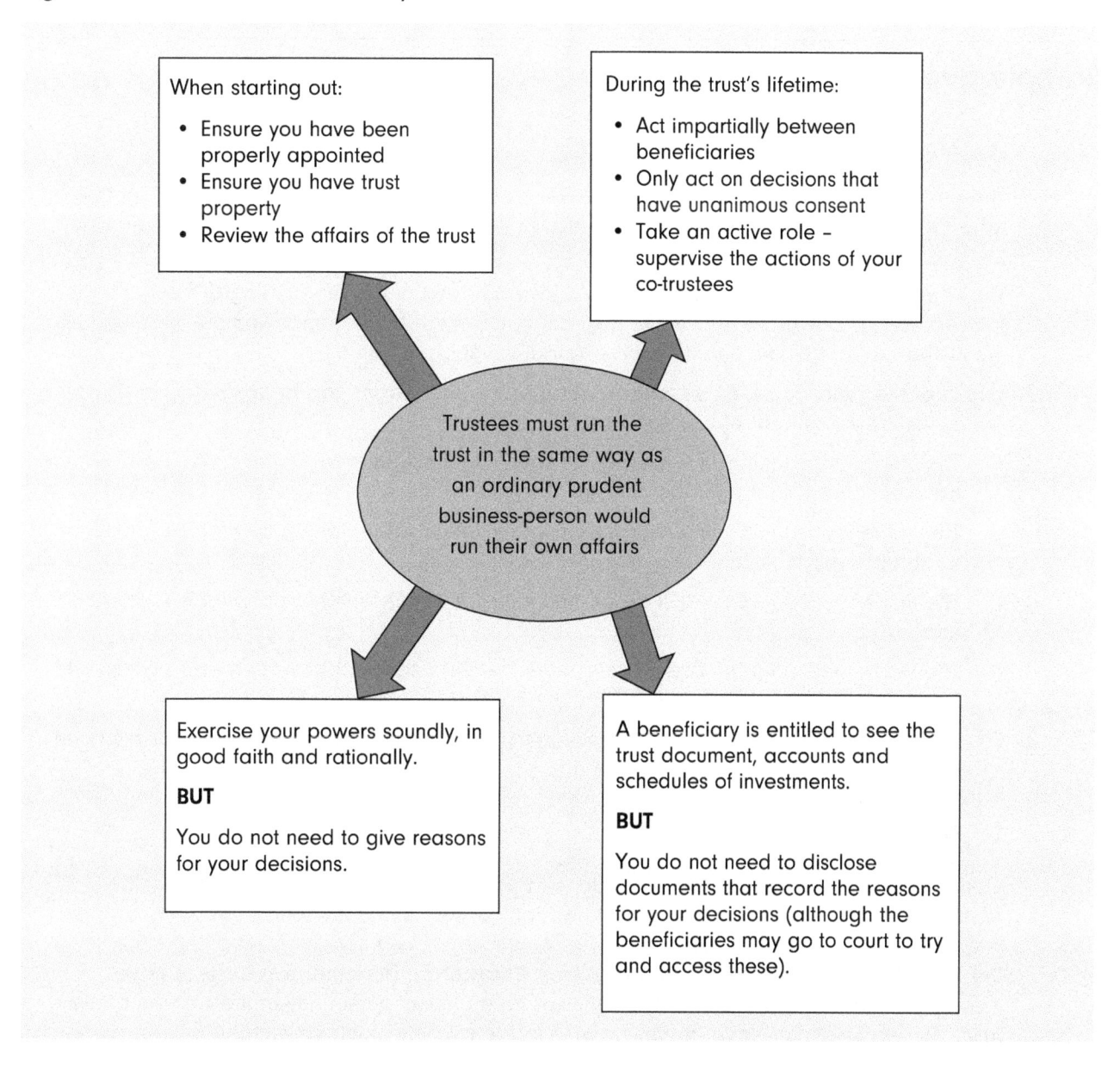

When starting out:
- Ensure you have been properly appointed
- Ensure you have trust property
- Review the affairs of the trust

During the trust's lifetime:
- Act impartially between beneficiaries
- Only act on decisions that have unanimous consent
- Take an active role – supervise the actions of your co-trustees

Trustees must run the trust in the same way as an ordinary prudent business-person would run their own affairs

Exercise your powers soundly, in good faith and rationally.

BUT

You do not need to give reasons for your decisions.

A beneficiary is entitled to see the trust document, accounts and schedules of investments.

BUT

You do not need to disclose documents that record the reasons for your decisions (although the beneficiaries may go to court to try and access these).

Summary

In this chapter you have considered the trustees' duty of care when running a trust:

- *Standard of care.* When running a trust, a trustee is held to the same standard as an ordinary prudent business-person who is managing their own affairs.
- *Duties when running a trust.* Trustees must take decisions unanimously and personally. They must be active in the running of the trust and must supervise the actions of their co-trustees. When exercising powers, the decisions that trustees take are a matter for their own discretion, but that discretion must be exercised rationally and in good faith.
- *Reasons and documents.* Trustees do not need to give reasons for the decisions they take or the powers they exercise. Beneficiaries are entitled to see the trust document and some

associated core documents (such as accounts), but cannot demand sight of documents that record the decisions that trustees have taken (such as minutes of meetings). If beneficiaries want to see such documents, they will need to apply to the court.

Sample questions

Question 1

Three trustees – a man, woman and a lawyer – have been appointed to administer a trust for a (female) life tenant and a remainderman. There are no relevant express provisions in the trust deed.

The trustees agreed that the lawyer should take all decisions in the running of the trust. The lawyer recently advanced 90% of the trust capital to the remainderman without informing his fellow trustees or the life tenant. The life tenant is unhappy with this.

Which of the following best describes whether the life tenant can bring a claim arising out of the advancement of capital?

A   The life tenant cannot bring a claim, because the trustees were under a duty to advance capital to the remainderman.

B   The life tenant cannot bring a claim, because the advancement of capital is a matter for the trustees in their sole discretion.

C   The life tenant cannot bring a claim, because the advancement of capital was lawfully undertaken.

D   The life tenant can bring a claim, because the life tenant's prior written approval should have been obtained, but only against the lawyer.

E   The life tenant can bring a claim, because the life tenant's prior written approval should have been obtained, and can bring that claim against all the trustees.

Answer

Option E is correct. The lawyer has breached trust because he advanced capital to the remainderman without first obtaining the written consent of the life tenant, who has a prior interest and whose written approval to the advancement is a condition set out in s 32 of the TA 1925 to the exercise of this power (see **Chapter 8**). The other two trustees have also breached their duties because they have failed to act personally in the running of the trust. Their passivity means that they have failed to supervise and correct the actions of the lawyer. All the trustees therefore are in breach of trust.

Options A to C largely required you to remember and apply material covered in **Chapter 8**.

Option A is wrong. The advancement of capital is a power exercisable by the trustees, not a duty.

Options B and C are wrong. Whilst it is correct to say that the advancement of capital is largely a matter for the trustees' discretion, if the trustees are thinking of advancing capital under s 32 of the TA 1925, they must first ensure that all the relevant statutory conditions are satisfied, which is not the case here. The life tenant did not provide her prior written consent to the advancement.

Option D is wrong. All the trustees are in breach of trust and a claim can therefore be brought against all of them.

Question 2

The trustees are holding property on trust valued at £500,000 for the settlor's grandchildren who reach the age of 25 years. There are currently two grandchildren both under the age of 25 years. There are no relevant express provisions in the trust deed.

The grandchildren are unhappy with the way that the trustees have run the trust to date. In particular, two years ago, each grandchild requested that the trustees advance the sum of £10,000 to them for different purposes. The trustees discussed these requests at a meeting ('the Advancement Meeting') and agreed to advance £10,000 to one grandchild, but not the other. The grandchildren are starting to make various demands of the trustees.

Which of the following best describes what documentation (if any) the trustees must provide to the beneficiaries?

A   The trustees must, upon request, supply the beneficiaries with copies of the trust deed, accounts, schedule of investments and the minutes of the Advancement Meeting.

B   The trustees must, upon request, supply the beneficiaries with copies of the trust deed, accounts and schedule of investments.

C   The only document to which the beneficiaries are entitled is the minutes of the Advancement Meeting.

D   The trustees need not supply any documents or information to the beneficiaries.

E   The trustees need not supply the minutes of the Advancement Meeting, but in the interests of fairness must give reasons as to why they advanced capital to one beneficiary but not the other.

Answer

Option B is correct. The beneficiaries are entitled to see the trust deed, accounts and information about investments as of right. The trustees cannot refuse to hand over such documents.

Option E is wrong. The trustees are under no duty to give reasons for their decisions (and this is unlikely to be a case where the beneficiaries have a legitimate expectation that such reasons be given).

Options A and C are wrong for similar reasons. The beneficiaries are not entitled to documents that record why trustees exercised their powers in a particular way, such as the minutes of the Advancement Meeting (although the beneficiaries could go to court and attempt to secure the disclosure of those minutes under the court's inherent supervisory jurisdiction).

Option D is wrong. The beneficiaries are entitled as of right to those documents listed in option B.

Question 3

A man executed a trust deed 20 years ago for 'such of my children, grandchildren and great-grandchildren and in such shares as my Trustees in their discretion see fit'.

As at today's date, there are four such children and five such grandchildren. Over the past 20 years, various children and grandchildren have written to the trustees to request monies from the trust fund, but have received no response. No distribution from the trust fund has been made to anyone in the past 20 years.

One of the grandchildren is about to start a trek across the Australian Outback. Six months ago, he asked the trustees to distribute part of the trust fund to him to help meet the costs. The trustees have not responded. The grandchild has recently found out that the trustees have never met over the past 20 years.

Which of the following best describes whether the trustees are in breach of trust?

A   The trustees cannot be in breach of trust because they have exercised their discretion not to distribute money from the trust to the grandchild.

B   The trustees are in breach of trust because they have failed to consider over the past 20 years whether they should distribute money from the trust.

C   The trustees are in breach of trust because they have failed to give any reasons for their refusal to distribute any money to the grandchild.

D   The trustees cannot be in breach of trust because they have an absolute discretion over whether money from the trust fund will be distributed.

E   The trustees are in breach of trust because the grandchild had a legitimate expectation that he would receive money from the trust.

Answer

Option B is correct. The trust is a discretionary trust. This trust imposes a duty on the trustees to consider from time-to-time whether they should exercise that discretion to distribute property to selected individuals within the class. Given that there have been a number of requests for property to be distributed over the past 20 years, none of which the trustees have responded to, it would appear that the trustees are in breach of this duty.

Option A is wrong in that it misrepresents the facts of the scenario. As the trust is discretionary, it is correct to say that the trustees cannot be in breach of trust for deciding not to distribute money to an individual. However, that does not appear to have happened on the facts. Rather, the trustees appear not to be taking any decisions at all.

Option C is wrong. Trustees are generally under no duty to give reasons for their decisions.

Option D is wrong. The trustees of a discretionary trust do not have an absolute discretion over whether trust money should be distributed. They have a discretion in relation to whom money can be distributed – but they must distribute the trust money.

Option E is wrong. There is nothing on the facts to suggest that the grandchild had a legitimate expectation that his request for money would be accepted. This is the first time that he has made such a request.

10 Trustee Duties: Investment

10.1	Introduction	130
10.2	Investments, objectives and strategy	131
10.3	Express provisions in the declaration of trust	133
10.4	Authorised investments	133
10.5	Duties when purchasing investments	134
10.6	Delegation	136
10.7	Summary flowchart	138

SQE1 syllabus

This chapter will enable you to achieve the SQE1 assessment specification in relation to functioning legal knowledge concerned with the following core principles:

- Trustees' duty to invest (and powers in relation to investment).

Note that for SQE1, candidates are not usually required to recall specific case names or cite statutory or regulatory authorities. Cases are provided for illustrative purposes only.

Learning outcomes

By the end of this chapter you will be able to apply relevant core legal principles and rules appropriately and effectively, at the level of a competent newly qualified solicitor in practice, to realistic client-based and ethical problems and situations in the following areas:

- establishing what forms of investment trustees can purchase;
- identifying what criteria trustees use when assessing whether to purchase specific investments;
- establishing what process trustees must follow when deciding whether to invest;
- establishing what standard trustees will be held to when investing; and
- advising on whether trustees can delegate their investment powers to a suitably qualified agent and the process for doing so.

10.1 Introduction

As an absolute owner, as and when I have some money left over, I look to invest it. I do this for various reasons:

(a) I want my money to grow. Generally, the price of goods and services rises over time and the purchasing power of money falls over time. This is known as inflation. If I had £10,000 in savings at the end of the tax year and stuffed this money in my mattress for 10 years, I would still have the nominal sum of £10,000 in 10 years' time, but due to the ravages of inflation, that sum of money might only pay for the equivalent value of £7,500 in goods and services. In real terms, the value of my money has slumped because inflation has lessened its purchasing power.

(b) I want some additional income. Income is a regular receipt of money derived from capital. If I put my £10,000 in a savings bank account I might get some interest, but if this rate of interest is low, I might think of purchasing something else that is likely to produce more income, eg shares in a company with a good track-record of paying regular dividends.

Before deciding what to invest in, I ask myself what I want to achieve in the short-, medium- and long-term. By thinking of my objectives and the timescales I have to achieve those objectives, I can then start to identify the right kinds of investments that I need to buy.

Trustees manage property on behalf of the beneficiaries. As part of that management (and subject to any contrary provision in the trust deed), they must duly and promptly invest all trust capital and income not being distributed to or applied for beneficiaries, and the trustees may become liable for any losses arising out of trust funds being left uninvested for an unreasonable period of time.

But how to invest those trust funds? Some beneficiaries, such as the life tenant, may need a constant stream of income. Other beneficiaries, such as contingent beneficiaries, may not become entitled to a capital share for a number of years, but will expect the trustees to have grown the value of the trust fund so that when they do become entitled to their share, the trust fund will have kept up with, if not beaten, inflation. Just as I try to identify my objectives before choosing how best to invest my own money, when thinking of investing trust money, the trustees must identify the objectives of the trust and the likely requirements of the beneficiaries.

Investments can be a confusing area for most people. Even people who claim expertise in the financial markets can get things wrong. Trustees who are not financial experts may find this duty to invest daunting. The law therefore tries to strike a balance:

(a) given that the trustees are investing on behalf of the beneficiaries, the beneficiaries must have some ability to recover any losses caused by the trustees' failure to act properly; but

(b) if trustees follow the right process when selecting investments, the fact that those investments then perform badly is not generally something that beneficiaries can complain about;

(c) as a matter of best practice, trustees must generally take expert advice when thinking about investing trust property and can also delegate their investment functions down to a more suitably qualified agent.

This chapter looks at:

- some common forms of investments and some common questions that must be asked before purchasing those investments;
- the forms of investment that trustees are authorised to purchase on behalf of the trust;
- the criteria that trustees must use when deciding whether to purchase investments;
- the need to review investments with the benefit of advice;

- the standard of care trustees must adopt when purchasing and reviewing investments;
- the need to act impartially between beneficiaries and secure the best return for beneficiaries; and
- the ability to delegate investment functions to someone else.

10.2 Investments, objectives and strategy

Before we consider the legal framework that trustees must consider when thinking about investments, we will first consider more broadly the types of things that trustees should be thinking about before investing and the types of investments that are available.

10.2.1 Objectives

Trustees should tailor their investment strategy according to the particular trust they are dealing with. Trustees should consider:

(a) What sort of interests do beneficiaries have?

(b) What are the circumstances of the individual beneficiaries?

(c) How long will the trust last for? Are they investing for the short-term or the long-term?

(d) What is the size of the trust fund?

(e) What is the tax position of the trust and the beneficiaries?

⭐ *Example*

The trustees are managing a trust fund currently valued at £500,000 for Philip for life, remainder to Rachel. Philip is currently aged 47 years.

While Philip is alive, he will receive trust income. When he dies, Rachel will receive the trust capital. For this trust, it is important to invest some of the trust fund in income-producing investments for Philip and some of the trust fund in capital-growth investments for Rachel. Whilst some investments are capable of producing both income and capital growth, often one form of return comes at the expense of the other – an investment that produces a good rate of income usually produces low capital growth and vice-versa. A balance will therefore need to be struck between Philip's interests and Rachel's interests.

Philip might live for another 40 years, so this trust is likely to run for a long time. As a general rule, the longer you have to invest, the more risk you can afford to take in the early years because you have time to ride out any downturns. Generally speaking, the greater the risk, the greater the return. So initially, the trustees may want to take a riskier approach when investing for capital growth. As Philip gets older, the trustees might then start to 'de-risk' the trust fund, switching into less risky forms of investment to keep the trust fund safe and secure for Rachel.

The trust fund is relatively large. The larger the trust fund, the greater opportunity there is to buy a mixture of investments (known as 'diversification'). Trustees should consider buying a mixture of investments wherever possible to ensure that they do not 'place all their eggs in one basket' – if some investments show a loss, this can be compensated by the profit hopefully showing on other investments. Also, the larger the trust fund, the more risk you can afford to take when investing part of that fund because you can, and should, be buying some safer investments by way of security.

Trusts

10.2.2 Investment types

An investment is something that is expected to produce an income return, a capital return or both. Some common types of investments are summarised in **Table 10.1**.

Table 10.1 Common types of investments

Investment type	Returns	Things to consider
Shares	Income = dividend payments Capital = any rise in the value of the shares	Historically over any 10-year period, there is likely to be an increase in the capital value of shares rather than a loss. The longer you invest in shares, the more likely that you will achieve a greater capital return. However, the value of shares can go down as well as up, so they are not without risk. Companies operate in various sectors and geographies. It is worth spreading investments in shares across companies operating in different lines of business and in different parts of the world. Some companies (known as 'blue chip companies') tend to be relatively safe, but better returns might be obtained by investing in higher risk companies such as those operating in emerging geographic markets (the fact that these markets are often less regulated and that any returns are at the mercy of currency fluctuations accounts for some of the higher risk). Many people who want to purchase shares will invest in public companies that trade their shares on a stock exchange. Shares in private companies (Ltd) are also forms of investment and some can be quite profitable. However, as a general rule, there is often less information available about how well a private company is doing financially and less opportunity to buy and sell shares.
Bonds	Income = the coupon (the interest that runs on the loan) Capital = many bonds are often viewed primarily as income-producing investments, but can generate capital growth when sold on secondary markets	Bonds are provided in exchange for money lent to governments and companies. The bond states when the loan will be repaid and the amount of interest that will be paid back to the investor each year. Some bonds are riskier than others, but gilts (which represent loans to the UK government) are often a safe and secure form of investment as there should be little chance of the government defaulting on the loan.
Property (real estate)	Income = rent if let Capital = the rise in property values	Generally, property values rise over time, but occasionally there can be short and severe downturns. The rise in property values is usually lower and steadier than some other forms of investment, making property a relatively secure investment. However, land is an expensive asset to purchase.
Cash-in-bank	Income = interest Capital = there is no capital growth	Cash-in-bank is often the safest form of investment, generating regular (if small) amounts of income. A well-balanced investment portfolio will have some cash, but if you are investing for the long-term, cash should usually form a small proportion of the portfolio.

The following are examples of things that are not classed as investments:

(a) Purchasing a 'run-around' car. These cars depreciate in value over time and do not produce income. Purchasing classic cars or luxury, high-end items might produce a capital return in the long-term, but this would be a very risky form of investment for most trusts.

(b) Placing bets on the horses. You might win occasionally, but the expectation is that most people lose most of the time. This is not an investment.

(c) The law has historically taken the view that unsecured loans are not investments, and that trustees are not permitted to make unsecured loans unless the trust document contains a very clear, express provision to that effect.

10.3 Express provisions in the declaration of trust

As with a number of topics relevant to the running of a trust, the settlor may expressly identify in the declaration of trust the forms of investment that trustees can purchase and those they cannot. If they do so, those express provisions must be followed. The settlor can also insert exclusion clauses for the benefit of the trustees, excluding liability for any losses arising out of the investment choices they make.

In the absence of any express provision in the declaration of trust, the Trustee Act (TA) 2000 sets out the powers and duties trustees have when investing trust property.

For the most part, we will assume that the settlor has not made any express provision in relation to investments and has not modified or excluded the statutory powers or duties in any way.

10.4 Authorised investments

Sections 3 and 8 of the TA 2000 set out what investments trustees can purchase on behalf of the trust.

Under s 3 of the TA 2000, a trustee can make any kind of investment that they could make if they were absolutely entitled to the assets of the trust, save for investments in land, which are covered by s 8 of the TA 2000. Section 3 sets out what is known as the 'general power of investment'.

When it comes to land, s 8 of the TA 2000 provides that a trustee may acquire freehold or leasehold land in the UK either:

(a) as an investment;

(b) for occupation by a beneficiary; or

(c) for any other reason.

⭐ Example

Sienna and Tracy are trustees for two beneficiaries. They purchase a cottage in the Cotswolds for one beneficiary to live in and a villa in Benidorm, Spain, for the other beneficiary to live in. The trust deed contains no express clauses dealing with investments.

The purchase of the cottage in the Cotswolds falls within the trustees' powers of investment under s 8 of the TA 2000.

However, the purchase of the villa in Benidorm does not – s 8 of the TA 2000 only permits the trustees to purchase land in the UK, not abroad. By purchasing this villa, the trustees are in breach of trust.

10.5 Duties when purchasing investments

10.5.1 Statutory duties

When purchasing or reviewing investments, trustees must have regard to the 'standard investment criteria'. These are listed in s 4 of the TA 2000:

(a) The investments must be suitable for the trust. This is a two-step process.

Example

Trustees want to purchase shares in RSA Insurance plc.

Under step 1, the trustees should consider whether the trust should be investing in shares.

If the trustees decide that shares are a suitable investment, step 2 requires trustees to consider whether shares in RSA Insurance are a good choice. The trustees should consider the size of the trust fund and the size of the proposed investment, the risks attaching to the company and the risks attaching to the sector / geographical markets in which the company operates, the time-scale for investment, the interests of the beneficiaries and the taxation consequences.

(b) There is a need for diversification (insofar as is appropriate to the circumstances of the trust). We have already seen that it is important to purchase different types of investments where possible so as to minimise the chances of an investor losing all their money on one investment or one type of investment.

Example

Trustees are managing a trust fund worth £800,000. They are thinking of buying £700,000 worth of shares across three companies: Royal Dutch Shell, BP and Exxon Mobil.

It is unlikely that the trustees' current investment plans are diverse enough – they are putting a considerable amount of money in one investment type (shares) and all of that money is being invested in the oil and gas sector. It is possible that a downturn will affect all three companies in a similar way, exposing the investment portfolio to considerable future loss. The trust fund is large enough for the trustees to engage in more diversification and purchase a broader range of investments.

Trustees must review the investments of the trust from time-to-time. When doing so, they must have regard to the standard investment criteria to assess whether the investments should be varied.

How often the trustees must undertake this review is a question of fact and will depend on the circumstances of each trust. If the trustees are in the early days of managing a long-term trust, reviewing the investments every six months might be sufficient. However, if there is an economic downturn (eg a stock market crash), then the trustees should review the investments as quickly as possible.

Under s 5 of the TA 2000, when reviewing investments or thinking of selling/purchasing investments, trustees should obtain and consider proper investment advice from someone the trustees reasonably believe to be qualified to give such advice, unless the trustees reasonably conclude that in all the circumstances it is unnecessary or inappropriate to do so (such as where one of the trustees is a qualified financial adviser). The trustees must act reasonably when selecting an adviser, but there will be many independent financial advisers who will fit the bill. Whilst the adviser can advise the trustees on the exercise of their investment powers, the trustees must exercise those powers personally – the decision on what they will and will not invest in remains theirs.

When exercising any power or fulfilling any duty in relation to investments, the trustees must exercise such care and skill as is reasonable in the circumstances (TA 2000, s 1). This is the overarching, objective 'duty of care' that applies to investment functions. Professional trustees (such as solicitors) will be held to a higher standard.

⭐ Example

Six months ago, Caitlin (a home-maker) and David (a plumber) were appointed trustees to run a trust for Usain for life, remainder to Venus and Whitney. Usain is currently aged 50 years, Venus is aged 20 years and Whitney is aged 15 years. The total value of the trust fund is £950,000 and is comprised of:

- *£200,000 in a variety of different current accounts;*
- *£400,000 house in Swindon, currently unoccupied;*
- *£150,000 shares in a family-run company called Gift Favours Limited; and*
- *£200,000 invested in shares in public companies trading in the technology sector.*

Caitlin and David are now reviewing the trust investments.

Caitlin and David should appoint someone suitably qualified to give them advice when reviewing the investments. Together with their appointed adviser, they should consider the standard investment criteria:

- *Suitability. Usain is interested in income, whilst Venus and Whitney will be interested in capital growth. These interests must be balanced. It is likely that the trust will continue for a number of years given Usain's age, so the trustees can adopt a longer-term view and could decide to adopt a few risks particularly if those risks are likely to give rise to larger capital growth for Venus and Whitney.*

    Turning to the individual investment types:

    - *There is a lot of money in current bank accounts. That money is not producing any capital growth and is unlikely to be producing much, if any, interest for Usain. Whilst it may be wise to keep a small reserve of cash in bank accounts, some of this money is probably better invested elsewhere.*
    - *The house in Swindon might well be a safe form of investment for Venus and Whitney, but if no-one is living there, it is not doing anything for Usain. It might be worth putting the house up for rent to generate some income.*
    - *More information is needed about the shares in the private company. Does the company regularly declare dividends? How well is the company doing financially? Are the shares likely to increase in value? Would the trustees be able*

to find a willing buyer for the shares? If the trustees are thinking of retaining this shareholding, then they should consider securing an appointment on the board of directors so that they can oversee and have some input into the management of the company (Bartlett v Barclays Bank Trust Co Ltd [1980] 2 WLR 430).

- *Diversification. There is a range of investments already, so the beneficiaries have some protection if one investment performs badly. However, there is a significant weighting of shares in technology companies, which can be a very volatile sector. It may be worth trading out of some of those shares and purchasing shares in different sectors. Caitlin and David will also need to consider diversifying into other investment types or investing in other sectors if they are going to use some of the cash-in-bank.*

10.5.2 Non-statutory duties

The following are some of the common duties outside of the TA 2000 to which trustees must have regard when exercising their investment powers:

(a) Trustees must act impartially between beneficiaries. In their choice of investments, trustees must strike a fair balance between the needs of all the beneficiaries, for instance a life tenant (who wants income) and a remainder beneficiary (who wants capital appreciation). Allowing one beneficiary the use of trust property without compensation for another beneficiary would also breach this duty.

(b) Trustees must secure the best return for the beneficiaries. This does not necessarily mean that the trustees must secure the *highest* return as that might entail accepting too much risk for the trust.

However, as most trusts are set up to provide financial benefits for the beneficiaries, the trustees are generally obliged to secure the best *financial* return – financial considerations must take precedence over other considerations. The trustees should not be guided by their own ethical or moral views about investments: these are generally irrelevant.

There are some circumstances, however, in which trustees may take ethical considerations into account when choosing investments:

   (i) if an investment in an ethical concern is likely to yield as good a return as an investment that is more morally dubious, the trustees can invest in the ethical concern;

   (ii) if the trust is charitable, the trustees can properly refuse to invest in things that might be at odds with the charitable purposes of the trust and that might alienate the charity's supporters; and

   (iii) the settlor can set out in the declaration of trust that trustees should not invest in specific sectors that the settlor considered to be unethical.

10.6 Delegation

Not all trustees will feel comfortable making decisions on what they should and should not invest in. Rather than making these decisions themselves, trustees can collectively delegate their investment functions.

Trustees can collectively delegate investment functions to either a third party (like an independent financial adviser) or to one of their number (so long as that trustee is suitably qualified to make investment decisions). However, they cannot collectively delegate these functions to a beneficiary. A third party agent can be paid reasonable remuneration for their services.

Trustees must comply with various processes when delegating investments (otherwise known as 'asset management functions') to someone else:

(a) They must retain the investment agent by written agreement.

(b) They must prepare a written statement (known as the 'policy statement') that gives guidance as to how the agent should exercise their asset management functions in the best interests of the trust.

The trustees must exercise reasonable care and skill in putting the policy statement together.

(c) The written agreement under which the agent is retained must include a term to the effect that the agent will secure compliance with the policy statement.

(d) The agent must comply with the same statutory and non-statutory investment duties that would otherwise apply to the trustees.

(e) The trustees must regularly review the arrangements under which the agent is acting and how those arrangements are working. That might include considering whether to revise or update the policy statement, or assessing whether the agent is complying with the policy statement and bringing the retainer to an end if they believe the agent is not.

(f) Importantly, the trustees must select a suitably qualified person to whom their asset management functions will be delegated. That selection must be made with reasonable care and skill.

Section 23 of the TA 2000 makes it clear that a trustee is not liable for any act or default of the agent, unless the trustee has breached any of the personal duties listed above and those breaches cause loss to the trust.

⭐ Example

Callum and Donna were appointed trustees over a £2 million trust fund. They quickly felt out of their depth so, last year, they asked their friend Eliot to be in charge of investing the trust fund. Eliot immediately put all of the money into shares of Fiasco plc, a company that was in financial difficulties at the time and that has now gone into liquidation. The beneficiaries are angry that Callum and Donna could have let this happen.

Callum and Donna will not be liable for the poor investment decisions that Eliot took, so long as they have not breached their own duties under the TA 2000. When advising Callum and Donna we should consider:

- *Did they properly retain Eliot? Was Eliot given a written policy statement identifying the beneficiaries and given guidance on what he should achieve? Was that statement put together with reasonable care and skill?*

- *Was Eliot the right person for the job? Did Callum and Donna select him because they reasonably believed he was suitably qualified, or did they select him because he was their friend?*

- *Did they keep Eliot's actions under review? If they simply let Eliot get on with things last year and have not met with him since to get an update on how the investments were performing, then they may find themselves liable for the losses that have been sustained.*

If Callum and Donna complied with their own duties when delegating their asset management functions down to Eliot, they should now think whether it is appropriate to take action against Eliot on behalf of the trust to secure compensation for the losses his investment decisions have caused. If Eliot is in the business of providing independent financial advice, he should hopefully have insurance that will ultimately pay out any damages that the trust is awarded should Eliot have acted negligently.

10.7 Summary flowchart

Figure 10.1 Investments summary flowchart

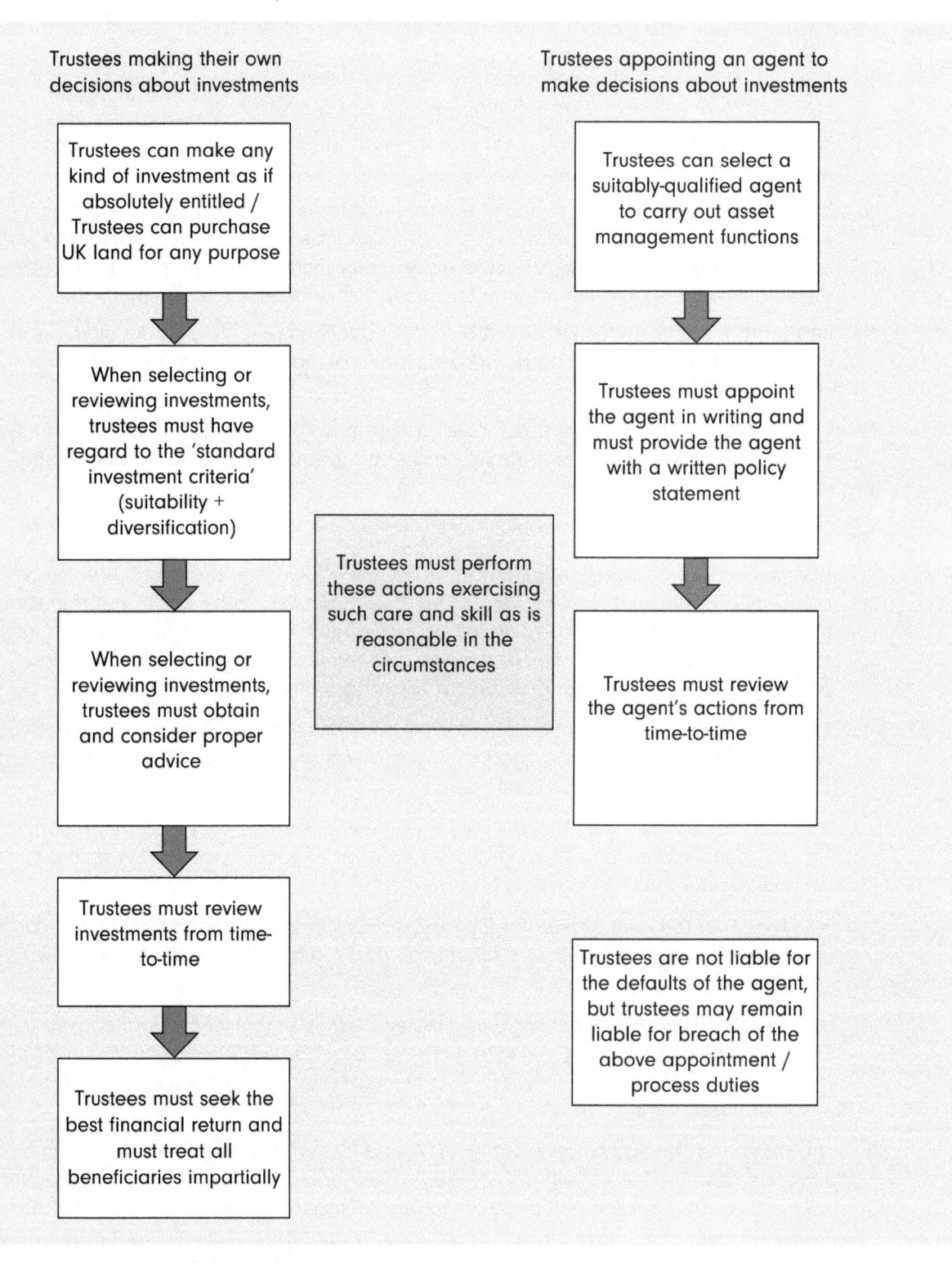

Trustees making their own decisions about investments

- Trustees can make any kind of investment as if absolutely entitled / Trustees can purchase UK land for any purpose
- When selecting or reviewing investments, trustees must have regard to the 'standard investment criteria' (suitability + diversification)
- When selecting or reviewing investments, trustees must obtain and consider proper advice
- Trustees must review investments from time-to-time
- Trustees must seek the best financial return and must treat all beneficiaries impartially

Trustees appointing an agent to make decisions about investments

- Trustees can select a suitably-qualified agent to carry out asset management functions
- Trustees must appoint the agent in writing and must provide the agent with a written policy statement
- Trustees must review the agent's actions from time-to-time
- Trustees are not liable for the defaults of the agent, but trustees may remain liable for breach of the above appointment / process duties

Trustees must perform these actions exercising such care and skill as is reasonable in the circumstances

Summary

In this chapter you have considered the trustees' duties and powers when investing trust property:

- *Power of investment.* Generally speaking, trustees can purchase any form of investment for the trust that they could purchase for themselves. The main exception is that trustees cannot purchase land overseas.

- *Duties when exercising investment powers.* Trustees must select investments with reference to the standard investment criteria (suitability and diversification), they must review investments from time-to-time, and they must select and review investments with the benefit of professional advice. They must do all this and choose appropriate investments with reasonable care and skill. Trustees must also act fairly between beneficiaries when choosing investments and should try to generate the best financial return for the trust.

- *Delegation.* Trustees can collectively delegate their investment decisions to an agent. They must comply with various duties when delegating these functions down to the agent, such as ensuring that they select a suitably qualified agent and produce a policy statement that correctly identifies the investment objectives of the trust. So long as trustees comply with these personal duties, they will not be liable for any losses caused by the decisions of the appointed agent.

Sample questions

Question 1

The trustees appointed to manage a large trust fund decide to delegate investment decisions to someone else. They ask their friends down the local pub for ideas and ultimately appoint the person ('the agent') with the most recommendations. The appointment is contained in a written agreement annexed to which is a written statement with guidance on how the agent should act in the best interests of the trust and provides that the agent must meet with the trustees to update them on the status of investments whenever required to do so.

Two years later, during one of their regular meetings to discuss investments, the agent advises that he purchased £325,000 worth of shares in a company that has recently gone into liquidation. The shares are now worthless.

Which of the following best describes whether the trustees will be liable for the loss in value to the trust fund?

A   The trustees may be liable if they failed to use reasonable care in selecting the agent.

B   The trustees will be liable if the agent was negligent in choosing to purchase the shares.

C   The trustees will be liable because the appointment of the agent can only last for a maximum of 12 months.

D   The trustees will not be liable because they appointed the agent in writing.

E   The trustees will not be liable because they arranged regular meetings with the agent to discuss investments.

Answer

Option A is correct. Trustees are not vicariously (or automatically) liable for the defaults of investment agents. However, trustees may remain liable if they have breached their own personal duties in appointing and supervising the investment agent. For instance, the trustees must take reasonable care and skill in appointing a suitably qualified agent, which is unlikely to have happened on the facts.

Option B is wrong. Just because the agent was negligent in choosing to purchase the shares does not mean that the trustees are automatically liable for any loss in value. Trustees are not vicariously liable for the negligence of their investment agents.

Option C is wrong. This option confuses collective delegation under the TA 2000 (which need not be time-limited in duration, but where the trustees must review the activities of their agent) and individual delegation under the TA 1925, where attorneys can only be in place for up to a maximum of 12 months (see **Chapter 7**).

Options D and E are correct insofar as they go – trustees must appoint investment agents in writing and they must supervise the activities of the agent from time-to-time. However, these are not the only personal duties that trustees owe when collectively delegating investment functions to an agent, so the fact that they got these things right does not necessarily make the trustees immune from any liability. These options therefore do not constitute the best advice to the trustees.

Question 2

Trustees are appointed to manage a trust fund worth £875,000 for the benefit of the settlor's grandchildren so long as they reach the age of 21 years. There are four grandchildren, all under the age of 21 years. There are no relevant express provisions in the trust deed.

One of the grandchildren – a grandson aged 19 years – asks the trustees to make an unsecured loan of some trust money. He wants the money so the company he has just set up can purchase a warehouse and promises to pay the money back to the trust with interest.

The trustees are unwilling to use their powers of advancement.

Which of the following best describes whether the trustees can use their investment powers to help the grandson?

A   The trustees must lend the money to the grandson as requested because the grandson is of full age and capacity.

B   The trustees can lend the money to the grandson as requested, but do not have to because how they invest trust property is a matter for them.

C   The trustees can lend the money to the grandson as requested, but only if they reasonably conclude this is a suitable use of money and they take a mortgage over the warehouse in exchange for the loan.

D   The trustees cannot lend the money to the grandson because, when exercising their investment powers in respect of land, that land must be either occupied or used by the beneficiary (and not a company belonging to the beneficiary).

E   The trustees cannot lend the money to the grandson because the only way that trust money can be given to a beneficiary before their interests vest is by the trustees exercising their powers of advancement.

Answer

Option C is correct. A loan secured on land is a type of investment that falls within the trustees' general power of investment, but the trustees must consider whether this loan is an appropriate use of trust money, by reference to the standard investment criteria (suitability and diversification) and whether they are treating all the beneficiaries impartially.

Option A is wrong. The decision to exercise powers of investment is a decision for the trustees. The beneficiaries cannot dictate to the trustees how to exercise those powers.

Option B is wrong. An unsecured loan is generally not considered to constitute an investment.

Option D is misleading – the investment is the loan secured on land (not the land itself). In any event, if the trustees were considering whether to purchase the warehouse as a form of investment for the trust, the fact that the warehouse is not being used by the beneficiary himself would not prevent the trustees from using their investment powers under s 8 of the TA 2000.

Option E is wrong. It is possible for the trustees to lend money properly secured to a beneficiary as opposed to exercising their statutory powers to advance capital to that beneficiary (under TA 1925, s 32). Whether that is an appropriate use of their investment powers is another issue.

Question 3

An independent financial adviser has been appointed a trustee for a management consultant for life and a student in remainder. The trust fund has been valued at more than £900,000. The trustee uses all of the trust fund to purchase shares in a large international company headquartered in India whose shares trade on the Dow Jones (New York stock exchange). The company's share-value has recently posted significant growth and the company has a reputation for paying significant dividends to its shareholders.

Which of the following statements best describes why the trustee is likely to be in breach of trust?

A   The trustee is only permitted to purchase shares in UK companies.

B   Shares are not an authorised form of investment.

C   The shares are not a suitable form of investment.

D   The shares do not represent a diverse form of investment.

E   The trustee failed to take proper investment advice before purchasing the shares.

Answer

Option D is correct. When purchasing investments, trustees must have regard to the standard investment criteria – suitability and the need for diversification. In this case, using the entire trust fund to purchase shares in one company does not respect the need for diversification. If the company gets into financial difficulties, the value of the trust fund may be materially and adversely affected.

Option A is wrong. The general power of investment contained in s 3 of the TA 2000 is not limited to the UK. Trustees can purchase investments based in any part of the world (so long as the trustee complies with the other investment duties in this chapter). This is different to purchasing land, where the power contained in s 8 of the TA 2000 is limited to land in the UK.

Option B is wrong. Shares are capable of producing both capital and income returns and are therefore a classic form of authorised investment.

Option C is wrong. Shares, in general, are a good investment for this trust. The trustee must consider the income needs of the management consultant and the capital needs of the student. Shares are capable of meeting these two needs. Focusing on the company itself, there is nothing on the facts to suggest that the company is a bad investment – it has a history of capital growth and dividend payments. The real issue here is one of diversification.

Option E is wrong. Whilst generally it is the case that trustees must take proper advice before purchasing investments, they do not need to do so when they reasonable conclude that it is unnecessary to do so. The trustee is an independent financial adviser and it is reasonable to conclude that the trustee can take investment decisions without needing assistance from someone else.

11 Fiduciary Duties

11.1	Introduction	144
11.2	Who can be a fiduciary	144
11.3	The core fiduciary duty	144
11.4	When trustees can make a personal profit	145
11.5	Breaches of fiduciary duty	146
11.6	Remedies	150
11.7	Summary flowchart	151

SQE1 syllabus

This chapter will enable you to achieve the SQE1 assessment specification in relation to functioning legal knowledge concerned with the following core principles:

- The fiduciary relationship and its obligations
- The duty not to profit from a fiduciary position
- Trustees must not purchase trust property
- The fiduciary should not put themselves in a position where their interest and duty conflict

Note that for SQE1, candidates are not usually required to recall specific case names or cite statutory or regulatory authorities. Cases are provided for illustrative purposes only.

Learning outcomes

By the end of this chapter you will be able to apply relevant core legal principles and rules appropriately and effectively, at the level of a competent newly qualified solicitor in practice, to realistic client-based and ethical problems and situations in the following areas:

- identifying the types of people who might be classed as a fiduciary;
- recognising the main objectives of the fiduciary relationship;
- providing examples of breaches of fiduciary duty;
- identifying the defences available to someone who has breached a fiduciary duty; and
- advising on the remedies available for breach of fiduciary duty.

11.1 Introduction

A trustee has all the powers available to them under common law to manage property. To the outside world the trustee looks for all intents and purposes as if they were the absolute owner of trust property. Whilst they need this array of powers to properly manage and administer property for the benefit of the beneficiaries, it also raises the prospect of abuse – the trustee could be tempted to exploit their control over trust property or the running of the trust to make a profit for themselves.

The fiduciary relationship, and the duties that underpin that relationship, are designed to stop this abuse from happening. The duties are applied in a very strict manner and are designed to deter a trustee from putting their own self-interest above the interests of the trust.

This chapter looks at:

- who can be a fiduciary;
- what are the main objectives and characteristics of the fiduciary relationship;
- examples of the ways in which fiduciary duties can be breached;
- the defences available for a breach of fiduciary duty; and
- the remedies available for breach of fiduciary duty.

11.2 Who can be a fiduciary

A fiduciary is someone 'who has undertaken to act for or on behalf of another in a particular matter in circumstances that give rise to a relationship of trust and confidence' (*Bristol and West Building Society v Mothew* [1998] Ch 1).

The people who fall within this definition include:

(a) trustees, who owe fiduciary duties to beneficiaries;

(b) company directors, who owe fiduciary duties to their company;

(c) business partners, who owe fiduciary duties to each other;

(d) agents, who owe fiduciary duties to their principal;

(e) senior employees with access to confidential information, who owe fiduciary duties to their employer; and

(f) solicitors, who owe fiduciary duties to their client.

Given that many people can end up being a fiduciary, lawyers in departments other than private client have to be aware of fiduciary relationships and the duties they import. In all cases, the duties are based on the cases and principles summarised in this chapter, although in some cases the duties have now been codified in statute (eg company director duties are now contained in the Companies Act 2006, see the **Business Law and Practice Manual** for more information) or regulation (eg solicitor duties are set out in the SRA Codes of Conduct, see the **Ethics and Professional Conduct Manual** for more information).

For most of this chapter, we shall focus on trustees as fiduciaries.

11.3 The core fiduciary duty

While trustees are controlling and managing the trust, they will have countless opportunities to prefer their own interests:

(a) they might own a house that they are having trouble selling. They may decide to sell it to the trust for an inflated price, thinking that no-one will be any the wiser;

(b) they might pay themselves a large sum from trust funds in remuneration for the work they are doing; or

(c) they may get investment tips from the trust's advisers that they decide to use for themselves rather than passing them on to the trust.

To safeguard against this, the fiduciary must not:

(a) put themselves in a position where their own interests conflict with the interests of their principal (the 'no conflict' rule); and

(b) make an unauthorised personal profit from their position or use their principal's property to make such a profit (the 'no profit' rule).

The fiduciary relationship is a relationship of loyalty. The trust is entitled to the single-minded loyalty of the trustee. The trustee must 'not make a profit out of his trust; he must not place himself in a position where his duty and his interest may conflict; he may not act for his own benefit ... without the informed consent of his principal [the beneficiaries]' (*Bristol and West Building Society v Mothew*).

In the case of Bray v Ford [1896] AC 44, Lord Herschell characterised the nature of the fiduciary relationship in this way:

> It is an inflexible rule of a Court of Equity that a person in a fiduciary position ... is not, unless otherwise expressly provided, entitled to make a profit; he is not allowed to put himself in a position where his interest and duty conflict ... I regard [this] as being based on the consideration that, human nature being what it is, there is a danger, in such circumstances, of the person holding a fiduciary position being swayed by interest rather than duty, and thus prejudicing those whom he was bound to protect.

If the trustee acts for their own benefit rather than the trust's and makes a personal profit, the trustee will be obliged to account for that profit, ie pay it over to the trust.

When deciding whether a trustee has breached their fiduciary duty, the court will not enquire into the merits of the case: the honesty of the trustee is irrelevant as is the amount of effort the trustee has put in to secure a personal profit. Nor does it matter that the trust was not willing to take up the opportunity for itself and has not lost anything. Liability is applied strictly, the justification being that this will then act as a deterrent – if trustees know that they cannot keep profits in any circumstances, they will not try to make a personal profit in the first place. This ensures that the trustee is always motivated by the best interests of the trust.

11.4 When trustees can make a personal profit

Before looking at examples of how the core fiduciary duty might be breached, it is worth quickly setting out the occasions in which trustees can keep a personal profit notwithstanding that they have acted in their own self-interest.

Trustees can keep personal profits if:

(a) this is authorised by the declaration of trust;

(b) all the beneficiaries are aged 18 years or over, know the full facts and consent; or

(c) this is authorised by a court order or by statutory provision.

11.5 Breaches of fiduciary duty

11.5.1 Self-dealing

A trustee may be tempted to sell to, or purchase property from, the trust. In these situations, the trustee is effectively selling trust property to, or purchasing trust property from, themselves. Remember that the trustee is the legal owner of trust property and is the person who has the power to sell it.

If a trustee sells property to, or purchases property from, the trust, the trustee will put themselves in a position of conflict. For instance, if the trustee is purchasing land from the trust:

- as seller acting in the interests of the trust, the trustee will want the purchase price to be as high as possible; but
- as buyer acting in their own self-interest, the trustee will want to the purchase price to be as low as possible.

If a trustee is involved in this kind of transaction, then the beneficiaries can set the transaction aside at a later date. This is known as the 'self-dealing rule'. The transaction is not automatically void, as the beneficiaries may decide that the transaction was a good deal as far as the trust was concerned. However, the beneficiaries can set the transaction aside for any reason within a reasonable period of time.

The self-dealing rule has been applied strictly. The courts do not consider whether or not the trustee has paid fair value for the property or whether the trustee was acting honestly.

⭐ Example

Imogen and Jane are appointed trustees for Kieran (aged 20 years) and Luke (aged 16 years). The trust property included a house in Beeston, which Imogen and Jane put on the market for £215,000.

However, the house did not attract any offers and after two years, Jane agreed to purchase the house for £180,000.

The local council have just announced the intention to build a new tramline and a stop will be located five minutes' walk away from the house. As a result, the house is now believed to be valued at £275,000.

Jane has been involved in self-dealing. She acted on both sides of the transaction – as one of the trustees selling the house, and as the purchaser. Kieran and Luke can therefore decide to set aside the transaction. They have a reasonable period of time to decide what to do (and given that Luke is currently aged under 18 years, that time period will be relatively generous).

If they do so, Jane must reconvey the house back into the joint names of herself and Imogen, and the trust must repay her the original purchase price of £180,000. The beneficiaries will therefore gain the benefit of the house's increase in value.

The fact that Jane's purchase may have represented a good deal for the trust at the time (given that there was no interest in the house from any third party) and that she may have acted honestly and in good faith is irrelevant to the beneficiaries' ability to set the transaction aside.

A trustee cannot get around the self-dealing rule by retiring from the trust before purchasing trust property. If the trustee has retired with the object of purchasing trust property, then they will still be caught by the rule and the beneficiaries will still be able to set the transaction aside.

11.5.2 Competition with the trust

Where the trust includes a business, the trustee must not set up their own business in competition. If they do so, they will be liable to account for any profits made by their competing business. If the beneficiaries become aware that the trustee is planning to set up a competing business, they can obtain an injunction to prevent this from happening.

11.5.3 Remuneration of trustees

Trustees cannot demand payment for their services from trust funds unless authorised by:

(a) Express provision in the trust deed. Trustees can charge fees if there is a clause authorising remuneration in the declaration of trust. It is relatively common for trust deeds and wills to contain such clauses. They are often referred to as 'charging clauses'.

(b) The beneficiaries consenting. If the beneficiaries are all 18 years or above, they can agree to pay the trustees remuneration. However, the agreement must be fair and the trustees must make full disclosure of all relevant facts, otherwise the beneficiaries can set aside the agreement at a future date.

(c) Court order. The court should order remuneration if it is in the interests of the beneficiaries because, for instance, the trust needs the skill of the trustee in question and their fees are not excessive compared with those of other professionals.

(d) The TA 2000. Save where the trust deed makes any provision about remuneration:

   (i) a trust corporation, or

   (ii) a trustee who acts in a professional capacity and who is not a sole trustee, and where the other trustees have agreed in writing,

   is entitled to receive reasonable remuneration. A trustee acts in a professional capacity if they act in the course of a profession or business that consists of or includes the provision of services in connection with the management or administration of trusts. What is reasonable to charge will depend on the individual facts of each case. That will include considering the nature of the services to be provided, the size of the trust and the attributes of the trustee who is seeking to charge.

⭐ Example

Mark and Naoko have been appointed as trustees over a family trust. Mark is a financial adviser and Naoko is a dental hygienist. Mark and Naoko want to charge for their time working on the trust. They have checked the trust deed, which makes no provision for the charging of fees by trustees.

Mark is acting in a professional capacity. Financial advisers act in the course of a profession that can consist of services connected with the management or administration of trusts (primarily the giving of investment advice to trustees or, if the trustees collectively delegate this, undertaking the asset management functions of a trust). If Naoko agrees in writing that Mark can charge fees, then he will be able to charge reasonable remuneration. As a trustee, Naoko must act in the best interest of the beneficiaries and should not give this consent without proper consideration.

Naoko is not acting in a professional capacity for the purposes of the TA 2000 and therefore cannot rely on these provisions to secure remuneration. She will probably need to obtain the beneficiaries' consent to any fees she wishes to charge.

Whether or not a trustee is entitled to charge fees for their work, s 31 of the TA 2000 provides that the trustee can be reimbursed from the trust fund for any expenses properly incurred when acting on behalf of the trust (such as the cost of travelling to trustee meetings).

11.5.4 Incidental profits: commission

The above examples show how the fiduciary duty prevents trustees from making unauthorised profits from the trust. The fiduciary duty also prevents trustees from making incidental profits (the receipt of money from third parties). Trustees must not make unauthorised profits 'on the side'.

An example of an incidental profit is the payment of commission to a trustee when that trustee places trust business with a particular firm. The commission received by the trustee has to be accounted to the trust.

⭐ Example

Marta is a trustee and is also an employee in a firm of stockbrokers. The firm pays its employees commission if they introduce new business to the firm. Marta suggests that the trust employs her firm to carry out a valuation of the trust's shareholdings and the firm pays her commission.

Marta has to account to the trust for the commission unless she was authorised to keep it (eg under the terms of the trust deed). She profited from her position as trustee and placed herself in a position where her interests in receiving commission conflict with her duty to give the trust impartial advice on the choice of advisers (see Williams v Barton *[1927] 2 Ch 9).*

11.5.5 Incidental profits: director's salary

The trust might include a substantial shareholding in a company. The trustees should consider securing an appointment on the board of directors so that they can oversee and have some input into the management of the company.

However, what happens if the company then pays the trustee-director a salary? Can the trustee keep the salary or must they pay the salary over to the trust? In the absence of any authorisation from the trust deed, the beneficiaries or the court, the trustee must surrender their salary to the trust if they acquired the directorship only by virtue of being a trustee.

New directors are generally appointed at a shareholders' meeting. The appointment of a director requires over 50% of the votes cast to be in favour of the appointment. If the trust fund includes shares in the company, the trustees will be able to exercise the votes attached to those shares to vote themselves into office. If those shares were the reason why the trustee became a director, the trustee must surrender any salary they subsequently receive to the trust.

⭐ Examples

(a) *Natalie is a trustee. The trust holds shares in Gamma Corp Limited. The trust shares comprise 35% of all the shares in the company.*

At a shareholders' meeting, 90% of the attending shareholders by value vote in favour of Natalie becoming a director. Gamma Corp subsequently pays Natalie a salary.

Natalie can keep her salary. She became a director independently of the trust's shareholding. Even if you ignore the votes attached to the trust's shares (or, putting it another way, you hypothetically assume that those shares voted against her), Natalie would still have secured sufficient support amongst the other shareholders to be appointed a director.

(b) Let us take the same facts, but now assume that only 65% of attending shareholders by value voted in favour of Natalie becoming a director. In this case, it is assumed that Natalie only became a director by virtue of her trusteeship (if you ignore the trust's shareholding or assume that those shares voted against her, Natalie would not have secured the majority needed to become a director – only 30% of independent shareholders were in favour of her appointment). She has become a director by virtue of her position as trustee. She has also put herself in a position where her own interests in keeping the salary conflict with those of the trust. The trust would no doubt prefer that she undertook her directorship for free thereby keeping monies in the company, increasing the potential for dividend payments or future capital growth, either of which will stand to benefit the trust. Natalie will have to account to the trust for her salary (Re Macadam [1946] Ch 73).

If someone was a director of a company before they became a trustee of a trust that has shares in the company, the director can keep their salary. They did not become a director by virtue of the trust.

11.5.6 Use of information or opportunity

A trustee is liable to account for any profits they receive where they received that profit by exploiting an opportunity that belonged to the trust. Likewise, a trustee who makes use of confidential information for their own personal gain when they only became aware of the information due to their trusteeship will have to account for any profits they receive. This is the case whether or not the trust could have taken advantage of the opportunity or was interested in the information.

In Boardman v Phipps [1967] 2 AC 46, Thomas Boardman was a solicitor acting on behalf of the trustees of a family trust. The trust fund included a substantial shareholding in a company that was not doing well financially. In his capacity as solicitor for the trustees, Mr Boardman gained valuable information about the company (information that was not otherwise in the public domain) and advised the trustees on how they could turn around the fortunes of the company, which would require the trust to purchase additional shares. The trustees had no power to purchase additional shares, and whilst they could have applied to the court for authorisation, the managing trustee, Mr Fox, said he would not have considered doing so. Mr Boardman therefore asked Mr Fox and another active trustee whether he (Mr Boardman) could purchase the shares in his own name out of his own funds. The trustees did not object. Mr Boardman purchased the additional shares and was able to turn the company's affairs around, making a tidy profit for both himself and the trust. A beneficiary then complained that Mr Boardman should not be allowed to keep his profit for himself and that his personal profit also belonged to the trust.

The majority of the House of Lords held that Mr Boardman had to surrender his personal profit to the trust. He had gained information about the company and the opportunity to make a personal profit by virtue of his fiduciary position. Indeed, according to some of the judges, the fact that Mr Boardman only obtained information about the company through acting on behalf of the trust made that information trust property. He had therefore used trust property to gain a personal profit and had to account that profit back to the trust.

A further ground for the House of Lords' decision was the 'no conflict' rule. Mr Boardman had placed himself in a position where his interest might conflict with that of the trust. They maintained that the slightest possibility of a conflict makes trustees liable to pay their personal profits over to the trust. In this instance, had the trustees asked Mr Boardman whether they should apply to court for power to buy the additional shares, he could not have given impartial advice (as he was conflicted by his own plans to purchase the shares for himself). The fact that the trustees did not appear minded to go to court was immaterial.

Mr Boardman therefore had to surrender his personal profit to the trust, but as he had acted with complete honesty and had invested a great deal of time and skill in changing the fortune of the company, which had in turn greatly benefited the trust, the court awarded Mr Boardman generous remuneration for his work.

In the above case, Mr Boardman was solicitor to the trustees – he owed his fiduciary duties to the trustees – so he should have sought prior authorisation from the trustees who were his principals. (Whilst he did seek authorisation from the two active trustees, there was a third trustee from whom he did not seek consent.) In the case of a trustee looking to exploit opportunities that properly belong to the trust, the trustee will need the authorisation of the beneficiaries.

Example

Peter is a trustee. He is told by the trust's financial adviser of an opportunity to buy some shares in Silky Swirls Limited. He informs his fellow trustees of this opportunity but they appear uninterested. Peter then asks the other trustees whether he can buy the shares himself, to which they consent. Peter buys the shares and, six months later, sells the shares when they have doubled in value.

Peter has used trust property (the information about the shares) and his position as trustee to secure a personal profit. He has put himself in a position where his own interests conflicted with the interests of the trust. The fact that the other trustees were unwilling to purchase the shares and Peter apparently acted honestly is irrelevant. If Peter wanted to ensure that he could retain any personal profit from the shares, he should have either sought consent from the beneficiaries (assuming they were all aged 18 or over) or authorisation from the court.

11.6 Remedies

If a trustee breaches their fiduciary duty and they have not obtained authorisation to keep any personal profit, the beneficiaries are entitled to bring either:

(a) a personal claim that the trustee pays over their unauthorised profit. The trustee must surrender their personal profit to the trust. Note that this claim does not follow the usual loss measures that appear in contract or tort. The trustee is not making good any loss that their actions have caused; indeed, the trust may not have suffered any loss. If commission is paid by a firm to a trustee for the placement of trust business and the firm's services result in significant profits for the trust, the beneficiaries are still entitled to bring a personal claim against the trustee for the surrender of the commission even though the trust has not suffered any loss. The trustee must surrender any unauthorised personal profits they have secured by virtue of their position; and/or

(b) a proprietary claim. A proprietary claim will seek to recover property owned by the trustee that represents the personal profit they received. For instance, if a trustee made an unauthorised profit of £400,000 by exploiting an investment opportunity that properly belonged to the trust, and used this money to buy shares in Astrid plc, the beneficiaries could require that the trustee convey the shares over to the trust. This would be particularly attractive if the shares have gone up in value, because the trust would get the benefit of that increase. We will consider proprietary claims in more detail in **Chapter 13**.

11.7 Summary flowchart

Figure 11.1 Fiduciary duties (trustee) summary flowchart

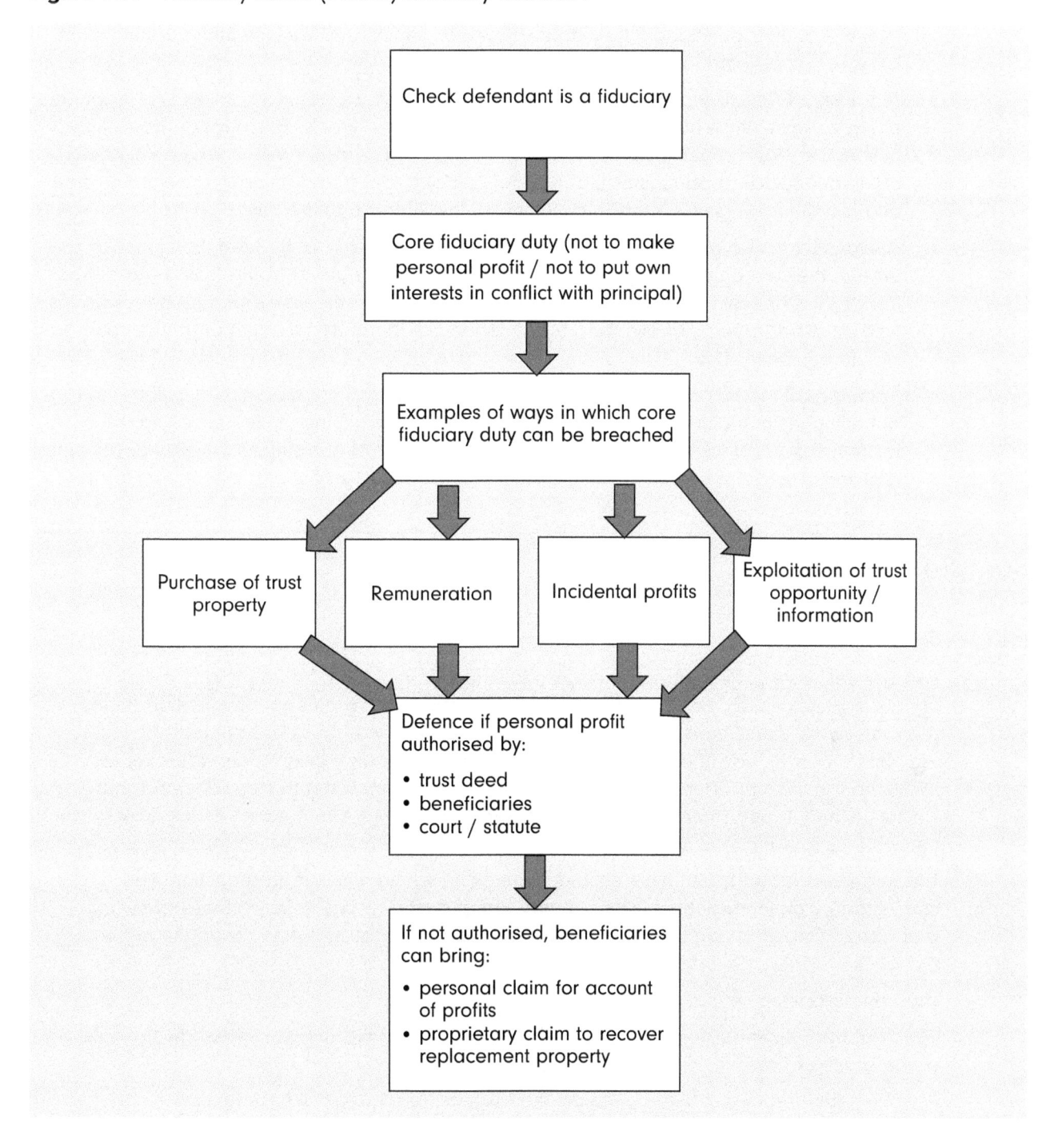

```
Check defendant is a fiduciary
              ↓
Core fiduciary duty (not to make
personal profit / not to put own
interests in conflict with principal)
              ↓
Examples of ways in which core
fiduciary duty can be breached
    ↙         ↓         ↓         ↘
Purchase of   Remuneration  Incidental   Exploitation of trust
trust property              profits      opportunity /
                                         information
    ↘         ↓         ↓         ↙
Defence if personal profit
authorised by:
 • trust deed
 • beneficiaries
 • court / statute
              ↓
If not authorised, beneficiaries
can bring:
 • personal claim for account
   of profits
 • proprietary claim to recover
   replacement property
```

Summary

In this chapter you have considered the fiduciary relationship and its obligations:

- *Who can be a fiduciary.* Fiduciary relationships extend far beyond trusts. Solicitors acting in commercial, corporate and employment departments have to have a good working knowledge of fiduciary duties.

- *The core fiduciary duty.* A fiduciary relationship is one of the utmost loyalty. A fiduciary must work whole-heartedly and solely for their principal. A trustee's attention and effort must be concentrated wholly on the trust. They must not use their position as fiduciary to secure a personal profit. They cannot allow their own self-interests to conflict with the interests of their principal. If they do so, however honest and well-intentioned they might be, they will be held to account.

- *Breaches of fiduciary duty.* Over the years, the courts have come across various examples of the ways in which trustees can prefer their own self-interests. These range from purchasing trust property, to the receipt of profits from third parties, to the exploitation of information or opportunities that properly belong to the trust. In each case, the trustee allowed their own self-interest to conflict with the interests of the trust.

- *Authorisation as a defence.* If the trustee secures a personal profit from their position as trustee, they will only be allowed to keep that personal profit if (a) the trust deed allows this, (b) the beneficiaries consent (the trustee must secure the consent of all beneficiaries, who must be 18 years or over and fully informed of the material facts) or (c) the court or statute authorises this.

- *Remedies.* If the trustee obtains a personal profit in breach of fiduciary duty, the beneficiaries can either (a) bring a personal claim against the trustee requiring the trustee to account for their profits (whether or not the trust has suffered a loss) or (b) bring a proprietary claim if the trustee has used their personal profits to purchase property.

Sample questions

Question 1

Two trustees were appointed to manage a trust fund comprising the freehold of a block of flats in Lincolnshire. The trustees secured an independent, professional valuation on the premises, which concluded that the current freehold value was £425,000 but that the local real estate market was in difficulty and that the value was likely to drop considerably in the future. Having considered the interests of the beneficiaries, the trustees decided that it would be in their best interests to sell the freehold and buy other investments more likely to generate capital growth.

The trustees decided to sell the freehold at auction two months ago. The auction was conducted by an independent, professional firm of auctioneers with experience of selling real estate. One of the trustees decided to take part in the auction and made the highest bid for the property at £450,000.

The beneficiaries have just found out about this.

Which of the following best describes whether the beneficiaries can set aside the sale of the block of flats?

A The sale must be set aside because the trustees failed to get the beneficiaries' prior approval.

B The sale can be set aside by the beneficiaries, so long as they do so within a reasonable timeframe.

C The sale cannot be set aside by the beneficiaries because the trust has not suffered a loss, the purchase price being higher than the current market value for the property.

D The sale cannot be set aside by the beneficiaries because the trustees secured professional advice on the valuation of the property and its sale.

E The sale cannot be set aside by the beneficiaries because the property was sold by auction, which ensures that the trust got best value for the sale.

Answer

Option B is correct. This is an example of 'self-dealing' – one of the trustees has sold trust property to themselves. The transaction can be set aside at the request of the beneficiaries, so long as that decision is taken within a reasonable timeframe.

Option A is wrong. Whether or not the beneficiaries set aside the transaction is a matter for them – they are not obliged to do so (and might not given that the purchase price was higher than current market value).

Options C, D and E are wrong. Beneficiaries are allowed to set aside a 'self-dealing' transaction regardless of how honest the trustee's actions were or how fair the transaction is. Such matters are irrelevant. The fact that the trust has not suffered a loss, that professional advice was obtained and that the sale was conducted via auction do not provide the purchasing trustee with any kind of defence.

Question 2

Three trustees have been appointed to manage trust property: an accountant, a piano teacher and a solicitor. At their first trust meeting held six months ago, the trustees agreed in writing that the accountant and the solicitor could each charge the trust £150 for every hour spent on trust business and that the piano teacher could charge the trust £100 for every hour spent on trust business.

The trust deed contains no provisions about whether trustees can or cannot charge fees.

Which of the following best describes whether the trustees can charge the fees they have agreed?

A All the trustees can as they are all entitled to be paid reasonable remuneration for services they provide and have agreed this in writing.

B The accountant and the solicitor can so long as £150 an hour is reasonable.

C Only the solicitor can because only the solicitor is a professional trustee entitled to charge remuneration.

D Only the piano teacher can as her agreed charge-out rate is lower than the others.

E None of the trustees are entitled to be paid remuneration for services they provide.

Answer

Option B is correct. In the absence of any express provision in the trust deed, professional trustees are entitled to reasonable remuneration for their services, so long as there is more than one trustee in office and the agreement to charge fees is in writing. The accountant and the solicitor are both likely to satisfy the statutory definition of a 'professional trustee' (both acting in the course of a profession or business that consists of or includes the provision of services in connection with the management or administration of trusts).

Options A and D are wrong. The piano teacher is not a professional trustee and therefore cannot rely on the TA 2000 to authorise the payment of her fees. In the absence of beneficial consent or court authorisation, the piano teacher will not be allowed to charge fees to the trust.

Option C is wrong. Both the accountant and the solicitor are likely to satisfy the definition of a professional trustee, and therefore both should be able to rely on the statutory authorisation to charge fees as set out within the TA 2000.

Option E is wrong. Trustees can only be paid remuneration from the trust fund if this has been authorised. Such authorisation can be provided by the TA 2000 (the trust deed does not contain any express provision excluding the operation of the Act).

Question 3

Three trustees – an actuary, a business analyst and a chartered accountant – are appointed to manage a large trust fund. The trust owns various retail buildings in the local town centre. At a trust meeting last month, the trustees agreed (with the benefit of advice from an external adviser) that they were happy with the investments in the trust fund and were not minded to make any changes to the current portfolio over the next six months.

As the meeting was coming to a close, over coffee, the external adviser told the chartered accountant that an office block next door to one of the trust's retail buildings was going to come on the market in a few weeks. The external adviser told the chartered accountant that the office block was in a prime location and that if the chartered accountant got in before it went on the market, he could probably purchase it at a discounted price. The chartered accountant spoke to the trust's solicitor, who advised that there was no reason why he could not buy the office block himself. After some quick negotiations with the owners, he did so. The other trustees have just found out and are unhappy with the course of action taken by their fellow trustee. They claim that they would have been interested in buying the office block had they known about it.

Did the chartered accountant breach a fiduciary duty?

A   Yes, because he has allowed his own personal interests to conflict with those of the trust.

B   Yes, because he has engaged in self-dealing.

C   No, because his actions could not reasonably be regarded as likely to give rise to a conflict of interest.

D   No, because the trust's solicitor authorised him to purchase the office block.

E   No, because the trustees had just agreed not to purchase any further investments for the time being.

Answer

Option A is correct. As a trustee, the chartered accountant must ensure that his own interests do not conflict with the interests of the trust. He became aware of the opportunity to purchase the office block at the end of a trust meeting – that information properly belonged to the trust. He has therefore used trust property to gain a personal advantage. He should have shared that opportunity with his fellow trustees to see whether they wanted to take advantage of the opportunity on behalf of the trust.

Option B is wrong. This is not a case of self-dealing. Self-dealing occurs when a trustee sells property to or purchases property from the trust. Neither has happened here.

Options C and E are wrong. These options suggest that there has been no breach of fiduciary duty given that the facts imply that the trust was unlikely at the time to have taken advantage of this opportunity had the other trustees known about it, and therefore any potential conflict is more hypothetical than real. However, a trustee can still breach a fiduciary duty by taking advantage of an opportunity that properly belonged to the trust, even when the facts suggest that the trust would not have taken advantage of that opportunity or was not interested in it. In this situation, the chartered accountant should have tried to persuade the other trustees that the opportunity was a valuable one for the trust, failing which, if he wanted to purchase the property himself, he should have secured authorisation from the beneficiaries or the court.

Option D is wrong. The approval from the solicitor to purchase the office block is not a valid form of authorisation allowing the chartered accountant to do so. In the absence of anything set out in the trust deed, the only people who could provide the required authorisation would be the beneficiaries or the court.

PART 3
BREACH OF TRUSTS AND EQUITABLE REMEDIES

12 Remedies Against Trustees: Personal Claims

12.1	Introduction	158
12.2	Personal claims	158
12.3	Breach of trust	159
12.4	Which trustees can be the subject-matter of a personal claim?	160
12.5	Causation	160
12.6	The value of the personal claim	161
12.7	Defences	162
12.8	Indemnity and contribution	163
12.9	Summary flowchart	165

SQE1 syllabus

This chapter will enable you to achieve the SQE1 assessment specification in relation to functioning legal knowledge concerned with the following core principles:

- Breach of trust
- Measure of liability
- Protection of trustees
- Limitation period

Note that for SQE1, candidates are not usually required to recall specific case names or cite statutory or regulatory authorities. Cases are provided for illustrative purposes only.

Learning outcomes

By the end of this chapter you will be able to apply relevant core legal principles and rules appropriately and effectively, at the level of a competent newly qualified solicitor in practice, to realistic client-based and ethical problems and situations in the following areas:

- establishing what is a personal claim and when you would advise such a claim to be brought;
- identifying what kinds of actions and omissions constitute a breach of trust;
- recognising against which trustees a personal claim can be brought and for how much;
- establishing what kinds of defences are available; and
- advising on how trustees can apportion liability between themselves in the case of a successful personal claim for breach of trust.

12.1 Introduction

In **Part 2** of this manual, we considered the duties with which trustees must comply when running the trust. In **Part 3**, we will consider the types of claims that can be brought on behalf of beneficiaries should the trustees breach those duties.

Claims brought by beneficiaries can be divided into two main categories:

- Personal claims. These are claims for monetary compensation brought against the wrongdoing trustee(s). The claim is 'personal' because the wrongdoing trustee(s) must satisfy the claim from their own property or funds. We will consider these types of claims in this chapter.
- Proprietary claims. In these claims, the beneficiary is seeking the return of property owned by the trust (or, more usually, property in the hands of the trustee that represents trust property). The claim is 'proprietary' because the beneficiary is going after specific property. In order to identify property that now represents trust property, the beneficiary utilises so-called 'tracing rules', which trace trust property into the hands of the trustee. We will consider these types of claims in **Chapter 13**.

This chapter looks at:

- the nature of a personal claim and when a beneficiary would bring such a claim against wrongdoing trustee(s);
- when a beneficiary can bring such a claim (ie what constitutes a breach of trust);
- against which trustees the beneficiary can bring a claim;
- the degree of liability of the wrongdoing trustee;
- the defences that might be available for the trustee(s); and
- the ability of one trustee to apportion liability amongst their co-trustees by way of indemnity or contribution.

12.2 Personal claims

If a trustee's wrongdoing causes the trust to suffer a loss, the beneficiaries can seek compensation for the trust. This claim is against the trustee personally (sometimes referred to as a claim 'in personam'). The trustee will be required to satisfy the claim from their own property or funds. A personal claim is only as good as the financial solvency of the trustee. Before bringing such a claim, the beneficiary should ideally assess the financial standing of the trustee. If the trustee has pockets deep enough to pay any compensation that might be awarded, then a personal claim should be considered.

A personal claim may not be appropriate or advantageous in the following circumstances:

(a) If the trustee is insolvent (ie cannot pay their own debts when they fall due), a personal claim will be of little use. The beneficiary will rank as an unsecured creditor in any bankruptcy, whose claims generally come 'at the back of the line' when there is very little money left. The beneficiary will recover little, if anything, on behalf of the trust.

(b) The trustee may have used trust property to buy themselves something that the beneficiary considers attractive. For instance, the trustee may have stolen £100,000 from the trust fund and used this money to purchase shares that have since doubled in value. In this case, the beneficiary should assert a proprietary claim to recover the shares. If successful, all of those shares will belong to the trust and the trust will be able to take advantage of their increase in value. By contrast, if the trustee has spent trust money on something other than tangible property (eg paying off their credit card bills or going on a luxury cruise), then a proprietary claim will not be possible.

(c) The trustee's wrongdoing may have happened some time ago. As we shall see, personal claims are sometimes statute-barred six years after the date of breach. After that time period, the beneficiary can no longer bring a personal claim. However, proprietary claims are not subject to any statutory limitation period and might therefore remain available if the wrongdoing happened more than six years ago.

⭐ Examples

(a) *Breesha has been appointed a trustee over a large family trust. Three years ago, she decided to sell £250,000 worth of trust investments to purchase shares in Haemorrhaging plc. She took this decision without taking proper financial advice and, since then, has not reviewed how these shares were doing. Fynn, the beneficiary, has just found out that the shares are now worthless.*

If Fynn wants to recover the lost value of the trust fund from Breesha, he must bring a personal claim against her. He will have to assert that her failure to take proper financial advice and review the investments from time-to-time constituted wrongdoing (ie a failure to comply with the statutory investment duties set out in the TA 2000) and that such failure caused the trust to suffer a loss. He cannot bring a proprietary claim because Breesha has not taken any property 'out of the trust'. Fynn is not seeking the return of property owned by the trust – the worthless shares continue to be owned by the trust.

(b) *Asher is a trustee. Two years ago, he used £25,000 of trust money to buy a painting by Igor Prokop. Asher has just been declared bankrupt. Iona, one of the beneficiaries, has been told that Igor Prokop's work is currently very much in demand and the painting may have substantially increased in value.*

Whilst Asher's actions will probably constitute wrongdoing, there is little practical point in Iona bringing a personal claim against him. He is bankrupt and therefore will unlikely have the personal funds available to satisfy such a claim.

Instead, Iona should consider bringing a proprietary action to recover the painting. If she can establish that the painting belongs to the trust, then the painting will not be distributed as part of Asher's bankruptcy. The painting is not owned beneficially by Asher, and therefore it is not available to his creditors. If the painting does belong to the trust, then the trust will also get the benefit of any increase in value in the painting.

(c) *Let us take the same facts as the above example, but this time let us assume that Asher is still solvent and has not been declared bankrupt.*

In this case, Iona should still consider bringing a proprietary action to recover the painting. However, if it turns out that the advice she received about the value of the painting was wrong and the painting is now only worth £20,000, she can still bring a personal claim against Asher to recover the balance of the loss that the trust suffered (ie the remaining £5,000 plus interest).

12.3 Breach of trust

In order to bring a personal claim against a trustee, the beneficiary must identify a breach of duty (often referred to as a 'breach of trust'). The trustee must have done something wrong in the running of a trust, as covered in **Chapters 8** to **10** inclusive.

⭐ Examples

Susan and Yvonne have been appointed trustees. Susan proposes that the trustees should sign blank cheques advising that this will help speed up trust business in the future. Yvonne agrees and countersigns the cheques. Susan uses the cheques to steal £50,000 from the trust and then disappears.

Susan has clearly breached the trust by stealing trust money. However, there may be little point in bringing a claim against her if we cannot find her.

*The beneficiaries may instead decide to bring a claim against Yvonne. A trustee must act as an ordinary prudent business-person would act and must supervise the activities of their co-trustees (see **Chapter 9**). By agreeing to sign blank cheques, Yvonne has breached these duties of care and therefore will also be liable for breach of trust.*

As we shall see in **section 12.5**, when it comes to investments, identifying a breach of trust can be difficult.

12.4 Which trustees can be the subject-matter of a personal claim?

In order to bring a personal claim against a trustee, that trustee must themselves be in breach of trust. Trustees are not vicariously, or automatically, liable for the defaults of their co-trustees. However, if a trustee has breached trust (and that breach has caused loss to the trust), that trustee can be named as a defendant to a personal claim.

If more than one trustee has breached trust, their liability is joint and several. This means that the beneficiaries can choose either to bring a claim against all of them, or bring a claim against an individual trustee. In either case, the claim will be for the full loss suffered. Beneficiaries therefore may decide to bring a personal claim for the full loss against the wealthiest trustee or against a professional trustee who is more likely to be backed by insurance.

⭐ Example

Rose and Matthew have been appointed trustees of a trust that expressly prohibited investing in any companies registered outside the UK. Rose is a partner in the banking department of a top-25 law firm. Shortly after their appointment, she told Matthew (a home-maker with no independent source of income) that he should leave the running of the trust to her. Matthew was more than happy to do so. Rose purchased shares in various South American companies that have since gone insolvent. The shares are now worthless.

Rose has breached trust by failing to follow the instructions set out in the declaration of trust, ie purchasing investments that were expressly prohibited in the trust deed.

Matthew has also breached trust by failing to act personally in the running of the trust and by failing to supervise and correct Rose's actions.

Rose and Matthew are jointly and severally liable for the loss that the trust has suffered. The beneficiaries could sue both of them or one of them for the full loss. In this case, the beneficiaries may decide to bring the claim against Rose given that she is likely to have significantly more personal wealth than Matthew.

12.5 Causation

In order to successfully claim compensation, the beneficiaries must establish causation – they must establish that the trustees' breach of trust caused the loss suffered. In order to do so, the beneficiaries must satisfy the 'but for' test – they must show that the loss would not have occurred *but for* the breach of trust. If the loss would have happened anyway, the personal claim will fail.

⭐ Example

Let us go back to the example of Susan and Yvonne considered earlier. Susan proposed that the trustees should sign blank cheques advising that this would help speed up trust business in the future. Yvonne agreed and countersigned the cheques. Susan used the cheques to steal £50,000 from the trust and then disappeared.

Yvonne breached trust by failing to act personally. She had failed to supervise and take actions to correct Susan's conduct. Yvonne's failure enabled the loss to happen. Susan would presumably not have been able to steal trust money in the way she did but for Yvonne's breach of trust.

Whilst Susan is arguably more morally culpable for the loss than Yvonne, Yvonne is jointly and severally liable for that loss, because both Yvonne and Susan have breached trust. The beneficiaries could therefore bring a personal claim against Yvonne for the full loss suffered.

It can sometimes be difficult to bring a personal claim against trustees in relation to investment decisions they have taken.

In Nestle v National Westminster Bank plc [1993] 1 WLR 1260, Edith Nestle, the heiress to the Nestle family fortune, complained that the trustees had failed to make proper investments – had they done so, she would have received an inheritance four times greater than was the case. The Court agreed that the trustees had failed to acquaint themselves with their investment powers, had not taken legal advice on those powers, had not undertaken any regular reviews of trust investments and that the trustees had fallen 'woefully short of maintaining the real value of the fund, let alone matching the average increase in price of ordinary shares'. The Court of Appeal went so far to observe that '[n]o testator, in the light of this example, would choose this bank for the effective management of his investment'. Nevertheless, Edith's claim failed.

Edith had to show that the trustees had made decisions that they should not have made or failed to make decisions that they should have made (was there a breach of trust?) and that loss resulted therefrom (did that breach cause loss?). However, she failed to demonstrate that no other reasonable trustee would have invested in the same way. The trust had a complicated series of successive interests with different beneficiaries having different income and capital requirements, all of which had to be balanced. Other trustees faced with this complexity might have positively chosen similar investments (albeit for different reasons). The trustees' investment inactivity therefore did not amount to a breach of trust (another reasonable trustee may have invested in the same way) and their failure to take legal advice and review the investments did not cause any loss (there was no evidence that the trust fund would have been worth more under the management of a reasonable trustee who had undertaken regular reviews and taken advice). When it comes to investment decisions, a claim against the trustees may not succeed unless the beneficiaries can establish that the decision was one that no reasonable trustee could have made.

12.6 The value of the personal claim

So long as the beneficiaries can satisfy the above elements of a personal claim (and subject to any defences available to the trustees), they can recover compensation equal to the loss to the trust, plus interest from the date of breach. The rate of interest is at the discretion of the court, but is usually the rate allowed on the court's short-term investment account.

12.7 Defences

The following defences might be available to a trustee who is facing a personal claim for breach of trust:

(a) an exemption clause in the trust deed;

(b) knowledge and consent of the beneficiaries;

(c) s 61 of the TA 1925; or

(d) limitation and laches.

12.7.1 Exemption clauses

The settlor can include an express clause in the trust deed exempting trustees from liability for breach of trust. Such a clause can relieve trustees from liability for negligent or innocent breaches, but is void insofar as it tries to exclude liability for fraudulent breaches.

Professional trustees who cause a settlor to include a clause in a trust deed that has the effect of excluding or limiting liability must, before the creation of the trust, take such steps as are reasonable to ensure that the settlor is aware of the meaning and effect of the clause. Any ambiguity in the clause will be interpreted strictly against that professional.

12.7.2 Knowledge and consent of the beneficiaries

If the beneficiaries have all consented to a course of action that constitutes a breach of trust (whether before the action occurred or afterwards), they cannot subsequently bring a claim against the trustees. The consent must have been fully informed and freely given. The consenting beneficiaries must be adults and of full capacity – a minor cannot give valid consent.

If only one beneficiary consents to a breach of trust, that beneficiary can no longer bring any personal claim against the trustees, but the other non-consenting beneficiaries can.

12.7.3 Section 61 of the Trustee Act 1925

The court has a discretion to relieve trustees from liability, wholly or in part, if they acted honestly and reasonably, and ought fairly to be excused.

> *Example*
>
> *A trust has been created for such of my children who reach the age of 25 years. Sharon is my only child and is currently aged 21 years. She complains that Katie, the trustee, has not paid her any income from the trust as requested. Katie is a primary school teacher with no prior experience of running a trust. Katie claims that she thought about giving money to Sharon, but honestly thought that Sharon had no entitlement to any trust money until she reached the age of 25 years.*
>
> *Katie has committed a breach of trust. An adult contingent beneficiary is entitled to income as and when it arises due to the operation of s 31 of the TA 1925 (see **Chapter 8**).*
>
> *However, the court may excuse Katie from liability under s 61 of the TA 1925. Her refusal to pay income to Sharon appears to be an honest mistake and the court may sympathise that a lay trustee like Katie may not be aware of the intricate workings of the TA 1925. The court might be inclined to accept that Katie's refusal to pay Sharon any income was a reasonable mistake.*
>
> *By contrast, if Katie was a solicitor, it is extremely unlikely that Katie would secure much sympathy from the court. Even if the solicitor's area of practice did not involve the administration of trusts, the court might expect a reasonable solicitor to appreciate the need to access suitable legal advice in order to properly manage the trust.*

As a matter of public policy, the courts are reluctant to excuse passive trustees from the consequences of their inactivity, for fear that this might encourage future trustees to be passive in the management of trust business.

⭐ Example

Rima and Sarah are trustees. Sarah was a private client solicitor; Rima was a travel agent. Rima confessed to having no knowledge of investments and so left that to Sarah. Sarah invested the entire trust fund in Futile Limited. The company went insolvent four months later.

Sarah has possibly breached investment duties set out in the TA 2000 (such as failing to take proper investment advice, or by failing to take into account the standard investment criteria when investing). Rima has breached trust by leaving the management of the trust in Sarah's hands without enquiry and failing to watch over and correct her conduct. Sarah and Rima are jointly and severally liable for the whole loss.

If the beneficiaries bring a personal claim against Rima, it is unlikely that the court will exercise its discretion to relieve her from liability under s 61 of the TA 1925. Whether or not Rima has acted reasonably in leaving trust investments to Sarah, it is unlikely that the court would consider it fair to excuse her from liability. (Rima may, however, be able to claim an indemnity or contribution against Sarah for any compensation she has to pay the beneficiaries – see below.)

12.7.4 Limitation and laches

A personal claim for breach of trust is subject to a six-year limitation period; s 21 of the Limitation Act 1980. This period usually starts to run from the date of breach. However, as against a minor, time only starts to run when they reach the age of 18 years; and as against remainder beneficiaries, time only starts to run when their interest falls into possession (ie when the life tenant dies).

The six-year period does not run against trustees who have committed a fraudulent breach of trust.

Where there is no statutory limitation period, the court might still have regard to the equitable doctrine of laches. Laches will prevent a claimant from asserting a personal claim where:

(a) the claimant knows the facts that gave rise to the breach of trust;

(b) the claimant delays in taking action; and

(c) this delay either is deemed to constitute acquiescence in or waiver of the breach by the claimant, or causes detriment or prejudice to the trustee. Delay by itself is not usually a sufficient form of detriment; the court will want to see some evidence that prejudice has been caused. For instance, a defence of laches succeeded where the claimant took approximately 15 years to start proceedings, even though they knew of the matters complained of, and the defendant was able to argue that it would be difficult to prove their defence given the death of witnesses and destruction of documents in the intervening period (*Schulman v Hewson* [2002] EWHC 855 (Ch)).

12.8 Indemnity and contribution

We have identified that the liability between trustees in breach of trust is joint and several. The beneficiaries can choose to bring their claim against all of the wrongdoing trustees or merely one of them, but in each case they are entitled to recover the full loss that the trust has suffered. If one trustee is sued for the entire loss, can they share the burden of paying monetary compensation with the other trustees in breach?

There are two possibilities:

(a) the defending trustee may be able to claim the full amount of compensation from a co-trustee under an equitable indemnity; or

(b) the defending trustee may be able to claim a contribution towards the compensation from a co-trustee under the Civil Liability (Contribution) Act 1978.

12.8.1 Equitable indemnity

A trustee who is sued for breach of trust can recover a full indemnity from a co-trustee who:

(a) acted fraudulently when the others acted in good faith; or

(b) is a solicitor who exercised such a controlling influence that the other trustees blindly followed the solicitor's advice; or

(c) has benefited personally from the breach; or

(d) is also a beneficiary and benefited from the breach (in which case, the indemnity is limited to the value of their equitable interest, which will be impounded to meet the claim).

⭐ Example

A trust is created in 2008 for Aled and Fiona in equal shares. John, a solicitor, and Sadie, a waitress, are appointed trustees. The trust fund was valued at £500,000.

A year ago, the trustees advanced the sum of £200,000 to Aled. Fiona has only just discovered this and brings a personal claim against the trustees.

The trustees have breached trust in that, this being a trust created before October 2014, any advancement of capital was limited to half the value of each beneficiary's presumptive share (in this case, up to the value of £125,000). The liability of the trustees is joint and several.

Sadie argues that she wanted to be involved in the management of the trust but John told her that he would deal with things given that he knew best as a solicitor. She had only agreed to this advancement because John told her that it was the right thing to do and she should just sign the necessary paperwork and let him sort it out. In these circumstances, it may be that Sadie is able to claim an equitable indemnity against John. If so, John will ultimately bear the financial consequences of any monetary compensation awarded.

(It is also possible on these facts that Sadie might be entitled to a defence under s 61 of the TA 1925. She has not voluntarily chosen to be passive in the running of the trust, but has instead followed the advice given to her by a legally qualified co-trustee. In that situation, it is possible that she has acted honestly and reasonably, and ought fairly to be excused from liability.)

12.8.2 Contribution

Pursuant to s 1 of the Civil Liability (Contribution) Act 1978, the court can also order a co-trustee to make a contribution that is just and equitable having regard to the extent of that co-trustee's responsibility for the loss. That contribution can be anything up to 100% of the compensation ordered. In deciding how to exercise its discretion, the court will primarily reflect on the blameworthiness of the co-trustees.

12.9 Summary flowchart

Figure 12.1 Personal claims summary flowchart (assuming two trustees)

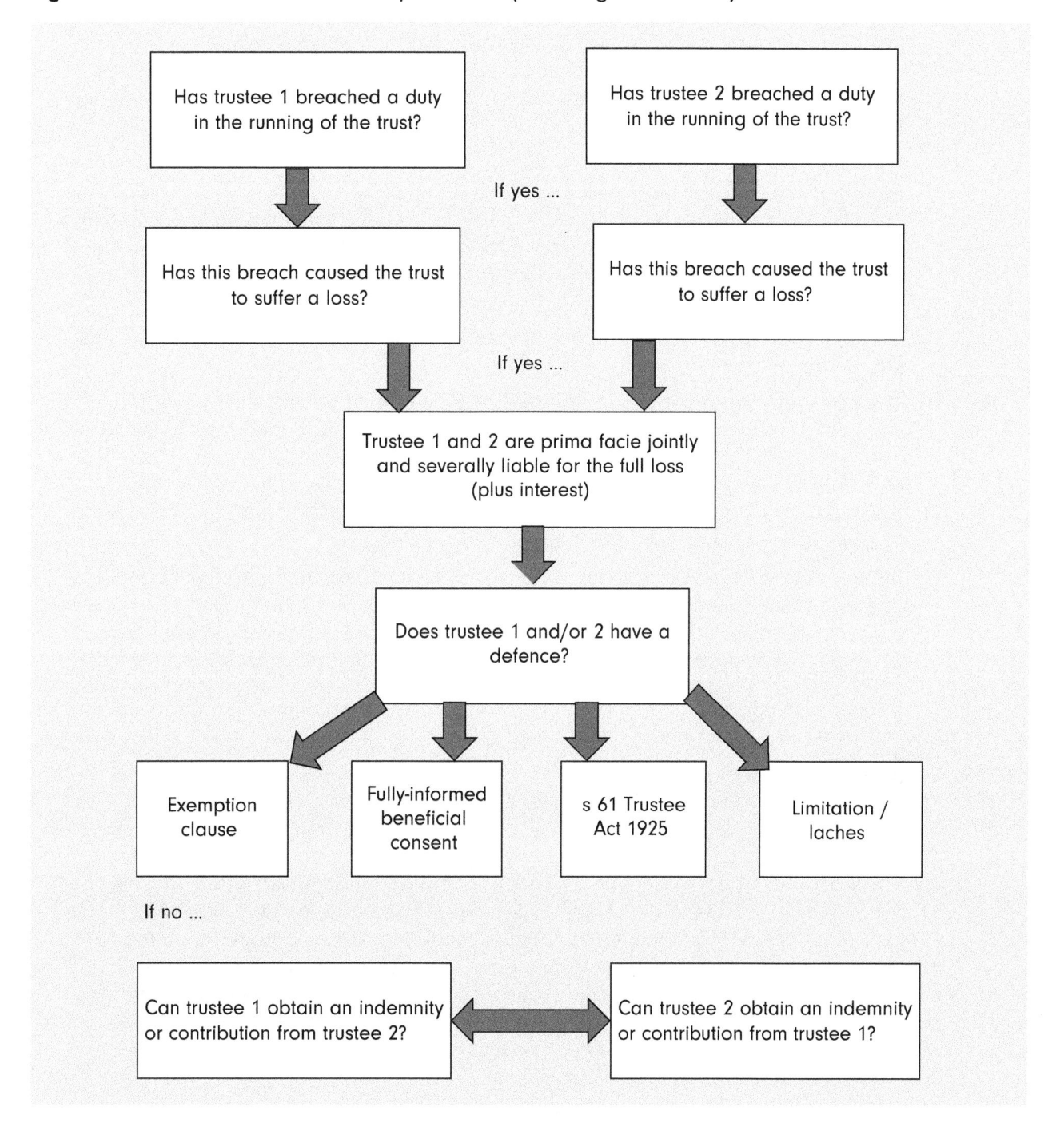

```
┌─────────────────────────────┐         ┌─────────────────────────────┐
│ Has trustee 1 breached a    │         │ Has trustee 2 breached a    │
│ duty in the running of the  │         │ duty in the running of the  │
│ trust?                      │         │ trust?                      │
└──────────────┬──────────────┘         └──────────────┬──────────────┘
               │           If yes ...                   │
               ▼                                        ▼
┌─────────────────────────────┐         ┌─────────────────────────────┐
│ Has this breach caused the  │         │ Has this breach caused the  │
│ trust to suffer a loss?     │         │ trust to suffer a loss?     │
└──────────────┬──────────────┘         └──────────────┬──────────────┘
               │           If yes ...                   │
               └──────────────────┬─────────────────────┘
                                  ▼
               ┌──────────────────────────────────────┐
               │ Trustee 1 and 2 are prima facie      │
               │ jointly and severally liable for the │
               │ full loss (plus interest)            │
               └──────────────────┬───────────────────┘
                                  ▼
               ┌──────────────────────────────────────┐
               │ Does trustee 1 and/or 2 have a       │
               │ defence?                             │
               └──┬──────────┬──────────┬──────────┬──┘
                  ▼          ▼          ▼          ▼
            ┌─────────┐ ┌─────────┐ ┌─────────┐ ┌─────────┐
            │Exemption│ │Fully-   │ │s 61     │ │Limitation│
            │clause   │ │informed │ │Trustee  │ │/ laches │
            │         │ │benefici-│ │Act 1925 │ │         │
            │         │ │al       │ │         │ │         │
            │         │ │consent  │ │         │ │         │
            └─────────┘ └─────────┘ └─────────┘ └─────────┘

If no ...

┌─────────────────────────────┐         ┌─────────────────────────────┐
│ Can trustee 1 obtain an     │◄───────►│ Can trustee 2 obtain an     │
│ indemnity or contribution   │         │ indemnity or contribution   │
│ from trustee 2?             │         │ from trustee 1?             │
└─────────────────────────────┘         └─────────────────────────────┘
```

Summary

In this chapter you have considered personal claims that beneficiaries can bring against trustees:

- *What is a personal claim.* Personal claims are claims for monetary compensation. The claim is brought against the wrongdoing trustee(s) and the compensation is payable out of their own personal funds. The viability of such a claim therefore depends on the trustees' solvency.

- *Which trustees are liable.* In order to bring a personal claim against a trustee, they must have breached trust (ie breached a duty in the running of the trust) and that breach must have caused the trust to suffer a loss. Trustees are not vicariously liable for the defaults of their co-trustees, but if a trustee has breached trust in a way that causes loss to the trust, that trustee will become jointly and severally liable for the full amount of loss that the trust has sustained.

- *For how much.* The trustees in breach of trust will be liable for the full loss that the trust has sustained, plus interest.

- *What defences are available.* The trustees may be able to defend themselves from a personal claim where (a) there is an express clause in the trust deed that exempts them from liability; (b) the beneficiaries gave fully informed consent to the trustees' course of action; (c) the trustees have acted honestly and reasonably and ought fairly to be excused; or (d) the personal claim is brought out of time either under the Limitation Act 1980 or by reference to the equitable doctrine of laches.

- *Indemnities and contributions.* The trustees in breach of trust can apportion liability between themselves either by claiming an indemnity from a co-trustee (in which case, the co-trustee becomes 100% liable for the loss suffered) or a contribution (where the court can order the co-trustee to pay an amount referable to their responsibility for the loss).

Sample questions

Question 1

A solicitor and a man are trustees of a trust fund worth £2.5 million. Two years ago, the solicitor proposed that the trust invest all its funds in the shares of a retail, high-street company. The man, who is a retired independent financial adviser, agreed. The trustees were so confident that the investment was a good one that they never reviewed the profitability of the company during the subsequent two years, notwithstanding numerous reports that suggested the company was losing out to online trade. The shares are now worthless. The beneficiaries have written to each trustee separately to advise that they intend to bring a claim to secure compensation.

Which of the following best describes who might be liable under any future claim brought by the beneficiaries?

A   The beneficiaries can only bring a claim against the solicitor because she was the person who suggested the investments.

B   The beneficiaries can only bring a claim against the retired financial adviser given that the subject-matter of the claim is a breach of investment duties.

C   The beneficiaries must bring a claim against both trustees and can secure 50% of the loss from each trustee.

D   The beneficiaries can bring a claim against the retired financial adviser for the full loss, but he will be entitled to an equitable indemnity against the solicitor.

E   The beneficiaries can bring a claim against the retired financial adviser for the full loss, but he may be entitled to a contribution from the solicitor.

Answer

Option E is correct. Both the retired financial adviser and the solicitor may be in breach of trust by failing to comply with those duties pertaining to investments set out in the TA 2000. Both trustees appear to have failed to consider the standard investment criteria (especially the need for diversification) before deciding to invest £2.5 million in a single company, and have failed to review that investment from time-to-time (see **Chapter 10**). As both trustees have breached trust, their liability for any losses caused is joint and several, enabling the beneficiaries to bring a claim against either or both trustees for the full loss.

If the beneficiaries bring a claim against only the retired financial adviser, he may be able to secure a just and equitable contribution from the solicitor under the Civil Liability (Contribution) Act 1978, the court having regard to the extent of the solicitor's responsibility for the loss.

Options A and B are wrong. As both trustees have breached trust, their liability is joint and several. The beneficiaries are not forced to bring their claim against only one of the trustees.

Option C is wrong. As both trustees have breached trust, their liability is joint and several. The beneficiaries can bring their claim against any one of the trustees for the full loss sustained.

Option D is wrong. It is very unlikely that the retired financial adviser will be able to secure an equitable indemnity from (ie pass on 100% of the loss to) the solicitor. The facts do not suggest that the solicitor exercised such an influence that the retired financial adviser blindly followed her investment proposals.

Question 2

A husband and wife are trustees of a trust fund created in 2018 for their nephew and niece should they reach the age of 25 years. The nephew is aged 23 years and the niece is aged 20 years. The trust fund is valued at £800,000. Six months ago, the husband and wife separated. The husband told the wife that whatever decisions she took in running the trust would be 'OK with me'.

The nephew has recently asked the trustees to advance him the sum of £500,000 to help start a business. The wife agreed and she arranged for the sum to be transferred to the nephew.

The niece is unhappy about this and has advised that she intends to bring a claim.

Which of the following best describes against whom the niece can bring a claim?

A   The niece can bring a claim against the husband; he has no defence; he may be entitled to a contribution from the wife.

B   The niece can bring a claim against the husband; he has no defence; he may be entitled to an equitable indemnity from the wife.

C   The niece can bring a claim against the husband; however, he will be able to successfully persuade the court that it should excuse him from liability.

D The niece can only bring a claim against the wife, as only the wife has breached trust.

E The niece cannot bring any claim, as there has been no breach of trust.

Answer

Option A is correct. Both the husband and the wife may be in breach of trust. The wife has advanced more capital than the nephew is entitled to (his entitlement is limited to the value of his presumptive share, being £400,000 in this case – see **Chapter 8**). The husband has remained passive in that breach and has failed to watch over the wife's running of the trust (see **Chapter 9**). As both trustees are in breach of trust, they are both potentially liable to a claim on a joint and several basis. The niece can bring a claim against the husband.

If the beneficiaries bring a claim against the husband, he may be able secure a just and equitable contribution from the wife under the Civil Liability (Contribution) Act 1978, the court having regard to the extent of the wife's responsibility for the loss.

Option B is wrong. The facts do not suggest that the husband will be able to secure an equitable indemnity against the wife.

Option C is likely to be wrong. The courts might excuse a trustee from liability under s 61 of the TA 1925 if that trustee has acted honestly and reasonably and ought fairly to be excused. As a matter of public policy, the courts are reluctant to excuse passive trustees from the consequences of their inactivity. The husband therefore is unlikely to secure the benefit of this defence.

Option D is wrong. The husband's passivity in the running of a trust is a breach of trust. He is therefore jointly and severally liable for the loss that the niece has suffered.

Option E is wrong. The £500,000 advancement to the nephew is a breach of trust because the trustees have advanced more than they should have under s 32 of the TA 1925.

Question 3

Ten years ago, a banker and an accountant were appointed as trustees of a trust fund for a teacher for life, remainder to the teacher's son. The teacher died last year, leaving everything she owned to her daughter. The accountant has recently been made personally bankrupt.

Upon their appointment, the trustees appointed a financial adviser in writing to invest the trust fund, having interviewed a number of potential candidates. The adviser made a series of investments and has subsequently met with the trustees at least once every six months to explain that in his view there was no need to change those investments.

The son recently requested a list of the trust's investments and has complained to the trustees that the trust fund has not been properly invested.

Which of the following best describes why a personal claim brought by the son against the accountant would fail?

A The accountant is bankrupt.

B Any breach of trust occurred while the mother was alive, such that her daughter is the only person entitled to bring a claim.

C The court will excuse the accountant from any liability.

D The claim is now time-barred.

E The accountant has not breached trust.

Answer

Option E is correct. Trustees are not vicariously liable for the investment choices made by an agent (see **Chapter 10**). Trustees are only liable if they have breached a personal duty when delegating such decisions (eg by failing to properly select or appoint an investment agent or by failing to review their performance). The banker and accountant do not appear to be in breach of such duties, and therefore no claim can be brought against the accountant.

Option A is wrong. If the son were able to bring a claim, the fact that the accountant is bankrupt has no bearing on the merits of that claim (although the son would need permission from the court to start proceedings). However, the fact that the accountant is bankrupt should make the son think again before bringing any claim. The son will, at best, be an unsecured creditor in the accountant's bankruptcy and therefore is unlikely to get much (if any) compensation even if the claim were to be successful.

Option B is wrong. Had the accountant done something wrong in appointing the financial adviser that caused a loss to the trust, the person who could bring proceedings would be the son (as a beneficiary under the trust) and not the daughter (who has no interest under the trust).

Option C is wrong. As the accountant has done nothing wrong, there is no liability to excuse him from.

Option D is wrong. The son's ability to bring a claim in these circumstances would not be time-barred because the six-year limitation period for bringing a claim for breach of trust would not start to run against him until his interests came into possession, which only happened last year when the teacher (the life tenant) died.

13 Remedies Against Trustees: Proprietary Claims

13.1	Introduction	172
13.2	Proprietary claims	172
13.3	Trustee holds original trust property	173
13.4	Trustee holds substitute property	173
13.5	Trustee mixes trust property with other property	174
13.6	Proprietary claims against other fiduciaries	185

SQE1 syllabus

This chapter will enable you to achieve the SQE1 assessment specification in relation to functioning legal knowledge concerned with the following core principles:

- The nature of equitable proprietary remedies
- The availability of tracing in equity

Note that for SQE1, candidates are not usually required to recall specific case names or cite statutory or regulatory authorities. Cases are provided for illustrative purposes only.

Learning outcomes

By the end of this chapter you will be able to apply relevant core legal principles and rules appropriately and effectively, at the level of a competent newly qualified solicitor in practice, to realistic client-based and ethical problems and situations in the following areas:

- establishing what is a proprietary claim and when you would advise such a claim to be brought;
- identifying what happens when the form of trust property changes and the tracing rules that enable beneficiaries to identify trust property;
- advising on the tracing rules that apply when a trustee mixes trust property with their own property; and
- advising on the tracing rules that apply when a trustee mixes two trust funds.

13.1 Introduction

In **Chapter 12**, we identified that beneficiaries can bring two different types of claims against wrongdoing trustees:

- Personal claims. These are claims for monetary compensation brought against the wrongdoing trustee(s). The claim is 'personal' because the wrongdoing trustee(s) must satisfy the claim from their own property or funds. We considered these types of claims in **Chapter 12**.
- Proprietary claims. In these claims, the beneficiary is seeking the return of property owned by the trust (or, more usually, property in the hands of the trustee that represents trust property). The claim is 'proprietary' because the beneficiary is going after specific property. In order to identify property that now represents trust property, the beneficiary utilises so-called 'tracing rules', which trace trust property into the hands of the trustee. We will consider these types of claims in this chapter.

This chapter looks at:

- the nature of a proprietary claim and when beneficiaries would bring such a claim against wrongdoing trustee(s);
- what happens if trust property changes form;
- what happens if a trustee mixes trust property with their own property; and
- what happens if a trustee mixes two (or more) trust funds.

13.2 Proprietary claims

Trust property ultimately belongs to the beneficiaries. If a trustee tries to assert absolute ownership over trust property (in breach of trust), the beneficiaries are entitled to call for that property back. They do so by asserting a proprietary claim (sometimes referred to as a claim 'in rem'), which enables them to recover the asset and bring the asset back within the trust's control.

If a trustee uses trust money to purchase something in their own name, the beneficiaries can assert a proprietary claim against that new asset so long as they can identify that the new asset represents trust property. This is easy to establish when a trustee withdraws cash from the trust's bank account and hands that straight over to the seller of the new asset. However, what if the trustee first transfers trust money into their own bank account, which already has some of the trustee's own money in it, before making a withdrawal to buy the asset? Does the new asset represent property belonging to the trust or the trustee? Whose money was used to buy it? In order to work this out, equity deploys various 'tracing rules' to trace the beneficiaries' equitable interests into new forms of property. Over the years, wrongdoing trustees have engaged in various different transactions with trust property, and equity has correspondingly developed a number of tracing rules to work out what the end result is. We will consider the most common rules in this chapter.

Whilst the trustee might be the defendant to a proprietary claim, the subject-matter of the claim is really the property that the beneficiary is seeking to recover. As a result, a proprietary claim is only as good as the property that the beneficiaries can trace into. Before bringing such a claim, the beneficiary should assess what kind of property the trustee has and how much it is worth. If the trustee has spent trust property in such a way that there is no longer any physical asset to trace into, such as the payment of credit card bills or using the money to go on holiday, there is no value in bringing a proprietary claim. In these scenarios, we say that the trust property has been 'dissipated'.

A proprietary claim may be appropriate or advantageous in the following circumstances:

(a) As we saw in **Chapter 12**, if the trustee is insolvent (ie cannot pay their own debts when they fall due), a personal claim will be of little use. The beneficiary will rank as an unsecured creditor in any bankruptcy, whose claims generally come 'at the back of the line'. The beneficiary will recover little, if anything, on behalf of the trust.

However, if the trustee still holds trust property (or something that represents trust property), then that property belongs to the beneficiary. They can recover that property in priority to anyone trying to recover money from the bankrupt trustee. The property does not belong to the trustee and does not form part of their bankruptcy estate – it cannot be used to satisfy any claims that the trustee's creditors might have.

(b) The trustee may have used trust property to buy themselves something that the beneficiary considers attractive. For instance, the trustee may have stolen £100,000 from the trust fund and used this money to purchase shares that have since doubled in value. In this case, the beneficiary should assert a proprietary claim to recover the shares. If successful, all of those shares will belong to the trust and the beneficiary will be able to take advantage of their increase in value.

(c) The trustee's wrongdoing may have happened some time ago. As we saw in **Chapter 12**, personal claims are sometimes statute-barred six years after the date of breach. However, proprietary claims are not subject to any statutory limitation period (although they are still governed by the equitable doctrine of laches) and might therefore remain available if the wrongdoing happened more than six years ago.

A proprietary claim does not work, however, where there is no property to recover.

13.3 Trustee holds original trust property

If a trustee still holds trust property in its original form, a proprietary claim will enable the beneficiaries to recover the property. No tracing is required here because the property is still identifiable in its original form.

⭐ Example

Nicholas and Miles are trustees of a trust that includes a farm in the Welsh Marches. The farm is conveyed into the sole name of Miles.

The beneficiaries can use a proprietary claim to order Miles to put the property back on trust (ie reconvey the farm into the joint names of Nicholas and Miles as trustees).

13.4 Trustee holds substitute property

If a trustee has sold trust property and purchased another asset with the sale proceeds, a proprietary claim will enable the beneficiaries to recover the new asset. This is often referred to as 'clean substitution' – there has simply been a swap between the original trust property and the new asset. The new asset is treated as if it belongs to the trust.

In this situation, the beneficiaries can choose either:

(a) to take the substitute property. The beneficiaries should take this option where the substitute property has increased in value; or

(b) to sue the trustee for compensation for the loss to the trust and take a charge (or 'equitable lien') over the property for the amount that the trust has lost. The beneficiaries should take this option where the substitute property has decreased in value.

⭐ Example

Caspar, a trustee, took £20,000 from the trust's bank account and used it to buy a painting that is hanging on his dining room wall. Eleanor, the beneficiary, has a proprietary claim to the painting. This is a case of 'clean substitution' – there has been a swap between trust property in its original form (money) and the new asset (the painting).

If the painting is now worth £25,000, Eleanor should elect to take the painting. She will therefore benefit from the painting's increase in value.

If instead the painting is now worth only £15,000, Eleanor should bring a personal claim against Caspar for £20,000 plus interest. She can, however, also assert an equitable lien over the painting, which will allow the painting to be sold (the lien is proprietary in nature because it fixes onto specific 'trust property' and ranks in priority over Caspar's unsecured creditors). The lien therefore provides Eleanor with security that she will receive £15,000 back should Caspar not have sufficient funds to satisfy the personal claim.

13.5 Trustee mixes trust property with other property

The position becomes slightly more complicated where a trustee starts to mix trust funds with either their own money or money belonging to someone else. Different tracing rules are used in different situations in order to identify trust property. In order to work out what the end result will be, you must first identify the relevant situation – how has the trust property been mixed – in order to then know what tracing rules you need to apply.

We will consider the following situations:

(a) The trustee buys an asset using partly their own money and partly funds wrongly drawn from the trust. The asset purchased in this way is often referred to as a 'mixed asset'.

(b) The trustee pays money from the trust into their own bank account, mixes that money with their own money, and then makes various withdrawals from the bank account. Here we need to use tracing rules to allocate the various withdrawals between trust money and the trustee's own money.

We will then consider similar situations, but this time identifying what happens if a trustee is running more than one trust and mixes together different trust funds, ie:

(c) The trustee buys a mixed asset using some money from Trust A and some money from Trust B.

(d) The trustee transfers money from Trust A and from Trust B and pays both sums into their own bank account, mixes those monies and then makes various withdrawals from the bank account. Here we need to use tracing rules to allocate the various withdrawals between the monies from Trust A and Trust B.

13.5.1 Mixed asset (trust + trustee funds)

A trustee wrongfully uses trust money to provide part of the cost of acquiring an asset, the balance coming from the trustee's own funds. This is a 'mixed asset' because the trustee has purchased the asset with a mixture of their own money and the trust's money.

In these situations, the beneficiary has the option of:

(a) claiming a proportionate interest in the mixed asset. The beneficiary should take this option where the mixed asset has increased in value; or

(b) suing the trustee for compensation for the loss to the trust and take a charge (or 'equitable lien') over the mixed asset for the amount that the trust has lost. The beneficiary should take this option where the mixed asset has decreased in value.

ⓞ Example

Stephan, a trustee for Lauren, took £10,000 from the trust and used this together with £5,000 of his own funds to buy £15,000 worth of shares in Sigma plc.

The shares are a mixed asset and tracing enables Lauren to assert a proprietary claim against them.

If the shares are now worth £24,000 (ie they have increased in value), then Lauren should claim a proportionate interest in the shares. The trust contributed two-thirds of the original purchase price. Lauren can therefore claim two-thirds of the value of the shares. This includes the increase in value, so the trust's interest is worth £16,000.

If the shares are now worth £12,000 (ie they have decreased in value), then Lauren should bring a personal claim against Stephan and assert an equitable lien over the shares. She can then insist that the shares be sold and that the trust recover all of its losses (£10,000) out of the sale proceeds.

As can be seen from the above example, equity tries to give the beneficiary the best result against the wrongdoing trustee whether the property has gone up or down in value.

13.5.2 Withdrawals from a mixed bank account (trust + trustee funds)

In this scenario, the trustee transfers money from the trust into their own bank account and then makes various withdrawals from that bank account.

For instance, a trustee takes £10,000 from the trust and pays it into their own bank account, which already contains £5,000 of their own money. From this bank account, they then buy some company shares and lose the rest of the money on an unsuccessful night out at the local casino. The beneficiary cannot bring a proprietary claim against the money lost at the casino – this money has been dissipated. The beneficiary therefore will want to bring a claim to recover the company shares. However, how does the beneficiary know whether the company shares were purchased using trust money or the trustee's own money? Equity uses a number of tracing rules to work out different end results, and then allows the beneficiary to cherry-pick between these rules – the beneficiary can choose the tracing rule that gives them the best end result.

13.5.2.1 Tracing rule 1: *Re Hallett*

The first tracing rule comes from *Re Hallett's Estate* (1880) 13 Ch D 696. This rule provides that the trustee is deemed to spend their own money first.

ⓞ Example

Patrick, a trustee for George, takes £25,000 from the trust and pays it into his own bank account, which already contains £10,000 of his own money. He then makes the following withdrawals:

- *He uses £10,000 to pay off his credit card bills; and subsequently*
- *He uses £25,000 to buy shares in Upsilon Limited.*

Ideally, George does not want trust money to have been used to pay off Patrick's credit card bill, as this represents dissipation. George would prefer trust money to be traced into the company shares.

The result of applying Re Hallett *is represented in* **Figure 13.1***.*

Figure 13.1 Application of *Re Hallett* (example 1)

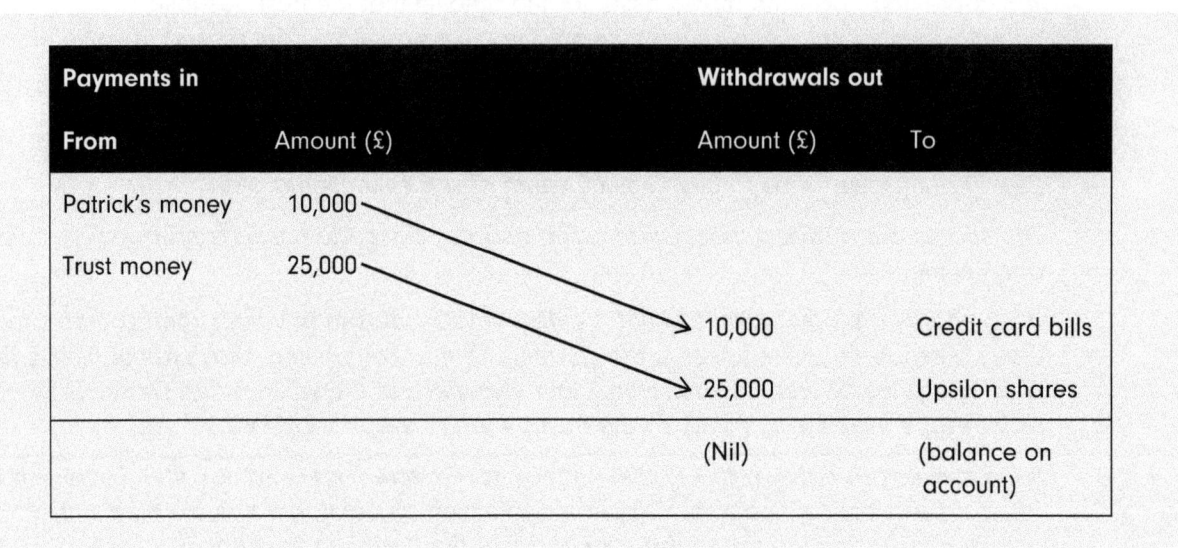

Payments in		Withdrawals out	
From	Amount (£)	Amount (£)	To
Patrick's money	10,000	10,000	Credit card bills
Trust money	25,000	25,000	Upsilon shares
		(Nil)	(balance on account)

Under *Re Hallett*, the trustee is deemed to spend their own money first. Patrick is deemed to spend his £10,000 on his credit card bills, enabling George to trace into and assert a proprietary claim over the Upsilon Limited shares.

The same result is achieved if we change the order of payments in, ie if Patrick pays in his own money only after the payment in of trust money (see **Figure 13.2**).

Figure 13.2 Application of *Re Hallett* (example 2)

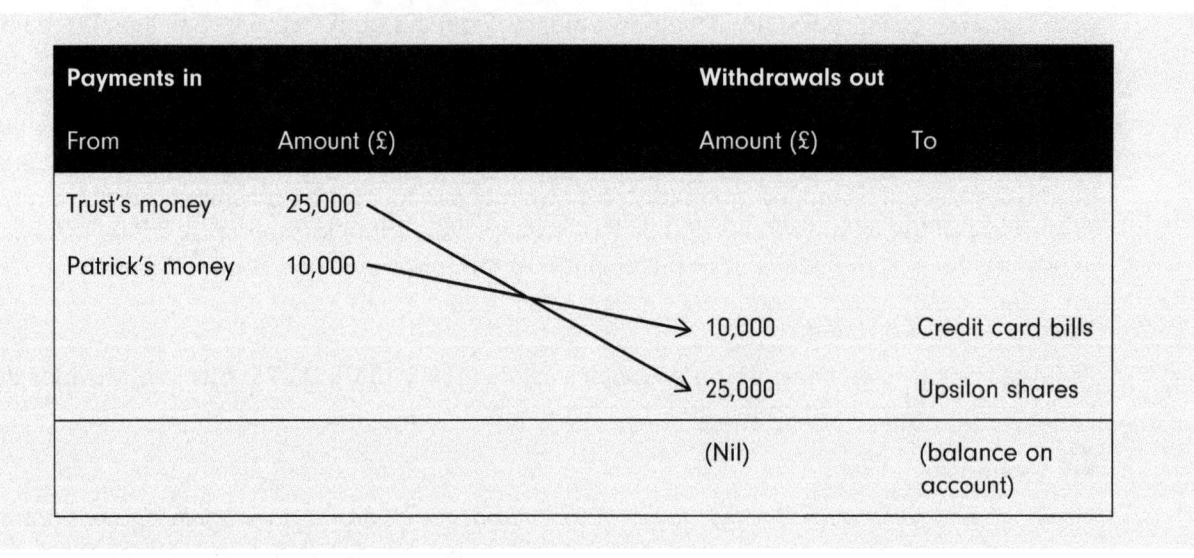

Payments in		Withdrawals out	
From	Amount (£)	Amount (£)	To
Trust's money	25,000	10,000	Credit card bills
Patrick's money	10,000	25,000	Upsilon shares
		(Nil)	(balance on account)

Let us now consider a slightly more complicated set of facts.

Example

Alexandra, a trustee for Niall, takes £25,000 from the trust and pays it into her own bank account, which already contains £10,000 of her own money. She then makes the following withdrawals:

- *She uses £8,000 to pay for a luxury cruise;*
- *She then uses £10,000 to buy shares in Omega plc;*
- *Leaving a balance on the account of £7,000.*

Ideally, Niall does not want trust money to have been used to pay for Alexandra's holiday, as this represents dissipation.

The result of applying Re Hallett *is represented in* **Figure 13.3**.

Figure 13.3 Application of *Re Hallett* (example 3)

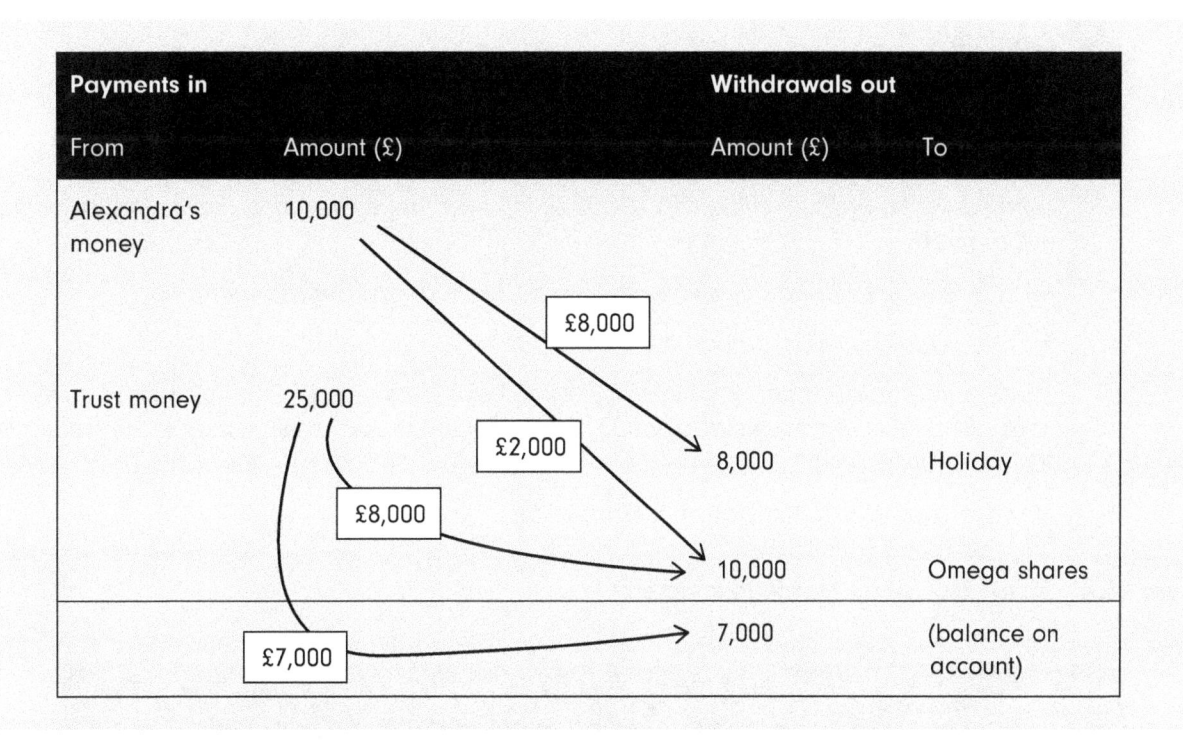

Payments in		Withdrawals out	
From	Amount (£)	Amount (£)	To
Alexandra's money	10,000	8,000	Holiday
Trust money	25,000	10,000	Omega shares
		7,000	(balance on account)

Arrows: Alexandra's £8,000 → Holiday; Trust £2,000 → Holiday; Trust £8,000 → Omega shares; Trust £7,000 → balance on account.

Applying Re Hallett *gives rise to the following results:*

- *The luxury cruise was paid for using Alexandra's money.*

- *£2,000 of the company shares were paid for by Alexandra, the balance of the purchase price (£8,000) came from the trust – Niall can therefore assert an equitable lien valued at £8,000 over the company shares.*

- *The balance on the account belongs wholly to the trust. (If there is a positive balance on the trustee's bank account,* Re Hallett *will trace trust money into that balance. Some commentators therefore describe the rule in* Re Hallett *as allowing the beneficiary, in a case where withdrawals have been made and spent by the trustee, to trace trust money into any credit balance remaining in the account.)*

What if the shares in the above example subsequently increase in value? Does Niall's proprietary claim extend to that increase in value?

For some time, it was difficult to say what the answer to this question would be. However, following obiter comments from the House of Lords in the case of *Foskett v McKeown* [2001] 1 AC 102, many commentators now suggest that the beneficiary can take the benefit of any increase in value in the assets into which they are tracing.

⭐ Example

Using the above example, if the shares in Omega plc are now worth £20,000, Niall should be entitled to claim a proportionate interest in those shares, including their increase in value. His proprietary claim would therefore be valued at £16,000 (given that the trust contributed 80% of the original purchase monies).

13.5.2.2 Tracing rule 2: *Re Oatway*

The first tracing rule in *Re Hallett* is particularly attractive where there is a healthy balance on the trustee's bank account, because the court will use the rule to trace trust property into that balance.

However, *Re Hallett* will not always work to the beneficiary's advantage.

> ⭐ **Example**
>
> Let us take the first example in the section on Re Hallett, but reverse the chronological order of the withdrawals.
>
> Patrick, a trustee for George, takes £25,000 from the trust and pays it into his own bank account, which already contains £10,000 of his own money. He then makes the following withdrawals:
>
> - He uses £10,000 to buy shares in Upsilon Limited; and subsequently
> - He uses £25,000 to pay off his credit card bills.
>
> Ideally, George does not want trust money to have been used to pay off Patrick's credit card bill, as this represents dissipation. George would prefer trust money to be traced into the company shares.
>
> However, now Re Hallett does not achieve this.

Figure 13.4 Application of *Re Hallett* (example 4)

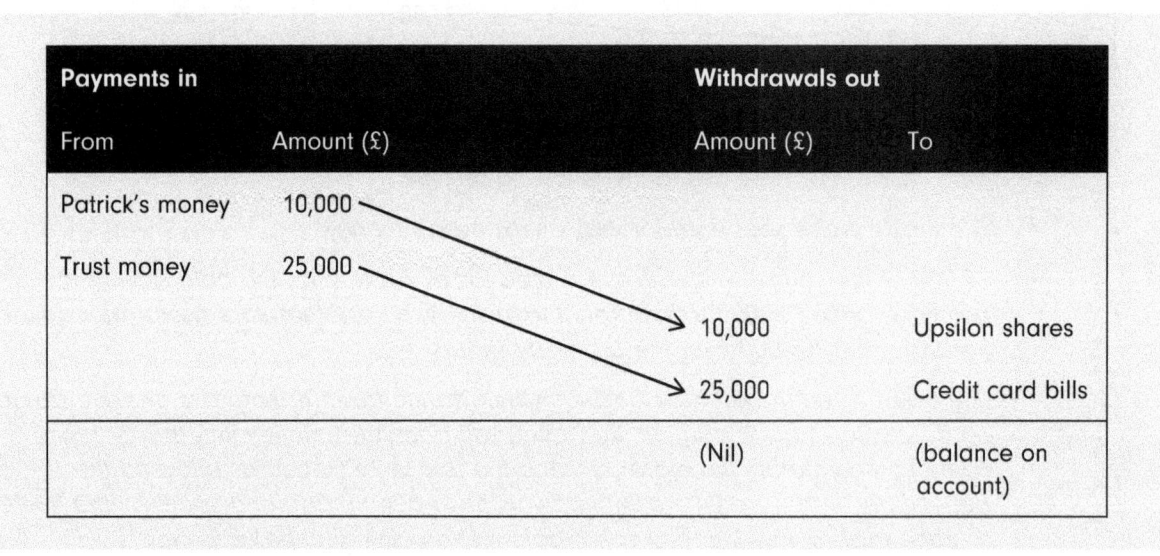

Payments in		Withdrawals out	
From	Amount (£)	Amount (£)	To
Patrick's money	10,000	10,000	Upsilon shares
Trust money	25,000	25,000	Credit card bills
		(Nil)	(balance on account)

> *Applying* Re Hallett *means that George cannot claim any interest in the only property left available – the company shares.*

The rule in *Re Hallett* is not an absolute rule, but is merely one application of the equitable maxim that 'everything is presumed against a wrongdoer'. If *Re Hallett* works to benefit the wrongdoing trustee, equity will apply another tracing rule to ensure a better result for the beneficiary.

This alternate tracing rule is set out in *Re Oatway* [1903] 2 Ch 356. This rule provides that the beneficiary has a first charge on the mixed fund (ie the amount sitting in the trustee's bank account) or any property that is purchased from that fund. In essence, the beneficiary gets 'first choice' and can therefore generally choose how best to satisfy their proprietary claim.

The trustee must wait until the beneficiary's claim is satisfied before the trustee can get any of the property. (Some commentators suggest that the tracing rule in *Re Oatway* provides that the trustee is deemed to spend trust money first, ie that the rule is the exact opposite of *Re Hallett*. Whilst this is often the result of *Re Oatway*, it is suggested that the rule is better understood as being an application of the more fundamental principle that the beneficiary is entitled to a first charge on the bank account and/or any withdrawals from that account.)

⭐ Example

Jack, a trustee for Bronwen, pays £50,000 of trust money into his account, which already contained £150,000 of his own money. Jack withdrew £150,000 to purchase a flat. He used the remainder to pay off debts that had accrued over a number of years.

If we apply Re Hallett, *all of the trust money would be dissipated on Jack's debts.*

Applying Re Oatway *gives a different result:*

Figure 13.5 Application of *Re Oatway*

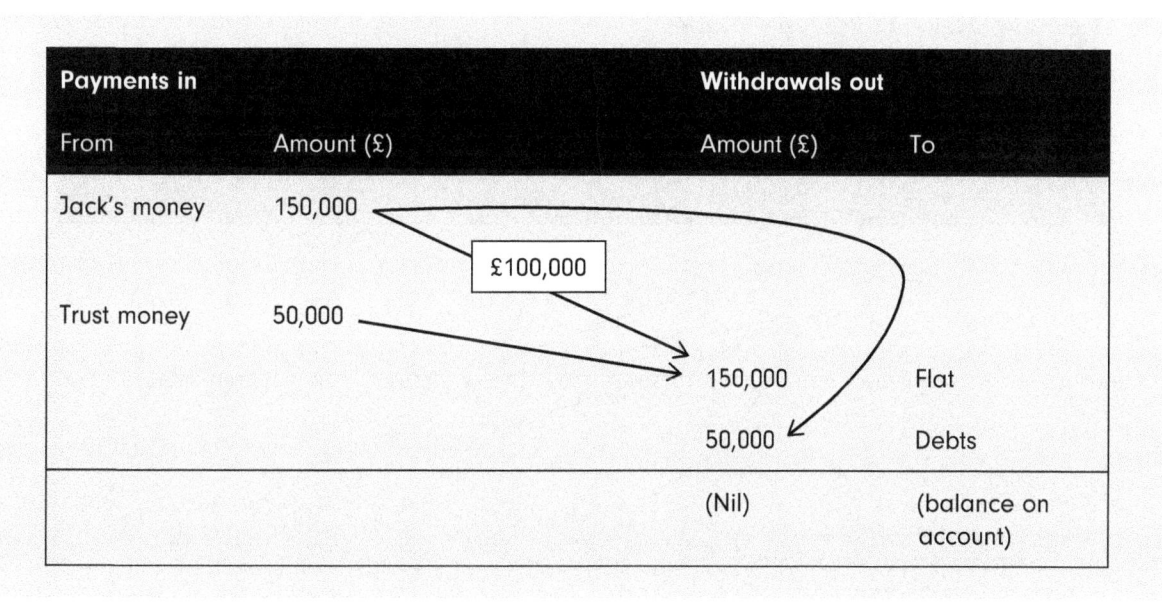

Payments in		Withdrawals out	
From	Amount (£)	Amount (£)	To
Jack's money	150,000		
		150,000	Flat
Trust money	50,000	50,000	Debts
		(Nil)	(balance on account)

£100,000

Under *Re Oatway*, the beneficiary gets 'first choice'. Bronwen can assert her proprietary claim through an equitable lien valued at £50,000 against the flat. Jack has to wait – once Bronwen has satisfied her claim, Jack's own money will be traced into the balance of the purchase price for the flat and will otherwise be dissipated, having been used to pay off the debt.

As is the case for *Re Hallett*, if an asset purchased partly with trust money increases in value, it is now believed that the beneficiary can also benefit from that increase in value (following the obiter comments of *Foskett v McKeown*). In the above example, the trust contributed one-third of the flat's purchase price. If the flat is now worth £180,000 (ie it has increased in value), it would seem that Bronwen can get a proportionate share of that increase, meaning that her proprietary claim would be valued at £60,000.

13.5.2.3 Limitation on the tracing rules: *Roscoe v Winder*

What if a trustee spends all the money in their mixed bank account, and then subsequently pays in some extra money into their account? Can the beneficiary trace any interest into that extra money?

⭐ Example

Carrie, a trustee, steals £40,000 trust money and pays it into her bank account, which already contains £10,000 of her own money. She spends £20,000 on a luxury cruise and a further £28,000 on private medical care, leaving a balance of £2,000 in the account. Her father then gifts her the sum of £3,000, which Carrie pays into her account.

In this case, Carrie has dissipated most of the money in her account, so there is nothing to trace into other than the balance sitting on the account. The gift from her father is not regarded as replacing the money she has stolen (unless it was specifically intended to replenish trust funds) – that gift is deemed to have come from sources other than the trust. The trust's interests cannot be traced beyond what is known as the 'lowest intermediate balance' – the lowest balance to which the account sank before extra money was paid in – confirmed in the case of Roscoe v Winder *[1915] 1 Ch 62.*

The trust's proprietary claim is therefore limited to the £2,000 balance on Carrie's account before her father made his gift, this being the lowest intermediate balance.

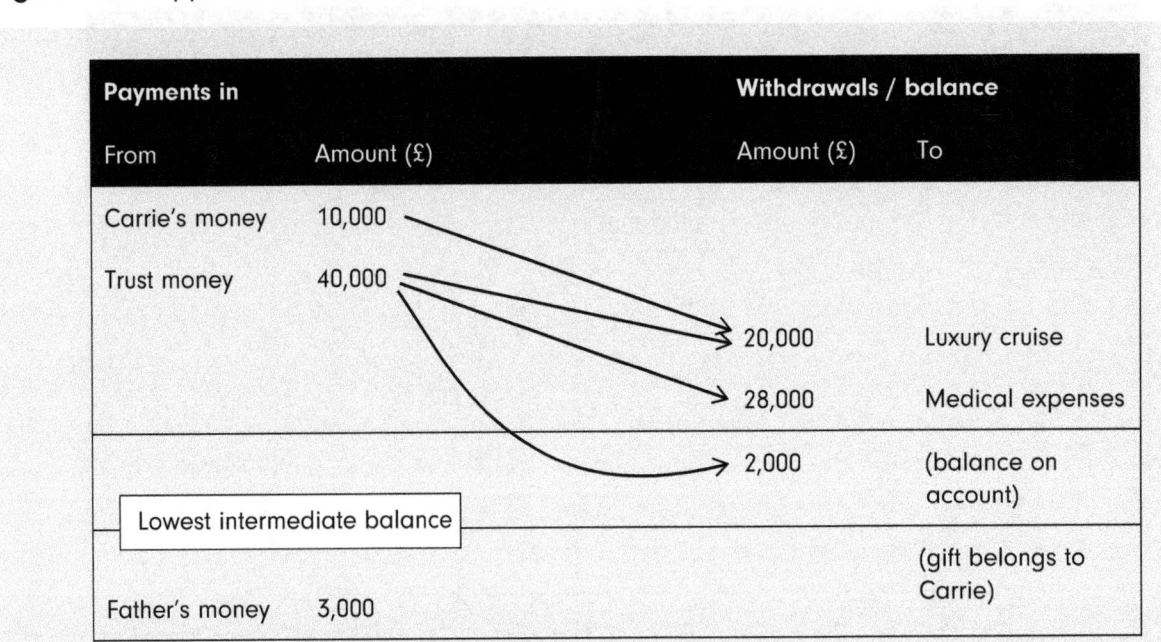

Figure 13.6 Application of *Roscoe v Winder*

Payments in		Withdrawals / balance	
From	Amount (£)	Amount (£)	To
Carrie's money	10,000	20,000	Luxury cruise
Trust money	40,000	28,000	Medical expenses
		2,000	(balance on account)
Father's money	3,000		(gift belongs to Carrie)

Lowest intermediate balance

13.5.3 Mixed asset (trust + trust funds)

'Everything is presumed against the wrongdoer'. As we have seen, if a wrongdoing trustee takes trust money and mixes it with their own, equity allows the beneficiary to cherry-pick the best outcome when identifying trust property using tracing rules. In these circumstances, tracing favours the innocent beneficiary.

An individual (such as a solicitor), however, may be a trustee of several trusts. It is possible that such a person could take money from a number of trusts in breach of trust and mix those together. In these circumstances, the beneficiary of each trust must use tracing rules to unravel what each trust owns. However, if each trust is innocent of the trustee's wrongdoing, then as between those trusts, equity must use a different set of tracing rules, which aim to treat each innocent trust in a more equal fashion. In these circumstances, tracing should not favour one set of beneficiaries to the disadvantage of others.

Let us first consider the scenario where the trustee takes money from one trust, mixes it with money from another trust, and then uses the entire mixed fund to buy an asset in their own name.

In these situations, the beneficiaries of each trust will share *pari passu* in the mixed asset purchased (ie rateably in the same proportion as their funds contributed to the purchase price).

⭐ Example

Stephan is a trustee for the Allan trust and the Barnes trust. He takes £10,000 from the Allan trust and £20,000 from the Barnes trust to buy £30,000 worth of shares in Sigma plc.

The shares are a mixed asset and tracing enables the beneficiaries of each trust to assert a proportionate interest in those shares.

If the shares are now worth £36,000 (ie they have increased in value), then the Allan trust's proprietary claim is now valued at £12,000, whereas the Barnes trust's proprietary claim is valued at £24,000.

If the shares are now worth £24,000 (ie they have decreased in value), then the Allan trust's proprietary claim is now valued at £8,000, whereas the Barnes trust's proprietary claim is valued at £16,000.

As between two innocent trusts, therefore, the outcome is always that each trust is entitled to a proportionate share in the mixed asset whether that asset has increased or decreased in value.

13.5.4 Withdrawals from a mixed bank account (trust + trust funds)

In this scenario, the trustee transfers money from one trust and money from another trust into their own bank account and then makes various withdrawals from that bank account.

⭐ Example

A trustee (John) pays £10,000 from the Chapman trust and later £20,000 from the Dawson trust into a newly opened bank account. From this bank account, John then uses £15,000 to pay off his credit card debts and, subsequently, uses the balance of £15,000 to purchase company shares.

How do the beneficiaries of each trust know whether the company shares were purchased using money from their trust fund or from the other trust fund?

13.5.4.1 Tracing rule 1: *Clayton's Case*

The first tracing rule comes from *Clayton's Case* (1816) 1 Mer 572. This rule states that, as between two or more innocents, the first money paid in is the first money paid out – First In, First Out (FIFO).

⭐ Example

Let us take the above example of John mixing money from the Chapman trust and the Dawson trust.

The result of applying Clayton's Case *is represented in* **Figure 13.7**.

Under Clayton's Case, *the first payment in is applied against the first payment out. In this scenario, the Chapman trust money has been dissipated on paying off John's credit card bills, whereas the company shares belong beneficially to the Dawson trust.*

Figure 13.7 Application of *Clayton's Case* (example 1)

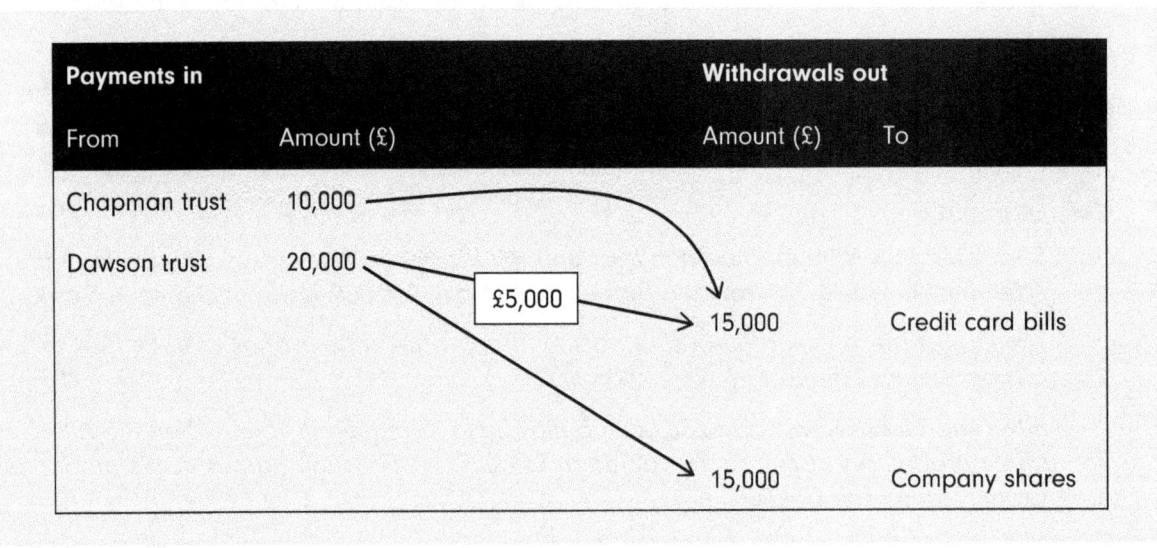

Payments in		Withdrawals out	
From	Amount (£)	Amount (£)	To
Chapman trust	10,000	15,000	Credit card bills
Dawson trust	20,000		
	£5,000	15,000	Company shares

13.5.4.2 Tracing rule 2: *Barlow Clowes v Vaughan*

The first tracing rule in *Clayton's Case* is a rule of convenience, and whilst it has been reaffirmed by subsequent cases, courts are often keen to indicate that the rule will only be applied if it does broad justice having regard to the competing claims that must be disentangled.

In *Barlow Clowes International Ltd (in liquidation) v Vaughan* [1992] 4 All ER 22, the Court of Appeal indicated that the FIFO rule in *Clayton's Case* can be departed from where:

- it is impossible to apply FIFO (eg where the records are so poor that ordering payments chronologically cannot be accurately undertaken);
- FIFO would result in injustice; or
- the application of FIFO would be contrary to the parties' intention.

It has subsequently been held that the general rule in *Clayton's Case* can be displaced by 'even a slight counterweight'. In those cases where the courts have departed from FIFO, the end result is that generally each investor (or trust) takes a rateable share in any remaining assets.

⭐ Example

If the court were persuaded to depart from Clayton's Case *in the Chapman / Dawson trust example above, the end result might be that each trust fund is entitled to assert a proportionate interest in the company shares rateable to the original amount of trust funds that were taken by John, ie:*

- *the Chapman trust can assert a proprietary claim against the shares valued at £5,000; and*
- *the Dawson trust can assert a proprietary claim against the shares valued at £10,000.*

13.5.5 Withdrawals from a mixed bank account (trust + trust + trustee funds)

The final situation we will consider is where the trustee takes money from two innocent trust funds and mixes that money with the trustee's own money, before making various withdrawals. In this situation:

(a) you should first apply the rules from **section 13.5.2** (*Re Hallett* and *Re Oatway*) with the aim of pushing as much of the trustee's own money into dissipation as possible ('everything is presumed against the wrongdoer'); and

(b) you should then apply the rules from **section 13.5.4** (*Clayton's Case* and *Barlow Clowes v Vaughan*) to allocate any remaining assets between the two (or more) innocent trusts.

⭐ **Example**

Daniel, a trustee, wrongfully transfers £20,000 from the Edis trust and £30,000 from the Fletcher trust to his own bank account, which already contains a balance of £10,000 of his own money.

Daniel then makes the following withdrawals:

- *£10,000 is used to pay off his credit card debts;*
- *£30,000 is then used to install a new kitchen at Daniel's home;*
- *£10,000 is then used to buy new artwork for Daniel's home; and*
- *£10,000 is applied towards a long holiday for Daniel and his family in Australia.*

Daniel then pays in £50,000, which represents an annual directorship salary from an independent company.

*We first apply the rules from **section 13.5.2**:*

Figure 13.8 Application of *Re Hallett* (example 5)

Payments in		Withdrawals out	
From	Amount (£)	Amount (£)	To
Daniel's money	10,000		
Edis Trust money	20,000		
Fletcher Trust money	30,000		
		10,000	Credit card bills
		30,000	Kitchen
		10,000	Paintings
		10,000	Holiday
		(Nil)	(balance on account)
Director salary	50,000		

Under Re Hallett, *the trustee is deemed to spend their own money first. Daniel is deemed to spend his own £10,000 on his credit card bills. This achieves the objective of trying to push the trustee into dissipation as much as possible, leaving assets or funds available into which the innocent trusts can trace.*

We then apply the rules from **section 13.5.4**:

Figure 13.9 Application of *Clayton's Case* (example 2)

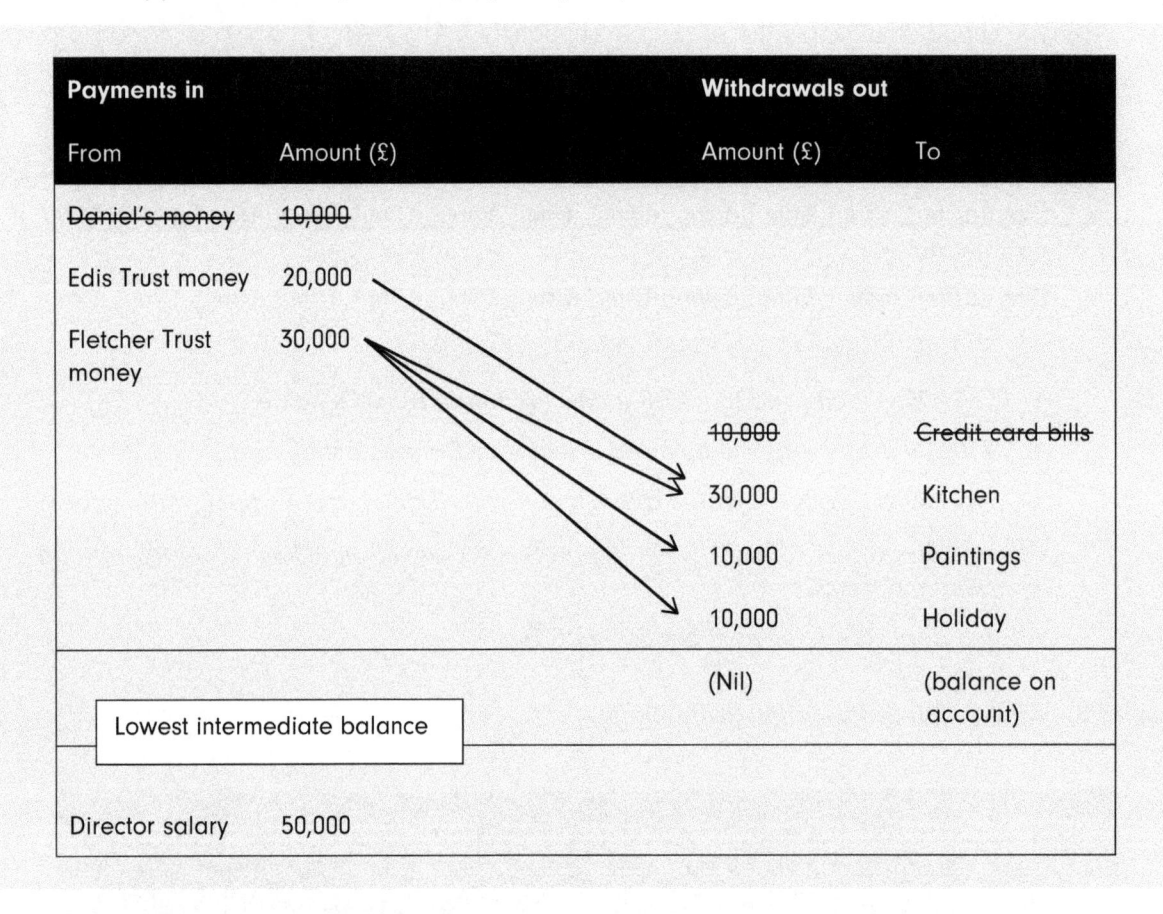

Payments in		Withdrawals out	
From	Amount (£)	Amount (£)	To
~~Daniel's money~~	~~10,000~~		
Edis Trust money	20,000		
Fletcher Trust money	30,000		
		~~10,000~~	~~Credit card bills~~
		30,000	Kitchen
		10,000	Paintings
		10,000	Holiday
Lowest intermediate balance		(Nil)	(balance on account)
Director salary	50,000		

Under Clayton's Case, the first payment in is applied against the first payment out. In this case, the Edis trust money is allocated against the payment to install the new kitchen (allowing the Edis trust to assert an equitable lien over that kitchen to the sum of £20,000). The Fletcher trust money is allocated:

- *£10,000 as against the new kitchen;*
- *£10,000 as against the new artwork; and*
- *£10,000 as against the holiday (which has therefore been dissipated).*

As in **section 13.5.4**, *the court may decide not to apply* Clayton's Case *if it would result in an injustice.*

Finally, you will note that by this stage all the trust money has been allocated against withdrawals. The nil balance on Daniel's account therefore represents the 'lowest intermediate balance'. The director's salary subsequently paid into the account belongs to Daniel.

13.6 Proprietary claims against other fiduciaries

The ability to bring a proprietary claim is not simply confined to beneficiaries. Principals of other fiduciary relationships can also bring proprietary claims to recover property that has been misappropriated by their fiduciaries. The existence of the fiduciary relationship enables the principal to use the equitable tracing rules set out in this chapter to identify their property even where it has been mixed by the fiduciary. If a director steals money from their company and uses the money to buy property, the company can assert proprietary claims against that property using the tracing rules set out in this chapter.

Summary

In this chapter you have considered proprietary claims that beneficiaries can bring against trustees:

- *What is a proprietary claim.* Proprietary claims assert rights over property. The claim is made in relation to any property now in the hands of the trustee, but which in fact belongs to the trust. The viability of such a claim therefore depends on whether the trustee is still holding trust property (or property that represents trust property).

- *Tracing rules.* Sometimes, the trustee will have taken trust property and changed its form or mixed such property with their own. In order to bring a proprietary claim, beneficiaries have to identify that the 'new' property belongs to the trust. This identification is carried out using different sets of tracing rules.

- *Clean substitution.* If a trustee has taken trust money and used that money to buy an asset in their own name, that asset will belong to the trust.

- *Mixed asset.* If a trustee has taken trust money and used that money together with some of their own money to buy an asset, the beneficiaries can choose to assert either a proportionate share in the asset (especially helpful where the asset has gone up in value) or an equitable lien over the asset (especially helpful where the asset has gone down in value). If a trustee has taken trust money from two separate trusts and uses that mixed fund to buy an asset, the beneficiaries of each trust can assert a proportionate share in the asset (whether the asset has gone up or down in value).

- *Withdrawals through a mixed bank account.* If a trustee pays trust money into their own bank account and mixes that money with their own money before making various withdrawals, the beneficiaries can use various different tracing rules (*Re Hallett* and *Re Oatway*) to identify what belongs to the trust. Under these rules, everything is presumed against the trustee and the beneficiaries can generally identify the more valuable items of property remaining as trust property. If a trustee pays money from two separate trusts into a bank account before making various withdrawals, the beneficiaries must use different tracing rules (*Clayton's Case* and *Barlow Clowes v Vaughan*) to identify what belongs to each trust. Under these rules, the courts try to apply a 'rough and ready' justice to both sets of innocent claimants.

Trusts

Sample questions

Question 1

A trustee takes £40,000 from a trust fund without authorisation and pays this into a bank account newly opened in his own name. He subsequently transfers £20,000 of his own money from another account.

He then withdraws (in order): £10,000 to buy company shares; £30,000 to spend on a painting; and £20,000 to pay off his debts. A month later, he receives the sum of £20,000 for completing some unrelated consultancy work. The company shares have subsequently increased in value to £15,000.

Which of the following represents the best available result for the beneficiaries should they bring a proprietary claim?

A   Two-thirds of the painting.

B   The painting.

C   The painting and the company shares.

D   One-third of the painting and the full balance now sitting on the account.

E   The company shares and the full balance now sitting on the account.

Answer

Option C is correct. The trustee has mixed trust funds with his own in a bank account and then made various withdrawals from that account. We must therefore use the tracing rules in *Re Hallett* and *Re Oatway* to work out the best result for the beneficiaries.

Re Oatway enables the beneficiary to assert a charge over the mixed fund and any withdrawals made from that fund. The beneficiary can choose to trace their interests into those withdrawals or funds that provide best value. Best value here is represented by option C. The appreciating company shares and the painting therefore represent the best possible outcome for the beneficiary.

Option A is wrong. This option identifies the end result if the beneficiary were to use *Re Hallett* to assert their proprietary claim. If the trustee is deemed to spend their own money first, the trustee will have paid for the company shares and one-third of the painting, meaning that some trust money has been used to pay off his debts (which means that money has been dissipated). This does not represent the best outcome for the beneficiary.

Option B is wrong. The beneficiary is best advised to trace into the company shares so that they can take advantage of the shares' increase in value.

Options D and E are wrong. The beneficiary cannot trace beyond the lowest intermediate balance and cannot therefore trace into the subsequent payment of £20,000 for the unrelated consultancy work.

Question 2

A woman is a trustee of a family trust and a charitable trust.

She takes £10,000 from the family trust without authorisation and pays this into a bank account in her own name, which already contains £20,000. She uses the balance of £30,000 to buy a car and subsequently closes the account. The car has depreciated in value and is now worth £24,000.

She takes a further £5,000 from the family trust and then £10,000 from the charitable trust without authorisation, paying each sum in turn into a separate bank account in her own name from which she makes the following withdrawals (in order): £10,000 to buy company shares; and £5,000 on a holiday.

Which of the following represents the best available result for the family trust?

A   100% interest in the car and 50% interest in the shares.

B   One-third interest in the car and 50% interest in the shares.

C   One-third interest in the car.

D   An equitable lien for £10,000 over the car and 50% interest in the shares.

E   An equitable lien for £10,000 over the car.

Answer

Option D is correct

The car represents a mixed asset (trust + trustee funds). As the car has gone down in value, the best result here is for the beneficiaries of the family trust to assert an equitable lien for £10,000 over the car so that the family trust can recover in full the £10,000 that was originally taken by the trustee. The company shares represent a withdrawal from a mixed bank account (trust + trust funds). Applying *Clayton's Case* and FIFO, the £5,000 taken from the family trust will be allocated against the company shares giving the family trust a 50% interest in those shares.

Option A is wrong. The car is a mixed asset and there is no way that the family trust can claim absolute ownership over it.

Option B is wrong. The car has depreciated in value. Asserting a proportionate one-third share in the car therefore does not represent the best available result for the family trust.

Options C and E are wrong. Both options omitted the possibility of claiming an interest in the company shares and therefore do not represent the best available result for the family trust.

Question 3

A management consultant and an insurance broker are trustees. The management consultant and insurance broker agreed that, in order to speed up the running of trust business, they should pay the trust fund into a bank account that allows withdrawals of any amount by only one signatory.

The management consultant takes £50,000 from the trust's bank account without authorisation and pays this into a newly opened bank account. He subsequently pays in £20,000 of his own money. From this account, he makes the following withdrawals (in order): £10,000 to pay for a luxury holiday; £10,000 to pay off personal debts; and £50,000 to purchase company shares.

The management consultant is now bankrupt. The company, whose shares he purchased, is now in insolvent liquidation.

Which of the following best describes whether the insurance broker can be named as a defendant to any claim that the beneficiaries might bring?

A   No claim will be brought against her because she did not commit a breach of trust.

B   No claim will be brought against her because she does not hold any property of value that the trust can trace into.

C   No claim will be brought against her because the beneficiaries are required to assert a proprietary claim against the company shares.

D   A claim could be brought against her for the £50,000 that the trust has lost plus interest.

E   A claim could be brought against her for the £50,000 that the trust has lost plus interest but she will be able to secure a sizeable contribution from the management consultant for the part he played in that loss.

Answer

Option D is correct.

This question is designed to remind you that beneficiaries can choose to bring personal and/or proprietary claims against their wrongdoing trustees.

Option D correctly identifies that the beneficiaries can bring a personal claim against the insurance broker for the full amount that her co-trustee stole from the trust. The insurance broker is in breach of trust. She agreed to pay the trust funds into an account that could be emptied by just one of the trustees. As such, she failed to act as an ordinary, prudent businesswoman and failed to supervise the activities of her co-trustee (see **Chapter 9**). This breach caused the loss that the trust has sustained.

Option A is wrong. The insurance broker did commit a breach of trust.

Option B is wrong. Whilst this option correctly identifies that the insurance broker is not holding any property of value that could form the basis of a proprietary claim, this does not prevent a personal claim being made against her.

Option C is wrong. The beneficiaries do not have to bring a proprietary claim. Indeed, on the facts, there would be no value in them doing so. The money used to pay for the holiday and the management consultant's debts has been dissipated. Given that the company is in insolvent liquidation, there is no value in the company shares, so there is no point in the trust seeking to recover them.

Option E is wrong. The insurance broker is unlikely to get a sizeable contribution from her co-trustee, notwithstanding that he is more responsible for the losses sustained. A claim for contribution under the Civil Liability (Contribution) Act 1978 is a personal claim and there is very little point in making such a claim now that the management consultant is bankrupt.

14 Remedies Against Third Parties

14.1	Introduction	190
14.2	Third party claims	190
14.3	Intermeddling	192
14.4	Equitable personal recipient liability (knowing receipt)	192
14.5	Equitable proprietary claims	194
14.6	Equitable personal accessory liability (dishonest assistance)	197
14.7	Claims arising out of a breach of fiduciary duty	199
14.8	Summary flowchart	200

SQE1 syllabus

This chapter will enable you to achieve the SQE1 assessment specification in relation to functioning legal knowledge concerned with the following core principles:

- Liability of strangers to the trust
- Establishing recipient liability
- Establishing accessory liability

Note that for SQE1, candidates are not usually required to recall specific case names or cite statutory or regulatory authorities. Cases are provided for illustrative purposes only.

Learning outcomes

By the end of this chapter you will be able to apply relevant core legal principles and rules appropriately and effectively, at the level of a competent newly qualified solicitor in practice, to realistic client-based and ethical problems and situations in the following areas:

- establishing what is meant by a 'stranger to the trust' and when you would advise that claims be brought against them;
- recognising claims that can be brought against strangers that have received property in breach of trust; and
- recognising claims that can be brought against strangers who have assisted a breach of trust.

14.1 Introduction

In **Chapters 12** and **13**, we considered the personal and proprietary claims that beneficiaries can bring against wrongdoing trustees.

However, it is possible that such claims will not adequately compensate the beneficiaries for any losses caused by the trustees' wrongful actions. The trustee may be bankrupt (and therefore unable to fund a personal claim) and may no longer be in possession of property belonging to the trust (and therefore there is nothing to recover by way of a proprietary claim). In these situations, there may be little point in bringing claims against the wrongdoing trustee.

Instead, the beneficiaries should be advised to consider whether claims can be brought against any third party. These third parties are often referred to as 'strangers to the trust' – this simply means that they have not been expressly appointed as a trustee.

Beneficiaries may be able to bring claims against those third parties who become entangled in a breach of trust or fiduciary duty. Third parties might become entangled in one of two ways:

- Recipient liability. It might be possible to bring a personal and/or proprietary claim against a third party if they are in receipt of trust property given to them in breach of trust or fiduciary duty.
- Accessory liability. It might be possible to bring a personal claim against a third party if they have assisted a trustee in a breach of trust or fiduciary duty.

This chapter looks at:

- the types of equitable claims that beneficiaries can bring against third parties and which claims should be brought in what circumstances;
- personal claims that can be brought against third parties who receive trust property in breach of trust or fiduciary duty;
- proprietary claims that can be brought against third parties who receive trust property in breach of trust or fiduciary duty; and
- personal claims that can be brought against third parties who assist with a breach of trust or fiduciary duty.

14.2 Third party claims

We will consider the following claims in this chapter:

- equitable personal actions against third parties who take it upon themselves to act as a trustee – known as 'intermeddling';
- equitable personal actions against third party recipients – the primary claim is often called 'knowing receipt';
- equitable proprietary actions against third party recipients; and
- equitable personal actions against third party assistors – the primary claim is often called 'dishonest assistance'.

Beneficiaries may also be able to require that their trustees bring common law claims against third parties, such as a claim in restitution. Common law claims are outside the scope of this manual.

We saw in **Chapters 12** and **13** that personal claims are only as good as the financial solvency of the defendant and proprietary claims are only as good as the property that you are able to recover using tracing rules. These same practical considerations should be used by the beneficiary when identifying which claims should be brought against third parties. The following flowchart suggests how a beneficiary can navigate their way through the various available claims.

Figure 14.1 Possible third party claims

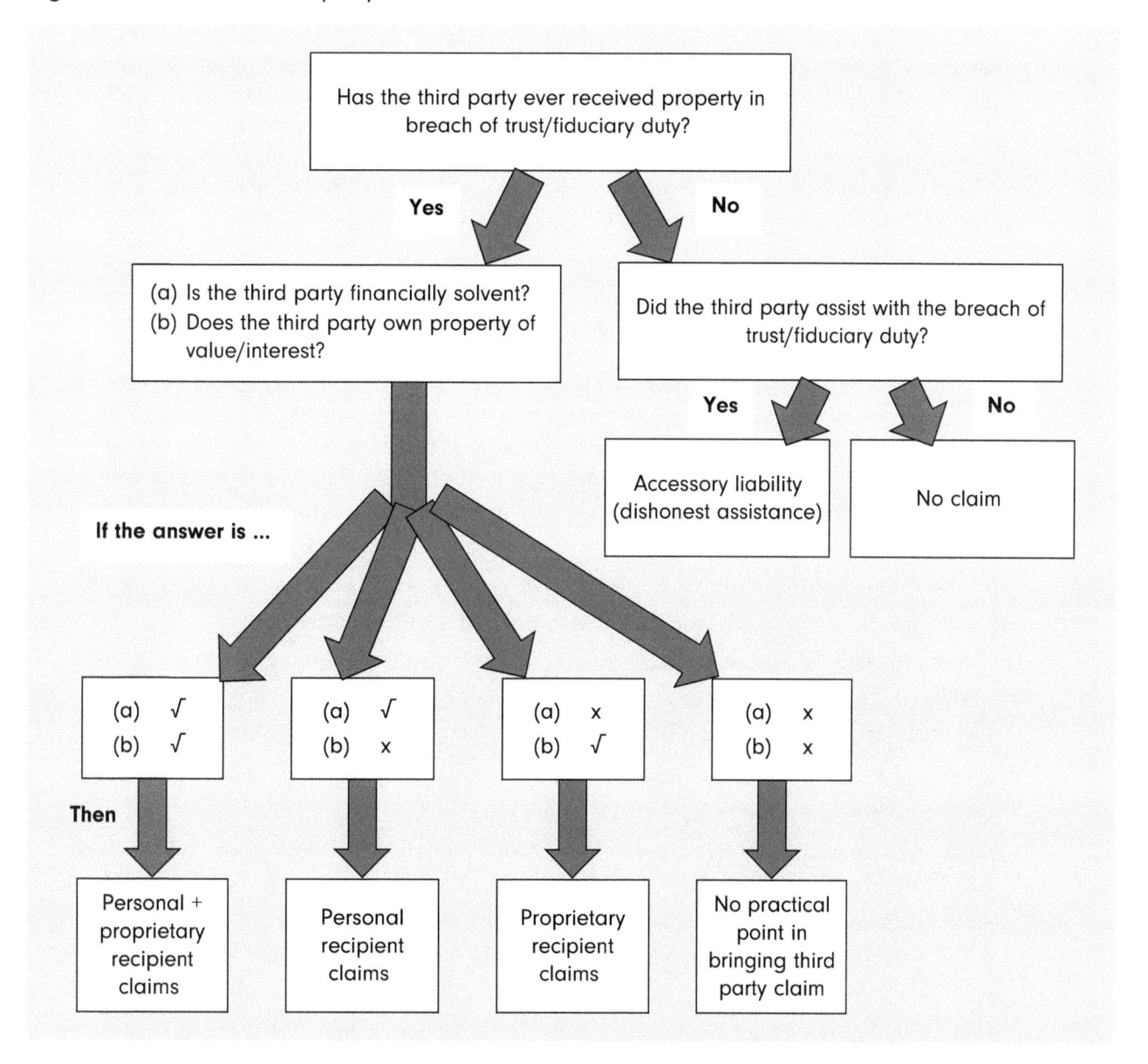

```
                    Has the third party ever received property in
                          breach of trust/fiduciary duty?
                         │                           │
                        Yes                          No
                         ↓                           ↓
        (a) Is the third party financially solvent?     Did the third party assist with the breach of
        (b) Does the third party own property of                 trust/fiduciary duty?
            value/interest?                              │                    │
                                                        Yes                   No
                                                         ↓                    ↓
                                                 Accessory liability      No claim
                                                 (dishonest assistance)

If the answer is ...

   (a) √          (a) √          (a) ×          (a) ×
   (b) √          (b) ×          (b) √          (b) ×

Then
   ↓              ↓              ↓              ↓
Personal +      Personal      Proprietary    No practical
proprietary     recipient     recipient      point in
recipient       claims        claims         bringing third
claims                                       party claim
```

This flowchart maps out the key practical questions that a beneficiary must ask when identifying which claims to bring against a third party. Having identified which claims they can bring, the beneficiary must then ask themselves whether those claims are made out on the facts. We will now address the key constituent elements of each claim.

14.3 Intermeddling

A third party who is not expressly appointed as a trustee, but takes it upon themselves to act as if they were, will be held personally liable for any losses caused by their actions as if they were an expressly appointed trustee. Such third parties are often referred to as a 'trustee de son tort' (a trustee of their own wrongdoing).

> In Lyell v Kennedy (No 4) *(1889) 14 App Cas 437*, an agent of a trustee collected rent from tenants of trust property and paid that rent into a separate bank account in the agent's name. The agent continued to do so after the death of the trustee, paying rent into the same bank account until, a few years later, the agent claimed that the money in the account belonged to him. The agent's mandate to collect rent ceased on the death of his principal (the expressly appointed trustee). He was therefore no longer acting as an agent. However, by continuing to collect the rent – ie handling trust income – the agent was doing acts characteristic of a trustee. The agent was therefore personally liable for his actions and had to account for the rent he had collected to the trust.

14.4 Equitable personal recipient liability (knowing receipt)

If a third party receives trust property, it may be possible to bring a personal claim against them up to the value of the trust property they received (plus interest from the date of receipt). A key element of this claim is that the third party's liability is fault-based – unless and until the third party was aware that they had received trust property, they are entitled to treat that property as if it were their own and spend it however they wish with no liability attaching to them.

The elements of this claim are as follows:

(a) the third party has received property in breach of trust or fiduciary duty;

(b) the third party has received that property for their own benefit; and

(c) while in receipt of the property, the third party has such knowledge that makes it unconscionable for them to retain or deal with the property as if it were their own.

A claim for knowing receipt will only succeed if the third party had the requisite degree of knowledge *while* in receipt of trust property. So, for example, a third party will be liable if:

(a) they receive trust property, knowing that property was transferred to them in breach of trust; or

(b) they receive trust property without providing consideration and without any knowledge that it belongs to the trust, but gain that knowledge while in receipt of the property and before they spend it.

However, the third party will *not* be liable where they only become aware that they received trust property after they have disposed of that property.

Example

> James, a trustee, wrongfully transferred £200 of trust funds to his girlfriend Katherine on her birthday saying that it was part of his birthday present to her. Katherine had no idea that the £200 had been stolen from the trust. She spent the money on a day out at a local spa. A month later, the beneficiaries of the trust write to Katherine saying that she had received trust property.

A claim for knowing receipt will not succeed in this case, because Katherine had no knowledge that she had received trust funds in breach of trust while she was in receipt of those funds.

For a claim in knowing receipt to be successful, the third party's state of knowledge 'must be such as to make it unconscionable for him to retain the [property]' (*Bank of Credit and Commerce International (Overseas) Ltd v Akindele* [2000] 4 All ER 221). Whilst this test has been criticised for being vague and uncertain, it will probably be unconscionable for a third party to retain and deal with trust property where one of the following applies:

(a) The third party knows that the property belongs to a trust.

⭐ Example

Ainka, a trustee, transferred £20,000 of trust funds to her girlfriend Elsa. Ainka told Elsa that she had taken the money from the trust without authorisation. Elsa will be liable for knowing receipt.

(b) The third party wilfully shuts their eyes to the obvious.

⭐ Example

Colin receives £20,000 from his husband, Matthew. Matthew tells Colin that the money came out of his bank account, but when Colin checks his bank statement, he sees that the money was paid by the 'Hardingham Trust Account'. Colin knows that Matthew is a trustee for a trust that Matthew's sister – Ms Hardingham – set up for her children. Colin decides to spend the money anyway.

Up until the point Colin checked his bank statement, he might have been able to deal with the money as he wanted. However, having checked his bank statement, Colin will in all likelihood be liable for knowing receipt having shut his eyes to the obvious source of the money.

(c) The third party deliberately decides not to ask any questions notwithstanding they have their suspicions about the origins of the property.

⭐ Example

Katrina receives £20,000 from her boyfriend, Dirk, who tells her that it is a present. Katrina is surprised by the amount of money because they have not been going out very long and Dirk has previously said that he did not have much money. Katrina remembers that Dirk once said he looked after money for some relatives. Nevertheless, she decides that it is best to simply take the money and spend it. She does not ask Dirk any questions because she is worried that, once she knows the truth, she might have to give the money back.

Katrina will be liable for knowing receipt.

What is less clear is whether a claim for knowing receipt can be made out where the third party asserts that they did not have any suspicions that the property belonged to a trust, but what they did know would have led a reasonable person to that conclusion (whether immediately or by putting that reasonable person on inquiry). Some judges have been willing to use this type of 'constructive knowledge' to ground liability for knowing receipt; others have not been so keen. Whether for or against, nearly all of these judgments were handed down before the Court of Appeal introduced the test of 'unconscionability' in *BCCI v Akindele*, and it is therefore difficult to say whether such judgments have any role to play in assisting our understanding. There is a significant amount of commentary on this point, which goes beyond the scope of this manual. What most commentators appear agreed on is we now need an authoritative answer on this point from the Supreme Court.

Let us take a look at a final example on recipient liability.

⭐ Example

Ruth was a beneficiary of a complex family trust arrangement. The trustees transferred some family heirlooms to her. Ruth sold them and spent the proceeds on living expenses and paying off numerous debts. The trustees subsequently discovered that under the complex terms of the trust, Ruth was not in fact entitled to the heirlooms.

Ruth has received trust property in breach of trust for her own benefit. However, it is unlikely that she will be held liable for knowing receipt. She did not actually know that she had received property in breach of trust and there appears to be no evidence that she deliberately shut her eyes to the obvious or had any suspicions. Would a reasonable person in Ruth's position have read the trust deed to check their entitlement? Unlikely, so even if 'constructive knowledge' was a relevant test, it seems unlikely that Ruth would be liable.

However, if Ruth knew that the heirlooms did not belong to her, she would be liable for knowing receipt even if the trustees did not know that they were transferring property in breach of trust. Recipient liability focuses on the conscience of the receiver – it is not necessary to show that the trustees knew that they were committing a breach of trust.

14.5 Equitable proprietary claims

Where a trustee has transferred trust property to a third party, and that third party still holds that property (in its original or replacement form), the beneficiaries may be able to assert a proprietary claim in order to recover that property. The practical advantages of asserting a proprietary claim against a third party are generally the same as those we encountered in **Chapter 13** (eg a proprietary claim will have priority if the third party has been made bankrupt).

The first step when bringing a proprietary claim to recover property held by a third party is to decide into which of the following three categories the third party falls:

(a) Bona fide purchaser for value without notice. If the third party paid for the property and had no idea that the property belonged to a trust, then the third party takes that property free from any equitable interests. No proprietary claim can be sustained against the third party in this scenario (as a result, this third party is often referred to as 'equity's darling'). Note that a personal claim in knowing receipt would also fail against equity's darling because they would not have the requisite degree of knowledge at the time of purchase to make any subsequent retention of the property unconscionable.

(b) Wrongdoing recipient. If the third party is an intermeddler or would have been guilty of knowing receipt on the grounds that their conscience is affected, then the beneficiaries can bring a proprietary claim against them to recover the property. As the third party is a wrongdoer, the harsher tracing rules relevant to a trustee apply ('everything is presumed against a wrongdoer').

(c) Innocent volunteer. If the third party has no knowledge or notice of the breach of trust and provided no consideration for the transfer of property, then a proprietary claim can still be brought, but the tracing rules are the kinder rules that are applied against innocent parties.

14.5.1 Wrongdoing tracing rules

When a beneficiary brings a proprietary claim against a third party guilty of recipient liability, the beneficiary will use the same tracing rules as they would use against a wrongdoing trustee. As a result, the following rules apply when identifying property in the hands of a wrongdoing recipient stranger:

(a) If the third party still holds trust property in its original form, the beneficiaries can assert a proprietary claim against that property to recover it.

(b) If the third party has used trust property to buy something new, the beneficiaries can assert a proprietary claim against that new property. This is a case of 'clean substitution' (see **Chapter 13.4**).

(c) If the third party has taken trust funds and mixed this with their own money to purchase property in their own name, the beneficiaries can assert a proprietary claim against that mixed asset. The beneficiaries can claim a proportionate share in the mixed asset or assert an equitable lien over the mixed asset, depending on whether the mixed asset has increased or decreased in value (see **Chapter 13.5.1**).

(d) If the third party has taken trust funds and paid this into their own bank account mixing it with money of their own, before making various withdrawals from that bank account, the beneficiaries will use the tracing rules of *Re Hallett* and *Re Oatway* to determine into what forms of property they can trace (see **Chapter 13.5.2**).

⭐ Example

Alastair transferred £30,000 of trust money to his boyfriend's (Robert's) bank account. Robert knew that Alastair was a trustee of a family trust and that the relationships between Alastair and the beneficiaries of that trust had become strained. Alastair had on previous occasions complained that he was not getting paid enough to deal with the many demands of the beneficiaries and said that he was minded to take money out of the trust to compensate him for his troubles with or without the beneficiaries' blessing. Robert suspects that Alastair has done just that, but decides not to ask any questions for fear that Alastair might turn against him.

Robert's bank account already contained £20,000 of his own money. He subsequently purchased a Jaguar XE car for £35,000 and used the balance on the account to pay off his credit card debts.

If the beneficiaries wish to bring a proprietary claim against Robert, they must first establish whether he is a wrongdoing recipient or an innocent volunteer. Robert has received trust funds in breach of the duties owed by Alastair, and Robert has received those funds for his own benefit. Given that Robert had his suspicions but deliberately decided not to ask any questions, it is likely that he had the requisite degree of knowledge as to the origins of the money to make it unconscionable to retain and deal with that money as if it were his own. As a result, it is likely that he is a wrongdoing recipient.

If that is the case, the beneficiaries will use the same tracing rules as they would against a wrongdoing trustee (such as Alastair). They will use these rules to try and trace into the Jaguar car – the payment of Robert's credit card debts constitutes dissipation, which the beneficiaries will want to avoid.

The beneficiaries will first of all apply the tracing rule from Re Hallett *– the wrongdoer is deemed to spend their own money first. However, this would mean that the Jaguar was purchased primarily from Robert's own money, splitting the trust money between the car and the credit card bills.*

*Instead, therefore, the beneficiaries will apply the tracing rule from Re Oatway, exercising a lien over the mixed fund and any assets purchased with it. As can be seen from **Figure 14.2**, this will allow the beneficiaries to assert that most of the value in the car belongs to them.*

Figure 14.2 Application of *Re Oatway* against a third party

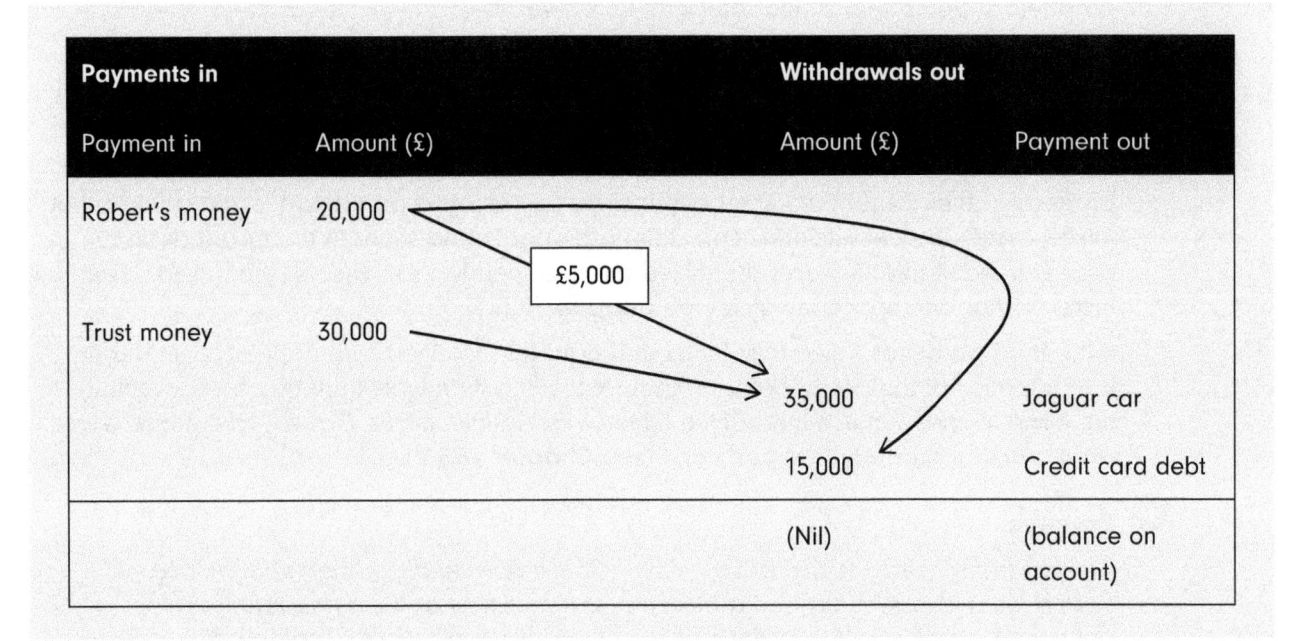

Payments in		Withdrawals out	
Payment in	Amount (£)	Amount (£)	Payment out
Robert's money	20,000		
		£5,000	
Trust money	30,000		
		35,000	Jaguar car
		15,000	Credit card debt
	(Nil)		(balance on account)

14.5.2 Innocent tracing rules

When a beneficiary brings a proprietary claim against a third party volunteer who had no knowledge or notice that the property belonged to the trust, the beneficiary will use the same tracing rules as they would when trying to assert their proprietary interests against other innocent parties. As a result, the following rules apply when identifying property in the hands of an innocent recipient stranger:

(a) If the third party still holds trust property in its original form, the beneficiaries can assert a proprietary claim against that property to recover it.

(b) If the third party has used trust property to buy something new, the beneficiaries can assert a proprietary claim against that new property. This is a case of 'clean substitution' (see **Chapter 13.4**).

(c) If the third party has taken trust funds and mixed this with their own money to purchase property in their own name, the beneficiaries can assert a proprietary claim against that mixed asset. The beneficiaries will claim a proportionate share in the mixed asset whether that asset has increased or decreased in value (see **Chapter 13.5.3**).

(d) If the third party has taken trust funds and paid this into their own bank account mixing it with money of their own, before making various withdrawals from that bank account, the beneficiaries will use the tracing rules of *Clayton's Case* and *Barlow Clowes v Vaughan* to determine into what forms of property they can trace (see **Chapter 13.5.4**).

However, when it comes to the mixing of monies in a bank account, the innocent volunteer might be able to assert a defence against the beneficiaries' proprietary claim. If an innocent third party receives trust money and uses that money to improve buildings they already own, then the beneficiary will not be able to trace any interest into that improvement. This is because either:

(a) that improvement has not increased the value of the third party's land, such that the trust money has in essence been dissipated; or

(b) that improvement has increased the value of the third party's land, but it would be inequitable to force the innocent third party to sell their property to realise the beneficiary's proprietary interest. If the beneficiary is allowed to enforce a lien over the innocent third party's land, the sale of the land will enable the beneficiary to recover their money but deprives the innocent third party of their land. Whilst the third party would get the balance of the sale proceeds, this is probably cold comfort for someone who might be thrown out on the street. Trying to enforce the beneficiary's proprietary interest will lead to an inequitable result, which defeats any proprietary claim. This is often referred to as the *Re Diplock* defence (following the Court of Appeal's judgment in *Re Diplock* [1948] Ch 465 where it was first established).

⭐ Example

Vida receives the sum of £15,000 in complete ignorance that this money came from a trust. She uses the money to install a new kitchen.

Vida appears to have had no knowledge that the money represented trust property. As a result, her conscience is unlikely to have been affected meaning that a claim for recipient liability is likely to fail.

It is quite likely that the new kitchen has added value to Vida's home. However, it would be inequitable for the beneficiaries to assert a proprietary claim against Vida's house, with the result that a proprietary claim will also fail.

The *Re Diplock* defence does not apply:

(a) as against wrongdoing recipients. If a third party guilty of knowing receipt uses trust money to improve their property, and this results in their property increasing in value, the beneficiaries are entitled to assert a proprietary claim against the third party's land (up to the increase in value caused by those improvements); nor

(b) in relation to mixed assets, even those purchased by innocent third parties. If an innocent third party takes trust money and combines it with their own to put down a deposit on a house, the beneficiaries can assert an interest in that house proportionate to their contribution.

14.6 Equitable personal accessory liability (dishonest assistance)

If a third party assists a trustee in the commission of a breach of trust or fiduciary duty, it may be possible to bring a personal claim against them up to the value of any loss their assistance has caused (plus interest). Once again, the third party's liability is fault-based – the third party must have acted dishonestly when providing that assistance.

The elements of this claim are as follows:

(a) there must have been a breach of trust or fiduciary duty. However, it is not necessary to establish that the trustee has acted dishonestly or intentionally in breaching the trust – all that is required is a breach of trust or fiduciary duty irrespective of how it has been committed;

(b) the third party must have assisted in that breach; and

(c) the third party must have acted dishonestly.

The assistance provided by the third party must be some kind of positive act – merely being passive in the commission of a breach of trust is unlikely to be sufficient.

So long as the third party takes some positive action, that will generally be sufficient to satisfy the element of 'assistance'. So, for instance:

(a) a solicitor could find themselves liable if they draft documents that help the trustee commit a breach of trust;

(b) an accountant could find themselves liable if they draw up accounts that help the trustee hide their breach of trust; and

(c) a banker could find themselves liable if they set up accounts to which trust monies are wired in breach of trust.

As can be seen from the above list, professionals who (wittingly or otherwise) provide services to a wrongdoing trustee are often the target of claims for dishonest assistance. The advantage of bringing claims against such defendants is that they are usually backed by insurance so have pockets deep enough to satisfy this type of personal claim.

Claims for accessory liability against third parties will only be successful if those third parties have acted dishonestly. The test for dishonesty in this area was first set out in the seminal Privy Council decision of *Royal Brunei Airlines v Tan* [1995] 2 AC 378. In his leading judgment, Lord Nicholls observed as follows:

> ... in the context of the accessory liability principle acting dishonestly, or with a lack of probity, which is synonymous, means simply not acting as an honest person would in the circumstances. This is an objective standard ... [However,] when called upon to decide whether a person was acting honestly, a court will look at all the circumstances known to the third party at the time. The court will also have regard to personal attributes of the third party, such as his experience and intelligence, and the reason why he acted as he did.

Notwithstanding the apparently clear guidance from the Privy Council, our understanding of what was meant by 'dishonesty' was muddied by subsequent authority from the House of Lords (such as in the case of *Twinsectra Ltd v Yardley* [2002] UKHL 12). However, more recent decisions appear to have restored Lord Nicholls' test of dishonesty, which the Court of Appeal has recently advised must now be 'treated as settled law'.

The test for dishonesty therefore requires the court to ask whether the ordinary honest person (imbued with the same experience and intelligence as the actual defendant) would have acted differently knowing what the actual defendant knew. If that honest person would have acted differently (eg by refusing to carry out the assistance requested of them, or refusing to act unless specific questions were answered) then the defendant's conduct is dishonest.

The test is primarily an objective one. The court is not concerned about whether the actual defendant thought that they were acting honestly. Instead, the court compares the defendant's actions to the objective standards of ordinary decent people.

Finally, the third party does not need to know that they are assisting in a breach of trust or fiduciary duty. Dishonest assistance will arise if the third party knows that they are actively assisting some form of illegal scheme.

Let us pull the elements of accessory liability together in the following example.

⭐ Example

Tessa is a newly qualified solicitor working in the private client department of a law firm. She is instructed by Vanessa, one of a number of trustees running a family trust, to draft the legal papers needed to convey a house owned by the trust into Vanessa's sole name. Vanessa advises that the purchase price for the house is £10 and that everyone, including the beneficiaries, has agreed to this. Tessa does as Vanessa instructs. The beneficiaries subsequently complain that they were never told about this house sale.

*The unauthorised sale of the house to a trustee is a breach of fiduciary duty (see the self-dealing rule in **Chapter 11**). By drawing up the necessary conveyancing documents, Tessa has assisted with that breach.*

If Tessa has acted dishonestly, she will be guilty of dishonest assistance and will be required to pay the trust compensation for any losses that have been sustained. The court will enquire as to Tessa's actual state of knowledge and belief and then compare her actions against the actions of an honest solicitor with the same knowledge and experience as Tessa. It is likely that an honest solicitor would not have acted on Vanessa's instructions (at least, not without asking more questions), and as such a claim for dishonest assistance against Tessa is likely to succeed.

14.7 Claims arising out of a breach of fiduciary duty

The ability to bring claims against third parties is not simply confined to beneficiaries. Principals of other fiduciary relationships can also bring the claims set out in this chapter where their fiduciaries have breached fiduciary duties they owe.

⭐ Example

Matthew is a director of Hudson Limited. He transfers the sum of £20,000 from the company's bank account to his husband Colin without authorisation. Matthew tells Colin that the money came out of his bank account, but when Colin checks his bank statement, he sees that the money was paid by Hudson Limited. Colin knows that Matthew is a director for Hudson Limited. Colin decides to spend the money anyway.

Up until the point Colin checked his bank statement, he might have been able to deal with the money as he wanted. However, having checked his bank statement, Colin will in all likelihood be liable having shut his eyes to the obvious source of the money. Hudson Limited, therefore, may be able to bring a claim against Colin for knowing receipt.

14.8 Summary flowchart

Figure 14.3 Third party claims summary flowchart

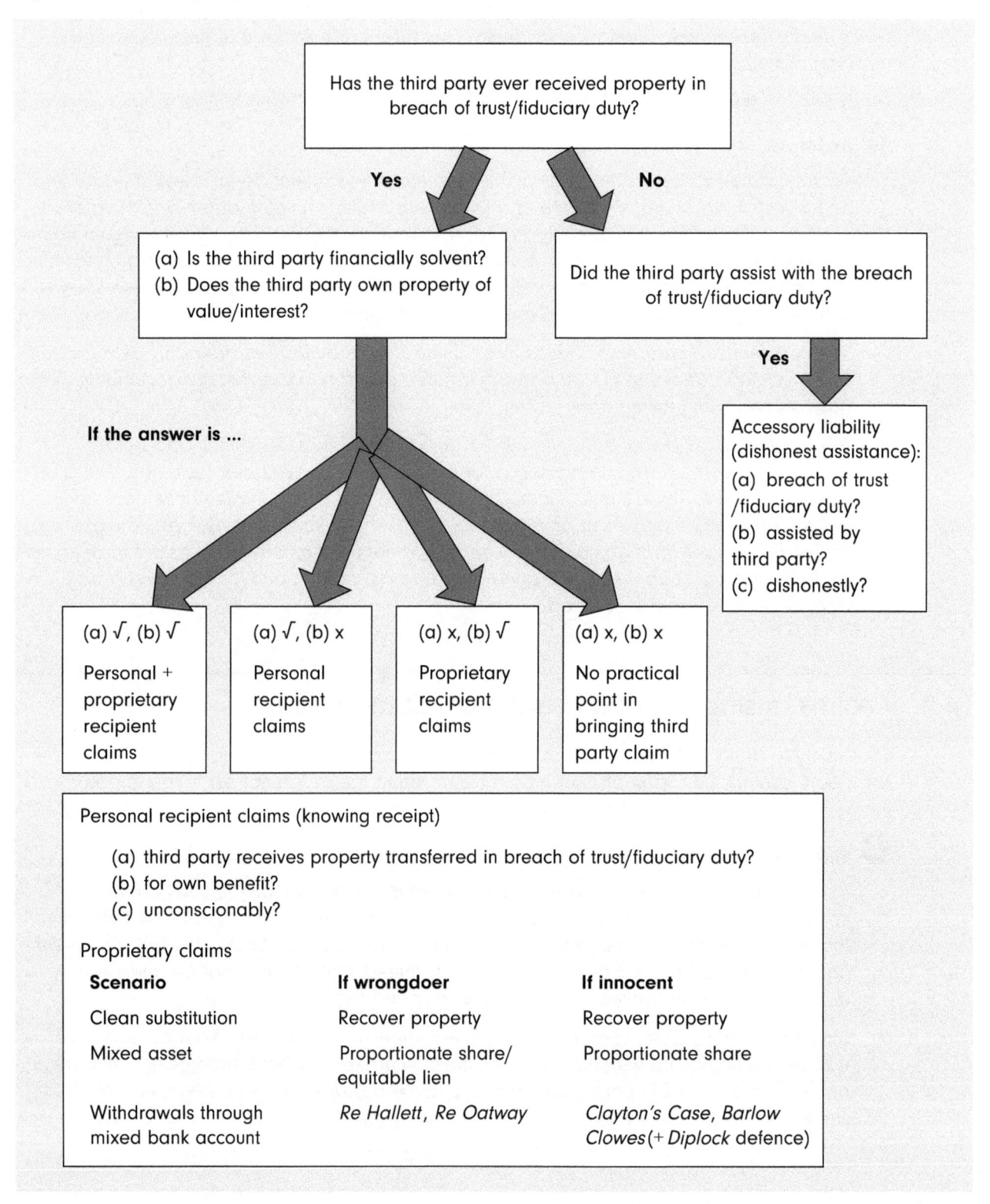

```
                 Has the third party ever received property in
                      breach of trust/fiduciary duty?
                    Yes ↓                    ↓ No
```

- (a) Is the third party financially solvent?
- (b) Does the third party own property of value/interest?

Did the third party assist with the breach of trust/fiduciary duty?

Yes ↓

Accessory liability (dishonest assistance):
(a) breach of trust /fiduciary duty?
(b) assisted by third party?
(c) dishonestly?

If the answer is ...

(a) ✓, (b) ✓	(a) ✓, (b) ✗	(a) ✗, (b) ✓	(a) ✗, (b) ✗
Personal + proprietary recipient claims	Personal recipient claims	Proprietary recipient claims	No practical point in bringing third party claim

Personal recipient claims (knowing receipt)

(a) third party receives property transferred in breach of trust/fiduciary duty?
(b) for own benefit?
(c) unconscionably?

Proprietary claims

Scenario	If wrongdoer	If innocent
Clean substitution	Recover property	Recover property
Mixed asset	Proportionate share/ equitable lien	Proportionate share
Withdrawals through mixed bank account	*Re Hallett, Re Oatway*	*Clayton's Case, Barlow Clowes* (+ *Diplock* defence)

Summary

In this chapter you have considered claims that beneficiaries can bring against third parties (strangers to the trust), for instance:

- *The third party has received trust property but dissipated it all.* The most relevant claim in this case is one for personal recipient liability (knowing receipt). You must ascertain whether the third party has received trust property for their own benefit with the requisite degree of knowledge that would render their retention of the property unconscionable. The third party must have sufficient financial solvency to be able to meet the claim.

- *The third party is still in receipt of trust property (or replacement property) but is bankrupt.* The most relevant claim in this case is a proprietary claim to recover the property. If the third party provided consideration for the transfer of property and had no knowledge/notice that the property belonged to a trust, then no proprietary claim can be maintained against them. If the property was a gift, you must ascertain whether the third party had knowledge/notice that the property belonged to the trust (in which case, you use the tracing rules you would apply as against a wrongdoing trustee) or had no such knowledge/notice (in which case, you use the tracing rules you would apply between innocent parties).

- *The third party did not receive any property but assisted with the breach of trust or fiduciary duty.* The most relevant claim in this case is one for personal accessory liability (dishonest assistance). You must ascertain whether the third party dishonestly assisted in the breach of trust or fiduciary duty by comparing their conduct against the conduct of an honest person (albeit one with the same knowledge and experience as the third party). The third party must have sufficient financial solvency to be able to meet the claim. Most defendants falling into this category are likely to be professionals and therefore will have insurance to meet the claim.

Sample questions

Question 1

A doctor is a trustee. He stole £50,000 from the trust and paid this into the bank account of an offshore company.

The doctor instructed the trust's accountant to draw up some 'inventive accounts'. She did so. These accounts have hidden the doctor's wrongdoing until now.

The offshore company has been wound up and the shareholders have since disappeared.

Which of the following claims is most likely to give the beneficiaries a positive outcome?

A A claim for knowing receipt against the accountant.

B A claim that the accountant has intermeddled in the affairs of the trust.

C A proprietary claim to recover any property that the accountant owns.

D A personal claim against the accountant for breach of trust.

E A claim for personal accessory liability against the accountant.

Trusts

Answer

Option E is correct. The accountant has positively assisted the doctor's breach of trust. If she has acted dishonestly (which seems likely given the facts – she was instructed to draw up 'inventive accounts'), a claim for personal accessory liability should be successful.

Options A and C are wrong. At no point has the accountant received trust property.

Option B is wrong. The accountant has not acted as if she were an expressly appointed trustee, so she cannot be liable for intermeddling.

Option D is wrong. The accountant is not an expressly appointed trustee, so she is not herself in breach of trust.

Question 2

A trustee steals £50,000 from a trust.

She transfers £20,000 of the money to her daughter who uses the money to pay off her credit card debts.

She transfers the remaining £30,000 to her son who uses the money as a deposit towards a flat.

The trustee and her son are facing bankruptcy proceedings.

Which of the following claims is most likely to give the beneficiaries a positive outcome?

A   A claim for personal recipient liability against both the daughter and the son.

B   A proprietary claim to recover trust property from both the daughter and the son.

C   A claim for personal recipient liability against the daughter; a proprietary claim against the son.

D   A proprietary claim against the daughter; a claim for personal recipient liability against the son.

E   A claim for personal recipient liability against the daughter; a claim for personal accessory liability against the son.

Answer

Option C is correct. The daughter has received trust property but has dissipated it by using it to pay off her credit card debts. There is no point bringing a proprietary claim against the daughter. However, depending on whether her state of knowledge as to the origins of the money she received made it unconscionable for her to spend that money, a claim for personal recipient liability might be successful.

The son has received trust property, which might be traceable into the flat. The beneficiaries should therefore assert a proprietary claim against the flat. However, the son is facing bankruptcy proceedings, and therefore there is unlikely to be any practical purpose in bringing any personal claim against him.

The son's bankruptcy means that bringing a personal claim against him would be practically worthless. As a result, options A, D and E are wrong. (Option E is also wrong because there is nothing on the facts to suggest that the son has assisted his mother's breach of trust.)

The fact that the daughter has dissipated the trust property she received renders meaningless a proprietary claim against her. As a result, options B and D are wrong.

Question 3

Two years ago, a trustee stole £80,000 from a trust fund.

She paid £40,000 into her boyfriend's bank account. She combined the remaining £40,000 with £40,000 of her own money to buy a Mercedes AMG coupe, which is now valued at £60,000.

Her boyfriend's bank account already contained £10,000 of his own money. He used £10,000 from the account to pay off his extensive gambling debts. He used the remaining £40,000 to purchase a sculpture for his garden. He was used to receiving large sums of money from the trustee, who was then independently wealthy but now has been made bankrupt, so he did not think anything was unusual when she transferred the sum of £40,000 to him.

Which of the following claims is most likely to give the beneficiaries the best outcome?

A   Asserting an equitable lien over the Mercedes AMG coupe; a proprietary claim asserting an equitable lien over the sculpture.

B   Claiming a 50% share in the Mercedes AMG coupe; a proprietary claim asserting an equitable lien over the sculpture.

C   A personal claim for breach of trust against the trustee.

D   Claiming a 50% share in the Mercedes AMG coupe; a claim for personal recipient liability against the boyfriend.

E   Asserting an equitable lien over the Mercedes AMG coupe; a claim for personal recipient liability against the boyfriend.

Answer

Option A is correct.

This question is designed to remind you that beneficiaries can choose to bring claims against both wrongdoing trustees and third parties as needed to ensure full recovery for the losses the trust has sustained.

The trustee has mixed some trust money with her own money to purchase the Mercedes. This car is a 'mixed asset'. Given that it has decreased in value, the beneficiaries are best advised to assert an equitable lien over the car to the full extent of their contribution towards that asset, ie £40,000.

The boyfriend still has property – the sculpture – that the beneficiaries can trace into. As he is an innocent volunteer (see below), the beneficiaries would have to use the kinder tracing rules set out in this chapter. The beneficiaries would start by applying *Clayton's Case* and FIFO, which in this scenario would mean that the boyfriend's own money was spent paying off his gambling debts, whereas the trust money was used to pay for the sculpture enabling the beneficiaries to assert an equitable lien over that sculpture.

Options B and D are wrong for suggesting that the beneficiaries should claim a 50% share in the Mercedes coupe. Given that the car has gone down in value, this does not represent the best outcome for the beneficiaries.

Option C is wrong. A personal claim against the trustee is now worthless given that bankruptcy proceedings have been opened against her.

Options D and E are wrong for suggesting that the beneficiaries can bring a claim for personal recipient liability against the boyfriend. The facts suggest that the boyfriend was used to receiving lavish gifts from the trustee. He may not, therefore, have had the requisite degree of knowledge about the origins of the money he received to have made it unconscionable to spend it. The chances of a claim for personal recipient liability being successful therefore look low.

Appendix 1   Equitable Remedies

When someone suffers a legal wrong, the primary remedy at common law is damages – the victim of the wrong is awarded money to compensate them for losses they have sustained. However, the person who has suffered a wrong might not always feel that damages provide adequate redress.

Equity has over the years supplemented the common law remedy of damages with additional remedies that may, in certain circumstances, better protect the innocent party. These remedies have some important principles in common:

(a) Damages must generally be inadequate. If you suffer loss which can be adequately compensated by money, then you will generally be limited to claiming damages.

(b) The remedies are discretionary, in the sense that they are awarded at the discretion of the court. This contrasts with damages at common law which are available as of right – if the claimant has a right recognised by the common law which has been infringed causing loss, the court must award damages. However, the fact that equitable remedies are discretionary does not mean that the courts are free to do what they want. Each equitable remedy is governed by a number of rules and principles which the court must consider and apply when deciding whether or not to grant the remedy sought.

(c) Equitable remedies are applied in accordance with various equitable maxims, most notably, 'he who comes to equity must come with clean hands'. A claimant who has acted unconscionably or improperly may find themselves without an equitable remedy notwithstanding that their rights have been infringed.

(d) Delay in pursuing an equitable remedy may prevent the claimant securing relief, particularly where the delay causes unfairness to the defendant or amounts to acquiescence.

The following equitable remedies are particularly significant.

Injunctions

An injunction is an order of the court that requires a party either:

(a) to refrain from doing something (prohibitory and *quia timet* injunctions); or less often

(b) to do something (mandatory injunctions).

Injunctions can be granted prior to the commencement of proceedings or at any time up to trial (interim injunctions) or at trial (final or perpetual injunctions). The court may grant an injunction in all cases where it is just and convenient to do so, and also has a discretion to award damages instead of an injunction where the injury to the claimant is small, capable of being estimated in money and where the grant of an injunction would be oppressive. Injunctions can be enforced by imprisonment, sequestration of assets or payment of a fine.

More detail on when injunctions are commonly sought can be found in the **Contract** and **Tort Manuals**, whilst the procedure to follow when applying for injunctions is set out in the **Dispute Resolution Manual**.

Specific performance

Specific performance is a court order which compels the defendant to perform a positive contractual obligation, ie do what they promised to do. Specific performance cannot compel the 'performance' of negative obligations (promises not to do something) – such obligations must be enforced by way of prohibitory injunction. Certain contracts do not lend themselves to specific performance (eg contracts for personal services and contracts which require constant supervision).

By contrast with injunctions, there is no power to make an interim order for specific performance. If a party wishes to secure an order for specific performance, they may need to apply for interim injunctions to 'hold the ring' allowing them to secure an order for specific performance at trial. Orders for specific performance can be enforced by imprisonment, sequestration of assets or payment of a fine. Alternatively, the claimant can seek an order that the contract be treated as discharged and proceed to claim damages.

More detail on specific performance can be found in the **Contract Manual**.

Rectification

Where a written document by mistake does not express the true agreement between the parties, it may be possible to use the remedy of rectification to change the written document so that it more properly reflects the parties' true agreement. This remedy only allows the parties to correct the written expression of their agreement – it cannot be used to change the agreement itself.

Common errors that are corrected include:

(a) the failure to match the correct parties with the correct contractual obligations (eg requiring a tenant to do something when the actual agreement was that the landlord would perform that activity);

(b) improperly defining the scope of the agreement's subject-matter (eg a lease might include the common parts within the scope of the demised premises when the common parts should have been excluded); or

(c) improperly recording the agreement as to price (eg by stating that the price was inclusive of VAT when the actual agreement was that the price excluded VAT).

The failure to record the true agreement between the parties must be a consequence of mistake, either:

(a) common – both parties mistakenly believe that the written document is correctly drafted; or

(b) unilateral – one party mistakenly believes that the written document is correctly drafted; the other party realises there is a mistake but stays quiet because that mistake will benefit them.

In the rough-and-tumble and disorder of many contractual negotiations, it can be difficult to subsequently find any cogent evidence that the parties held an intention different to the terms of the written document they have signed. It is also very difficult for a claim for rectification to succeed when the written document was drafted by lawyers. As a result, claims for rectification are often unsuccessful.

Other equitable remedies

(a) Appointment of receivers and managers – a receiver is appointed to collect and protect property for the benefit of those entitled to such property. A manager is appointed to continue someone else's trade or business. Receivers and managers may be appointed under the terms of a relevant security agreement (eg a mortgage or debenture) or by court order (eg in extreme cases where an injunction to prevent the defendant from dissipating property will not by itself provide sufficient protection).

(b) Actions of account – when someone has obtained a benefit to which they are not entitled, they may be ordered to account for that benefit. The most common example of an account being ordered is when a fiduciary makes a personal profit from a breach of fiduciary duty – the court will usually order the fiduciary to account for (quantify and pay) that personal profit to their principal. See **Chapter 11** for more detail.

(c) Rescission – this enables a party to a contract to have it set aside and to be restored to their pre-contract position. This commonly arises in cases of misrepresentation and undue influence. More detail on this remedy can be found in the **Contract Manual**.

Appendix 2   Charitable Purposes

The following is a summary of The Charity Commission's Guidance on Charitable Purposes published in 2013.

Charitable purpose (s 3(1) CA 2011)	Description	Examples
Prevention or relief of poverty	Relief of poverty/financial hardship of anyone who does not have the resources to provide themselves, either on a short or long-term basis, with the normal things of life which most people take for granted. Can include addressing the causes of poverty (prevention) and the consequences of poverty (relief)	Grants of money Provision of items such as furniture, bedding, clothing, food, fuel, heating appliances, washing machines and fridges Payment for services such as essential house decoration, repairs, laundering, meals on wheels, outings, utilities etc Provision of facilities connected with vocational training, technical skills, travelling expenses to help recipients earn their living, equipment and funds intended to bring the quality of life of beneficiaries to a reasonable standard
Advancement of education	Promote, sustain and increase individual and collective knowledge and understanding Includes formal and community education, physical education, training and life-long learning, research and the development of individual capabilities	Educational establishments: schools, colleges, universities Organisations supporting the work of educational establishments, such as parent-teacher organisations, prize funds, teacher training organisations, student unions Pre-school and out-of-school education, such as summer schools and homework clubs Organisations providing life skills training such as the Duke of Edinburgh award, Scouts and Guides Research foundations and think tanks Museums, galleries, libraries and learned societies (such as the Royal Geographic Society) Organisations which fund people's education

Appendix 2

Charitable purpose (s 3(1) CA 2011)	Description	Examples
Advancement of religion	Characteristics of religions include: • Belief in a god/goddess, supreme being or entity which is the object or focus of the religion • Relationship between the believer and being/entity by showing worship of that being/entity • Degree of cogency, cohesion, seriousness and importance • Identifiable positive, beneficial, moral or ethical framework	Provision of places of worship Raising awareness and understanding of religious beliefs and practices Carrying out religious devotional acts Carrying out missionary and outreach work
Advancement of health or the saving of lives	Prevent or relieve sickness, disease or human suffering as well as promote health. It extends beyond the treatment or provision of care to the provision of items, services and facilities to ease the suffering or assist the recovery of people who are sick or infirm. It includes conventional methods as well as complementary and alternative methods of healing.	Provision of medical treatment, care and healing Provision of comforts, items, services and facilities for people who are sick, eg Hospital Radio Medical research Services and facilities for medical practitioners, eg homes for nurses Provision of rescue services, such as lifeboats and first aid services Assisting the victims of natural disasters or wars Provision of life saving or self defence classes
Advancement of citizenship or community development	Support for social and community infrastructure	Promotion of civic responsibility and good citizenship Promotion of urban and rural regeneration Promotion of volunteering and the voluntary sector
Advancement of the arts, culture, heritage or science	Art includes abstract, conceptual and performance art (music, dance and theatre) Heritage includes local and national history and traditions, historic land and buildings Science includes scientific research and various learned societies	Art galleries and festivals Theatres, cinemas, choirs, orchestras, music/operatic/dramatic societies Promotion of crafts and local arts Local or national history or archaeology societies Preservation of ancient sites or buildings (whether specific or in general) Scientific research projects and learned societies, eg Royal College of Nursing
Advancement of amateur sport	Sports or games that promote health by involving physical or mental skill or exertion	Local sports clubs Multisports centres Local bridge clubs

Appendix 2

Charitable purpose (s 3(1) CA 2011)	Description	Examples
Advancement of human rights, conflict resolution or the promotion of religious or racial harmony, or equality and diversity	Resolving national and international conflicts and relieving suffering, poverty and distress by identifying the causes of conflict and seeking to resolve them Eliminating discrimination and promoting diversity in society	Promotion of human rights Promotion of restorative justice and other forms of conflict resolution Promoting good relations between persons of different racial groups and/or enabling inter-faith understanding Promoting equality and diversity through the elimination of discrimination
Advancement of environmental protection or improvement	Preserving and conserving the natural environment and promoting sustainable development Conservation of a particular species or wildlife in general	Conservation of flora, fauna or the environment generally Conservation of particular geographical areas or species Zoos Promotion of sustainable development and biodiversity Promotion of recycling and sustainable waste management Research projects into renewable energy sources
Relief of those in need because of youth, age, ill-health, disability, financial hardship or other disadvantage	Includes providing accommodation and care to persons falling under this head	Care and upbringing of children and young people (eg care homes and apprenticing) Relief of the effects of old age (eg specialist equipment, drop-in centres) Relief of disability (eg specialist equipment, providing access) Provision of housing (eg almshouses)
Advancement of animal welfare	Preventing or suppressing cruelty to animals or preventing/relieving the suffering of animals	Promoting kindness and preventing cruelty to animals Animal sanctuaries Provision of veterinary care and treatment Care and re-homing of abandoned and mistreated animals
Promotion of the efficiency of the armed forces or of the efficiency of the police, fire and rescue services and ambulance services	These services exist for public defence and security. It is charitable to promote the efficiency of the armed forces and other emergency services as a means of defending the country, preserving public order and protecting the public	Increasing technical knowledge and/or physical fitness of members of the services Supporting messes and institutes Providing memorials to fallen colleagues Providing associations which support a unit and enable serving and former members to mix together Encouraging recruitment to the services Provision of emergency air and sea rescue services

Appendix 2

Charitable purpose (s 3(1) CA 2011)	Description	Examples
Analogous charitable purposes		Provision of facilities for recreation and leisure-time occupation in the interests of social welfare Provision of public works and services and the provision of public amenities Promotion of industry, commerce and agriculture Gifts for the benefit of a particular locality, beautification of towns and civic societies Promotion of ethical standards of conduct and compliance with the law

Glossary

Absolutely entitled an adult beneficiary (or beneficiaries) who is (or are) entitled to the entire trust fund

Absolute owner someone who owns the legal and equitable title in property

Administrators people appointed other than by will to administer and distribute property after death (most commonly on intestacy)

Advancement (i) the passing of legal and equitable title to another for no consideration (ie a gift)

(ii) the giving of capital by a trustee to a beneficiary before the beneficiary is strictly entitled to call for such capital

Bankruptcy the legal process started by or against an individual who is insolvent

Bare trust trust for a sole adult, mentally capable beneficiary who has a vested interest

Beneficial interest the interest in property held by a beneficiary. Also referred to as the **equitable interest**

Beneficiary person who holds equitable title to trust property

Beneficiary principle the principle that states that trusts should generally benefit individuals

Capital the property held under trust

Chattels tangible property (such as jewellery, furniture, paintings etc)

Common intention constructive trust a form of constructive trust used to determine beneficial interests in the family home

Conceptual certainty the need for a class of people to be described clearly and objectively. Also referred to as **linguistic certainty**

Constitution the creation of valid express trusts. When the trustees are people other than the settlor, this involves putting legal title to trust property in the hands of the trustees

Constructive trust a trust that is implied in order to achieve fairness between parties or otherwise prevent the legal owner of property from behaving unconscionably

Contingent interest a conditional beneficial interest

Declaration of trust the terms of the trust. If in writing, this is commonly referred to as the **trust deed** or **trust document**

Discretionary trust a trust where the settlor identifies a group of people who might benefit but leaves it to the trustee(s) to decide which members of that group get what

Equitable title title to property enforceable in equity only. In a trust, this title is held by the beneficiary. Also referred to as **beneficial title**

Evidential certainty the need to have evidence to identify all the beneficiaries under a trust. Only required for fixed interest trusts

Executors people appointed under the terms of a will to administer and distribute property. A female executor is sometimes referred to as an **executrix**

Express trust a trust that the settlor expressly intends to create

Fiduciary a person who has an obligation of loyalty to another (their principal) and must put their principal's interests before their own. Common examples include trustees, company directors and solicitors

Fixed interest trust a trust in which the settlor fixes upfront which beneficiary gets what property

Implied trust a trust that arises on operation of law

Income a return paid on a regular basis that is derived from capital

Insolvency the situation in which a person (natural or corporate) cannot meet their debts as they fall due

Intestacy the process of administering and distributing a person's property if they die without executing a valid will

Joint and several liability where two or more persons are liable in respect of the same loss, the claimant being entitled to elect to sue all of them or one of them for the full loss

Glossary

Legal title title to property enforceable at common law. In a trust, this title is held by the trustee

Letter of wishes a document authored by the settlor of a discretionary trust that provides non-binding guidance to the trustees on how to exercise their discretion

Life interest trust a trust comprised of life tenants and remainder beneficiaries, being an example of a trust containing successive interests

Life tenant the person who receives income (or has the use and enjoyment of trust property) during their life

Lifetime trust a trust that is created during the lifetime of the settlor. Also referred to as an **inter vivos trust**

Liquidation the legal process started by or against a company that is insolvent

Minor someone under the age of 18 years. Also referred to as an **infant**

Objects (i) in the case of trusts for individuals, the people who might benefit from the trust; more specifically, those people who have not yet been selected by the trustees to receive property under the terms of a discretionary trust (once selected, such people become beneficiaries)

(ii) in the case of purpose trusts, the purpose that the trustees must achieve

Perpetuity rules the rules that provide that trusts cannot last forever

Personal claims claims for monetary compensation that the defendant must satisfy using their own personal funds. Also known as claims **in personam**

Personalty any property other than land

Proprietary claims claims that assert interests in specific forms of property. Also known as claims **in rem**

Proprietary estoppel an equitable mechanism that prevents a legal owner from denying proprietary rights to another when it would be unconscionable to do so

Purpose trust a trust where the trustees are obliged to achieve a purpose or attain an objective as opposed to distributing property directly to individuals. Examples include charitable trusts

Realty land

Remainder beneficiary the person who, under a life interest trust, receives trust capital once the life tenant has died

Residuary estate what remains of a testator's property once all debts, taxes and specific legacies have been paid. The person entitled to the residuary estate is known as the **residuary beneficiary**

Resulting trust (i) a trust that arises when property is transferred to another in circumstances where it is unclear who owns the beneficial interest

(ii) more specifically in the context of land: a trust that may arise when a person who is not the legal owner contributes directly to the purchase price of land, that person acquiring an interest proportionate to their contribution

Settlor person who creates a (lifetime) trust

Statutory next-of-kin the person entitled to someone's property if they have died intestate

Stranger someone who is not expressly appointed a trustee

Testator a man who executes a valid will. A woman who executes a valid will is known as a **testatrix**

Three certainties to be valid, a declaration of trust must comply with the three certainties: intention, subject-matter and objects

Tracing the ability of the original owner of property to identify and claim interests in property held by others

Transferee a person who receives property from another

Transferor a person who transfers property to another

Trust corporation corporate trustees that carry out trust business for profit

Trustee person who holds legal title to trust property for the benefit of the beneficiary

Trust property the property held on trust. Also referred to as the **trust fund** or **trust capital**

Unsecured creditor someone who is owed money and has not taken security or collateral for that debt

Vested interest an unconditional beneficial interest

Volunteer someone who has not provided consideration for the transfer of property

Index

A

absolute/outright ownership 2-3, 5-6, 48
account of profits 149, 150, 152
accounts 124, 126
additional trustees 103, 105
administration of trusts
    fiduciary duties 143-54
    investment duties 129-42
    maintenance and advancement, trustees' powers of 109-18
    running a trust 119-28
    trustees 99-107
advancement, presumption of 70, 73-4
advancement, trustees' powers of *see* maintenance and advancement, trustees' powers of
appointment of trustees 32-7, 100-1, 103-4, 105
attorney, delegation of functions to an 104, 105

B

bank accounts, withdrawals from mixed 175-80, 185
bare trusts 48-9
beneficial interests 43-54
    beneficiary principle 24, 57-8
    capital and income returns 44-5
    certainty of objects 17-18, 21-4, 76
    class of beneficiaries 21-3
    completely disposed, where beneficial interest is not 75-7
    conflicts with trustees 120, 122
    contingent interests 46, 47, 49
    creation of trusts 17-18, 21-3, 43-54, 76
    definition 4
    discretionary trusts 47-8
    fairly between beneficiaries, trustees' duty to act 122, 125, 136, 139
    family home 81-86
    fixed interest trusts 45-7, 49
    flowchart 51
    legal and beneficial ownership, separation of 3, 4-6
    non-charitable purpose trusts 57-8
    ownership of trust property 4-6, 81-6
    perpetuities 24
    quantification 88
    Saunders v Vautier, rule in 48-50, 76
    subject-matter, certainty of 20-1
    successive interests 46-7, 49
    summary tables 51
    vested interests 45-6
    youth, immaturity, health and vulnerability of beneficiaries 7
breach *see also* personal claims against trustees; proprietary claims against trustees
    fiduciary duties 146-50, 152
    trust, of 157-69, 172
but for test 161

C

capital 44-5, 58, 109-18
causation 161
certainties *see* three certainties
charitable trusts 58-63
    Attorney General, enforcement by 59
    charitable purpose, trusts must be for a 59
    Charity Commission 59
    creation of trusts 55-6, 58-63
    education, advancement of 59, 60, 63
    enforcement 59
    exclusively charitable purposes 61-2
    personal nexus test 60-1
    political purposes 61-2
    poverty, prevention of relief from 59, 60, 61, 63
    public benefit 59-60
    religion, advancement of 59, 60, 63
chattels, definition of 34
children, power to apply income for 110-11
classification of trusts 8-9
Clayton's case, rule in 181-3
cohabitees *see* family home
common intention constructive trusts 84-9, 92-3
    contributions 85, 8
    definition 9
    detrimental reliance 86-7
    flowchart 89
    implied trusts 84, 85-9
    inferred common intention 87-8
    joint ownership 85

common intention constructive trusts (*Continued*)
    proprietary estoppel 91
    quantification of beneficial shares 88
common law 2
common law marriage, myth of 83
compensation *see* personal claims against trustees
competition with the trust 147
confidentiality 124
conflicts of interests 120, 122, 143–4, 146, 150, 152
constitution of trusts 16, 31–41
    chattels, definition of 34
    declarations of trust 32, 37
    definition 16
    express trusts 16, 31–41
    flowchart 38
    land 33
    lifetime trusts 10, 31–41
    money 34
    self-constitute, lifetime trusts that 32, 39
    settlors as trustees 32, 37
    share transfers 33–4, 37
    trustees, appointment of 32–7
constructive trusts *see also* common intention constructive trusts
contingent interests 46, 47, 48
contribution and indemnity in person claims 163–4, 166
contribution to family home 84, 85, 87–8, 92–3, 163–4
creation of trusts
    beneficiaries 17–18, 21–3, 43–54, 76
    charitable trusts 55–6, 58–63
    express trusts 15–41
    family home 81–96
    lifetime trusts 3–4, 9–10
    non-charitable purpose trusts 55–8, 63–5
    ownership of trust property 4
    residuary estates 10
    next-of-kin, statutory 11
    resulting trusts 69–80
    settlor, definition of a 4
    three certainties 17–24, 27, 57, 76
    when trusts can be created 9–11
    will trusts 10
CREST system 33–4

D

damages, inadequacy of 2
death of trustees 104
declarations of trust 25, 32, 37, 121
    definition 16
    express trusts 16, 24–6
    flowchart 26
    formalities 24–6
    investment duties of trustees 133
    lifetime trusts 10
    maintenance and advancement, trustees' powers of 109–10
    non-charitable purpose trusts 57, 63
    oral declarations 24–5
    settlor, definition of a 4
    three certainties 17–23, 27, 76
    trustees 16, 100
    validity 16, 32, 57
    will trusts 10
delay defeats equity 91
delegation 104, 105, 136–7, 139
detrimental reliance 86–7, 89, 90–1, 93
disclosure of information 124, 125–6
discretionary trusts
    administrative unworkability 23
    capriciousness 23–4
    certainty of objects 22–3
    class 45–6
    complete list test 22–3
    definition 47
    express trusts 17
    fixed interest trusts 48
    given postulant test 22–3
    properly, duty to exercise discretions 123, 125
duties and powers, differences between 120–1
duty of care of trustees 120, 121, 135

E

education, charities for advancement of 59, 60, 63
emails *see* declarations of trust
equity *see also* maxims of equity
    common law 2
    equity, definition of 2
    equity follows the law 86
    residuary estate 10
estoppel *see* proprietary estoppel
exclusion clauses 133
excused, where trustees ought to be 162–3, 166
exemption clauses 162, 166
express trusts 15–41
    benefit individuals, trusts that will 8
    beneficiary principle 24
    constitution of trusts 16, 31–41
    creation of trusts 15–41
    declarations of trust 16–23, 24–6, 27, 76, 83–4
    definition 8, 16

discretionary trusts 17
family home 81, 83-5, 91-3
fixed interest trusts 16-17
perpetuities 24, 27
purpose, to achieve a 8
writing 83

F

fairness
   beneficiaries, trustees' duty to act fairly between 122, 125, 136, 139
   equity, definition of 2
   investment duties of trustees 136, 139
family home 81-96 see also common intention constructive trusts
   beneficial interests 81-6
   contributions 9, 84, 85, 87-8, 92
   creation of trusts 81-96
   express trusts 81, 83-5, 92-3
   joint ownership 82-3, 85, 86, 92-3
   joint tenants 82-3
   married couples/civil partnerships 81, 82-3
   ownership of the family home 82-3
   proprietary estoppel 81, 89-92, 93
   purchase price, contributions to 71-3, 84, 92
   resulting trusts 84, 92
   sole ownership 83, 85-8, 92-3
   tenants in common 82-3
   writing 83-4
fiduciary duties 143-54
   account of profits 149, 150, 152
   authorisation as a defence 152
   breaches of fiduciary duty 146-50, 152
   commission 148
   competition with the trust 147
   conflicts of interests 143-4, 146, 150, 152
   core fiduciary duty 143-4, 152
   definition 143
   director's salary 148-9
   flowchart 151
   information or opportunity, use of 149-50, 152
   personal claims 150, 152
   profit, when trustees can make a personal 145, 148-9, 150, 152
   proprietary claims 150, 152, 185
   remedies 150, 152
   remuneration and fees 147-8
   self-dealing rule 146-7, 152
   who can be a fiduciary 143, 151
fixed interest trusts
   beneficiaries 51-7, 49
   certainty of objects 1-2

   contingent interests 46, 47, 49
   discretionary trusts 48
   express trusts 16-17
   powers and duties, differences between 120-1
   successive interests 46-7, 49
formalities
   declarations of trust 26-7, 28
   land 57
   lifetime trusts 24
   oral declarations 24-5
   resulting trusts 77
   wills, formalities for 24-5
fraud 162-3, 164
future property 19

G

gifts 7, 19, 73-4

H

he who comes to equity must come with clean hands 2, 91
homes see family home

I

imperfect obligations, trusts of 64-5
implied trusts see common intention constructive trusts; resulting trusts
   definition 8-9
inalienability of capital, rule against 58
income and capital 44-5, 109-18
indemnity and contribution 163-4, 166
information or opportunity, use of 149-50, 152
insolvency 173
intention, certainty of 17-19, 27, 57
inter vivos trusts see lifetime (inter vivos) trusts
intestacy 11
investment duties of trustees 6, 120, 129-42
   authorised investments 133-4
   bare trusts 49
   care and skill 136-7, 139
   declarations of trust, express provisions in 133
   delegation 136-7, 139
   disclosure of information 124
   diversification 131, 136
   duty of care 135
   ethical considerations 136
   exclusion clauses 133
   expert advice 130, 135, 139
   fairly between beneficiaries, duty to act 136, 139

Index

investment duties of trustees (*Continued*)
    flowchart 138
    land, acquisition of 133-4, 139
    non-statutory duties 136
    objectives 130, 131, 139
    personal claims 163-4
    purchasing investments, duties when 134-6
    standard investment criteria 134, 139
    statutory duties 134-6
    types of investment 132-3

J

joint and several liability 160-71, 163, 166
joint ownership of family home 86, 92-3
    common intention constructive trusts 84-5
    joint tenants 82-3
    tenants in common 82-3

L

laches 159, 163, 166, 173
land *see also* family home
    formalities 57
    investment duties of trustees 133-4, 139
    registration 33
    voluntary transfers 71
legal and beneficial ownership, separation of 3, 4-6
legitimate expectations 123, 124
letters of wishes 124
lifetime (inter vivos) trusts 9-11
    constitution of trusts 10, 31-41
    creation of trusts 3-4, 9-10, 18
    declarations of trust 10, 24-5
    self-constitute, lifetime trusts that 32, 39
    trust, definition of 3-4
limitation periods and laches 159, 163, 166, 173

M

maintenance and advancement, trustees' powers of 109-18, 120
    capital to or for beneficiaries, power to pay 112-15
    declarations of trust, express powers in 109-10
    duty to pay income to certain beneficiaries 112
    education 110
    flowchart 115
    income or capital, payment of 109-18
    minors, power to apply income for 110-11
married couples/civil partnerships and family home 81, 82-3
matrimonial home *see* family home

maxims of equity
    delay defeats equity 91
    equity follows the law 86
    he who comes to equity must come with clean hands 2, 91
    vacuum, equity abhors a 76, 77
    volunteer, equity will not assist a 2, 34-7, 39
    wrongdoer, equity is presumed against the 178, 180
minors, power to apply income for 110-11
mixed assets 174-81
money 34

N

next-of-kin 11
non-charitable purpose trusts
    beneficiary principle 57-8
    creation of trusts 55-8, 63-5
    declarations of trust 57, 63
    flowchart 65
    imperfect obligations, trusts of 64-5
    individuals distinguished, trusts for 56-7
    intention, certainty of 57
    land, formalities for 57
    objects, certainty of 57
    perpetuities 57, 58
    Re Denley trusts 63-4
    resulting trusts 77
    subject matter, certainty of 57
    three certainties 57
    validity 63-5
number of trustees 100, 104, 122

O

objects, certainty of 17-18, 21-3, 57, 76
ownership of trust property 2-7
    absolute/outright ownership 2-3, 5-6, 48
    beneficial or equitable title going to beneficiary 4-6
    characteristics of legal and equitable title 5-6
    legal and beneficial ownership, separation of 3, 4-6
    trustees and title to property 4, 5-6

P

perpetuities
    beneficiary interests 24
    express trusts 24, 27
    inalienability of capital, rule against 58
    remoteness of vesting 24

personal claims against trustees 157–69, 172
    breach of trust 157–69, 172
    causation 161
    consent to breach 161, 162, 166
    defences 161–3, 166
    disadvantages 158–9
    excused, where trustees ought to be 162–3, 166
    exemption clauses 162, 166
    fiduciary duties 150, 152
    financial standing of trustees 158
    flowchart 165
    indemnity and contribution 163–4, 166
    investment duties of trustees 163–4
    knowledge and consent of beneficiaries 162
    limitation periods and laches 159, 163, 166
    proprietary claims 159
    subject-matter of claims, which trustees can be 160–1
    value of the personal claim 161
personally and unanimously, trustees' duty to act 122–3, 125
political purposes, charities for 59, 60, 63
poverty, charities for the relief of 59, 60, 61, 63
powers and duties, differences between 120–1
precatory words 18–19
professional trustees 100, 121, 135, 147, 153, 160, 162, 164, 198, 201
profits
    account of profits 149, 150, 152
    trustees' making personal profits 145, 148–9, 150, 152
property, ownership of *see* ownership of trust property
proprietary claims against trustees 171–88
    bank accounts, withdrawals from mixed 175–80, 185
    Clayton's case, rule in 181–4
    definition 158, 172, 185
    fiduciary duties 150, 152, 185
    insolvent, where trustee is 173
    limitation periods and laches 173
    mixed assets 180–1
    mixes trust property with other property, where trustee 174–80
    original trust property, where trustee holds 173
    personal claims 159
    substitute property, where trustee holds 173–4, 185
    tracing 172–85
proprietary estoppel
    assurance 90

common intention constructive trusts 91
detrimental reliance 90–1, 93
family home 81, 89–92, 93
flowchart 92
remedies 91
purchase money resulting trusts 71–3, 84, 92
purpose trusts *see* non-charitable purpose trusts

R

Re Denley trusts 63–4
reasons for using a trust 7–8
    gifts distinguished from trusts 7
    trustee, control and management of property by a 7
    youth, immaturity, health and vulnerability of beneficiaries 7
religion, charities for the advancement of 59, 60, 63
remedies *see also* personal claims against trustees; proprietary claims against trustees; third parties, remedies against
    account of profits 149, 150, 152
    damages, inadequacy of 2
    fiduciary duties 150, 152
    proprietary estoppel 91
removal and retirement of trustees 100–3, 104–5
remuneration and fees 147–8
residuary estates 10–11
resulting trusts 8, 69–80
    advancement, presumption of 70, 73–4
    certainty of objects 23
    completely disposed, where beneficial interest is not 75–7
    creation of trusts 69–80
    definition 8
    evidence 70–1, 73–4
    family home 84, 92
    flowchart 75
    formalities 77
    land, voluntary transfers of 71
    non-charitable purpose trusts 77
    presumptions 70–5, 77
    purchase money cases 71–3, 84, 92
    rebuttal of presumptions 74, 77
    voluntary transfer of personalty 70–1
running a trust, trustees' duties when 119–28
    appointment, following 121–2
    beneficiaries, conflicts with 120, 122
    control of property, taking 121, 122
    declarations of trust, express provisions in a 121

Index

running a trust, trustees' duties when (*Continued*)
    disclosure of information 124, 125-6
    discretions properly, duty to exercise 123, 125
    duty of care 120, 121
    fairly between beneficiaries, duty to act 122, 125
    flowchart 125
    personally and unanimously, duty to act 122-3, 125
    powers and duties, differences between 120-1
    reasons for exercise of a power 124, 125-6
    standard of care 120, 125

S

Saunders v Vautier, rule in 48-50, 76
self-dealing rule 146-7, 152
settlor, definition of
    declarations of trust 4
    trustees as settlors 4, 10, 32, 37
share transfers 33-4, 37
sole ownership of family home 83, 85-8, 92-3
standard of care 120, 125
Strong v Bird, rule in 36-7
subject-matter, certainty of 17-18, 19-21, 27, 57
substitute property, where trustee holds 173-4, 185
successive interests 46-7, 49

T

tenants in common 82-3
third parties, remedies against 189-203
    accessory liability 190, 197-9, 201
    breach of trust 190, 197-9, 201
    de son tort, trustees 192
    dishonest assistance 190, 197-9, 201
    fiduciary duties, breach of 190, 198-9
    flowchart 191, 200
    intermeddling 190, 191, 192
    knowing receipt 190, 192-4, 201
    personal claims, 190-4, 107-9, 201
    proprietary claims 190-1, 194-6, 201
    recipient liability 190, 192-4, 201
    tracing rules 195-7
three certainties 17-23
    creation of trusts 17-23
    declarations of trust 17-23, 27, 76
    intention 17-19, 27, 57
    lifetime trusts 18
    objects 17-18, 21-3, 57, 76
    non-charitable purpose trusts 57
    subject-matter 17-18, 19-21, 27, 57
    will trusts 18
tracing 172-85
trust corporations 100, 147
trust, definition of a 3-4
trustees *see also* fiduciary duties; investment duties of trustees; personal claims against trustees; proprietary claims against trustees
    appointment 32-7, 100-1, 103-4, 105
    attorney, delegation of functions to an 104, 105
    death of a trustee 104
    declarations of trust 100
    definition 4
    express powers 100-1, 109-10
    maintenance and advancement, trustees' powers of 109-18, 120
    number 100, 104, 122
    powers and duties 6, 16, 100-1, 109-18, 120
    reasons for using a trust 7
    removal and retirement 100-3, 104-5
    remuneration and fees 147-8
    selection of trustees 100
    settlor, definition of a 4, 10
    title to property 4, 5-6
    who can be a trustee 4, 100

U

unanimously and personally, trustees' duty to act 122-3, 125
unconscionability 193, 201
unmarried couples *see* family home

V

vacuum, equity abhors a 76, 77
vested interests 45-6
volunteer, equity will not assist a 2, 34-7, 39

W

will trusts 10-11, 18
wills, formalities for 24-5
writing 24-5, 83-4
wrongdoer, equity is presumed against the 178, 180